AUTOMOTIVE
PAINT HANDBOOK

Paint Technology For Auto Enthusiasts & Body Shop Professionals

John Pfanstiehl

HPBooks

HPBooks
Published by
The Berkley Publishing Group
A division of Penguin Putnam Inc.
375 Hudson Street
New York, New York 10014

First edition: August 1998

© 1998 John Pfansthiehl
10 9 8 7 6 5

Library of Congress Cataloging-in-Publication Data

Pfanstiehl, John.
    Automotive paint handbook : paint technology for auto enthusiasts
and body shop professionals / John Pfanstiehl. — Rev. ed.
        p.   cm.
  ISBN 1-55788-291-6
    1. Automobiles—Painting—Handbooks, manuals, etc.   I. Title.
TL255.2.P49   1998   97-45785
629.2′6—dc21   CIP

Cover Design by Bird Studios
Book Design & Production by Michael Lutfy
Interior photos by the author unless otherwise noted
Cover photo courtesy DuPont, Inc.

NOTICE: The information in this book is true and complete to the best of our knowledge. All recommendations on parts and procedures are made without any guarantees on the part of the author or the publisher. Tampering with, altering, modifying or removing any emissions-control device is a violation of federal law. Author and publisher disclaim all liability incurred in connection with the use of this information.

Technical information, updates and glimpses into the future came generously from many people in the industry. Special thanks go to Daryl Porter, Paint Platform Service Manager for Chrysler; John Hughes, Refinish Paint Technical Specialist for Ford; and Brian Dotterer, Senior Project Engineer, General Motor's Center Paint Expertise. It's been rewarding to see how much they care about the quality of automotive paint finishes and how effective they have been at improving refinish quality.

Thanks go also to many individuals at the major paint companies including American Standox's Keith Smith; BASF's Tony Aikens and Andy Ladak; DuPont's Lester Young and Paul Maiersperger; House of Kolor's Jon Kosmoski; ICI's Ron Klein and Mark Rapson; PPG's John Jeffrey; Sherwin Williams' Bill Warner; Spies Hecker's Brian Spenser and Jacqueline Connolly; and Valspar's Vern Cantwell.

A number of other manufacturers in this industry have also shared information and insights over the years. They include Meguiar's Barry Meguiar, Bondo/Mar Hyde's Terry Merrill & Debbie Sloneker and Automotive Interntional's Ron Ketchum.

What's a paint book without painters? One certainly deserves acknowledgement for his input: David SeCaur of Final Finish in Branford, Connecticut. I have had the pleasure to view and learn from his artistry for over 25 years. Others I've learned much from over the years are Bob Belling (the trucks shown are just a sample of the vehicles from his personal collection—all of which he's painted), Barry Pleasant, who has been specializing in innovative street rods, and Bill Bartenstein, the original founder of Corvette Center, who certainly can afford to have anyone paint his cars but enjoys doing it himself.

Finally, thanks go to Michael Lutfy, the Editorial Director of HPBooks, who sculpted the many kilobytes of information into a smooth flowing, complete source of information on automotive paint.

ACKNOWLEDGMENTS

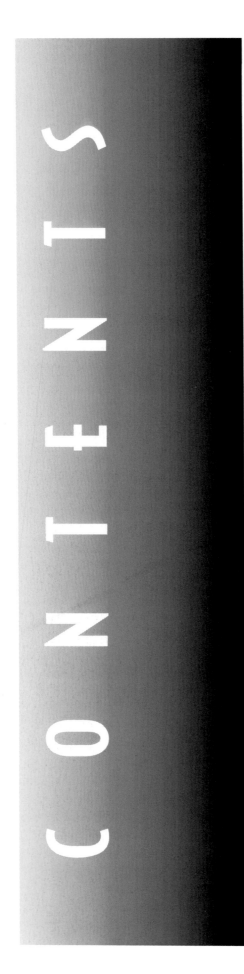

CONTENTS

It's been gratifying to see how well the first edition was received. The scope of information provided was new to this field, and the book was soon used by not only do it yourselfers and car enthusiasts but also by scores of professionals and industry leaders. After many reprintings, it was time for a second edition with major revisions and updating.

In writing this second edition, I have two things in mind. The first is to make the book understandable and enjoyable for readers. The second is to present the most up-to-date information on new paints, new application procedures, new tools, and new means to care for paint. In addition, you'll see how advances in measurement technology and true certification bring the promise of national quality standards in automotive painting to car owners.

A note on this book's format: each chapter is designed so it can be read by itself. That being said, Chapter 1, *Paint Basics*, and Chapter 2, *Current Technology*, provide a broader understanding for the other chapters. And if you want to get right to painting a car, read Chapters 1, 2, and 4, and then follow the procedures in Chapters 6 and 7.

Automotive painting is more involved than most people think. Are the rewards of automotive painting worth the effort? This photo of some of Bob Belling's trucks, all of which were restored and painted by him, tells the story better than words. As a hobby or as a profession, sculpting and crafting an unsightly wreck into a gleaming rolling work of art satisfies the soul. Courtesy Yankee Auto Truck, E. Hartford, CT.

INTRODUCTION

DEDICATION

To my wife, Kelly, who put up with the long hours and many months it took to research and write the first and second editions of the Automotive Paint Handbook. Fortunately, she loves cars, too.

To the individuals in this industry who strive to find new ways to improve the products and processes that affect us all.

Acrylic lacquer began to replace nitrocellulose lacquer in 1956. The 1957 Corvette was one of the first to wear it, although, at first, it was only available in Inca Silver. Photo courtesy *Corvette Fever* magazine.

Auto paint has only two purposes: to make the car look good and to protect the underlying metal or synthetic body panels from the harsh environment. During the past two decades, car owners have become more demanding in how their paint looks, and the environment has become harder on automotive finishes.

There have also been dramatic, fundamental changes in paint chemistry and application techniques mandated by environmental laws. Previous paints and their application methods have dumped thousands of tons of pollutants into the atmosphere every year. Unprecedented state and federal laws designed to change that unhealthy situation have already begun to be implemented, and that trend will continue.

The variety in today's auto paint goes beyond the simple choice of lacquer and enamel, although these are still the labels used for the major paint groups. More basic change has occurred in the field of automotive paint in the past ten years than in the past 50 years. And these changes are likely to stick because the environmental concerns will not go away. waterborne paints, base coat/clear coat systems, urethane top coats and plastic media blasting were exotic technologies ten years ago, but they will become the standard by the twenty-first century. Before getting into the very basics of paint technology, one more distinction needs to be made, and it is particularly of interest to owners of collector cars.

OEM vs. Aftermarket Paints—The composition of the paints that the factory uses are so chemically different from the paint which you or your body shop buys that paint manufacturers usually have two separate automotive divisions: the OEM (original equipment manufacturer), or OE for short, and the refinish (aftermarket) divisions. The types of automotive paint discussed here are the aftermarket kind which are used

Enthusiasts restoring cars of the early sixties can still repaint with acrylic lacquer, but lacquer today is not the lacquer of yesterday. Back then, auto paints were mostly low solids mixtures and had chromates, lead and other hard chemicals. Such chemicals are not used now for environmental reasons, but they did help produce durable paints in that era. Photo courtesy Musclecar Review

Paint is composed of the binder, the pigment (color), solvents and additives.

for repairing and repainting (refinishing) cars and trucks. The OEM paints are the ones the paint manufacturer supplies directly to the automaker, and you wouldn't want them, unless you wanted to disassemble your car and cure the paint in your oven like the factory does.

TYPES OF AUTOMOTIVE PAINT

Today's automotive paints are often grouped into two broad categories: lacquers and enamels. Lacquers were the first paints sprayed on cars, beginning in 1924. Several years later, enamels were also introduced in a form which could be sprayed on cars and trucks. Lacquer and enamels differ in their consistency and application. Enamels are thicker than lacquers when mixed for spraying and are applied with thicker but fewer coats. Enamels cure when they dry, by evaporation to some extent, but they also harden by the cross-linking of

their molecules. Lacquers dry primarily by evaporation, and therefore remain more susceptible to damage by solvents.

Lacquer Paints

Lacquer paint became more popular in the fifties, when a tougher acrylic lacquer made it more durable for automotive use. General Motors used acrylic lacquer for their more glamorous models and colors. Lacquer's image as the premium paint is still a common public perception, largely due to its use on custom cars with exotic paint jobs featured in auto shows and enthusiast magazines.

However, lacquer's glory days are over due to environmental concerns and the superior performance of the new two-part enamels. California, Texas and New Jersey have already passed laws which may, in effect, ban lacquers because as much as 85% of the thinned paint mixture in the spray gun goes into the atmosphere as the car is sprayed and as the paint dries.

Jon Kosmoski, the owner of House of Kolor, a premium custom paint manufacturer, reported that by the early nineties, less than 30% of his paint sales were lacquer-based. However, it is still available, and there are advantages and disadvantages to its use.

Advantages—Lacquer is the easiest paint to spray, and that's one reason why it is the choice of many beginning painters and hobbyists. Lacquer also dries quickly, which decreases the problem of dirt and bugs in a paint job. Such contamination happens even in the best paint booth, and it is much more of a problem for cars sprayed without a booth, such as in the home garage. If something falls, flies or walks into the car during painting, the intruder can be easily brushed off or lightly sanded out because lacquer dries so quickly.

Lacquer can be applied in thinner, drier coats which helps avoid the problem of massive drips or sags. A novice painter has to be very careful with the variation in the wetness of the paint because it will affect how metallics settle out and can easily make the paint look blotchy.

Lacquer facilitates some of the more advanced painting techniques and therefore lends itself to certain types of custom painting.

Lacquer is sometimes used for custom paint jobs because it is easy to work with, dries fast, and can be buffed to a high shine. However, it is not always durable. This fiberglass bodied Avanti was painted with acrylic lacquer, and although it is always garaged and seldom driven, the paint is beginning to crack.

is poured into the gun does not end up on the car.

Another disadvantage is that lacquer dulls down when it dries. That means you should wait at least several days before wet-sanding and buffing a lacquer paint job, however, this doesn't always happen in high-volume collision repair shops. As lacquer continues to dry, over a period of weeks, it will continue to sink and lose its gloss as the solvent evaporates. For the best custom paint jobs, professionals recommend that you wait as long as two months before buffing a new lacquer paint job to ensure nearly all solvent has evaporated.

*Equipment & Application—*Lacquer is one of the easiest paints for a hobbyist or backyard painter to apply. The lacquer dries so quickly that the overspray seldom sticks to other objects in the room. It's like

Another reason some people choose lacquer is that it was the original paint on many cars produced from the mid-twenties into the seventies, and in particular the popular GM cars of the fifties and sixties. When people restore these cars, they often choose lacquer so that the car will have the original type of paint. Actually, the lacquer they're buying today is not chemically identical to the stuff the factory applied. One final reason why many painters prefer lacquer is because it makes some spot repairs and blending easier.

*Disadvantages—*Lacquer can be a fragile paint. Even after months of drying in the sun, if a bird gets a direct hit on your car, you'll have problems. Not only bird droppings, but hard water, gasoline spills, acid rain and just about anything else will actually eat down into the paint. This may not be a problem for a show car or collector car which is usually kept garaged and covered, however, lacquer is a relatively delicate finish for cars which are driven daily.

Lacquer is already outlawed in several states, and may be outlawed in other states in the near future. The reason: more of lacquer paint goes into the atmosphere than any other type of paint. Most of the paint which

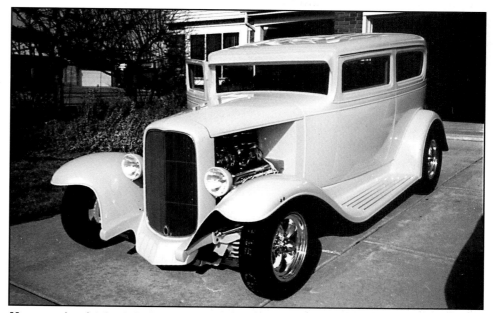

Many people mistakenly believe that lacquer which is applied in many layers and hand-rubbed provides the ultimate paint job. This may have been true at one time, but in reality, a multi-layered lacquer paint job, such as on the order of 36 coats, wouldn't last six months in the sun. Today's specialty custom painters seldom spray more than a few coats of lacquer, if they use it at all. Most have switched to two-part enamels. For example, the intense yellow which Brian Dotterer sprayed on his 1931 Chevy Tudor was a quick-setting urethane clear coat/base coat system.

People bent on restoring a car to "original, factory condition," will attempt to match the exact paint type and color originally sprayed by the factory. But paints applied at the factory, in the past as well as present, are chemically different than those available to body shops or restorers. Most factory paints are thermoset to cure in extremely hot ovens, so it is virtually impossible to reapply "original" paint to a restored car. Photo by Michael Lutfy

A new generation of paint, the two-part urethane, was introduced with DuPont's Imron brand in the early seventies. This pick-up truck was repainted with Imron in the mid-seventies and spent the next 15 years sitting outside, seldom washed, never waxed. The paint is still in good condition, because of the durability of two-part urethanes. The Studebaker is part of the working collection at Yankee Auto-Truck in E.Hartford, Connecticut which specializes in rust-roofing and preserving vehicles.

colored dust and can be easily wiped off most surfaces.

Air filtration for the painter is also a little less critical, at least compared to painting with the enamels, some of which are catalyzed with chemicals you definitely don't want to breathe. Many painters use only a throwaway particle mask when spraying lacquer, although a mask with a charcoal filter is strongly recommended.

Proper ventilation of the spray room or booth is recommended for any type of paint. Ventilation is, foremost, an important health concern. It also greatly affects the quality of the paint job because you can't see adequately what you're doing when the air is thick with paint. If you use fans, make sure they have fire-safe motors that don't emit sparks.

Enamels

In comparison to lacquers, enamels evaporate a much smaller portion of their chemistry into the atmosphere. They cure and chemically change from the liquid state in which they are sprayed to a hard solid film of paint. The newest enamels and spray systems are aiming for paints that will have less than 35% of their weight comprised of solvents which evaporate into the atmosphere.

Advantages—Regular one-part enamels are among the least expensive paints to apply. The labor of the paint job also costs less than lacquer painting because enamels don't require the labor costs for hours of wet-sanding and buffing after painting. Enamels dry glossy.

The durability of good one-part enamels, particularly alkyd enamels, is usually not as good as two-part enamels but they hold up better than most lacquers when subjected to the

Top coats need to stand up to harsh environmental conditions. Two-part enamels such as this clear by PPG are among the most durable automotive paints today. In addition, this new clear is low VOC and can be polished after only 15-20 minutes of forced drying at 140F. Photo courtesy PPG.

No, the photo is not out of focus. The distortion you see is "orange peel," found in the finish of virtually all new cars, regardless of the price. It can be caused by a variety of factors, such as very high solids paints, improper gun adjustment and techniques, drying or "flash" time, mixture of ingredients and wrong thinner or reducer. Orange peel is so common on new cars today, that the absence of it on a car just from the factory suggests it has been repainted. Judges may take points off a restored car if its finish is too perfect.

same conditions. Acrylic enamels, particularly when used with hardeners, can be quite durable under many conditions.

Alkyd enamels are often called synthetic enamels, because they were the first enamels to be made with a resin which was modified by synthesizing with petroleum products. The label "synthetic" has stuck, although it isn't really appropriate today because all modern paint resins are synthesized.

Disadvantages—Some bargain-priced enamels don't last long. Some really poor quality enamels have problems after just a few months in the sun. Also enamels are generally more difficult to apply than lacquers.

Equipment & Application—The spraying of enamel requires a little more practice because enamel is sprayed on wetter than lacquer. Also, shortly after it is sprayed on the car,

the enamel "flows out," which reduces surface texture problems like orange peel and increases the shine. However, when enamel flows out improperly it can run or sag. The painter has to anticipate what it will do after it is sprayed on—it's a fine line between ending up glossy or ending up runny.

A charcoal filter mask is recommended during spraying. Also look around the room and cover everything which you don't want to receive a color change. Enamel overspray is difficult to remove. Extremely thorough masking is particularly important to restorers because enamel overspray is often so hard to remove it can ruin irreplaceable parts or finishes. As always, ventilate the area and use a fresh air system if the enamel is catalyzed.

Two-Part Enamels

Although technically an enamel, two-part enamels have enough special qualities to warrant their own

category. Their best quality is that they are extremely durable. DuPont's IMRON brand polyurethane enamel, introduced in 1970, is one of the most well known of these extraordinarily tough new enamels. These are also called two-pack enamels or two-component enamels because they require the addition of a second component, an activator or hardener. Without the hardener, they won't dry, but with it they quickly undergo a chemical change. They'll even solidify inside the paint gun before they are sprayed if the painter waits too long.

Advantages—In addition to the fast set-up times, they also have strong advantages in durability. Many custom shops which used to paint exclusively with lacquer have switched to the new two-part enamels because of their ability to resist cracking and because they retain their gloss longer. Some are so tough that strong paint solvents can be poured on them with little effect. One proof of their superiority is that paint

Today's new metallic paints have reached an incredible degree of richness and intensity. In the past, the fine flakes were aluminum but now this is often achieved by mica particles, some of which can produce a shift in color depending on the viewing angle.

Many enamel paints today are two-part paints, and they require the addition of a special catalyst for hardening. These paints are also more dangerous to breathe, so a charcoal filtered mask or fresh air hood system is mandatory. Photo courtesy BASF

manufacturers only give written warranties to car owners on two-part enamels.

Another advantage is the speed of drying. This reduces the time the car is susceptible to dust contamination while it's wet. This also allows cars to be removed from the paint booth sooner.

Two-part enamels can be buffed very soon after painting. Many are buffed the next day. In fact, it may be a lot harder to buff them if you wait much longer than 24 hours. Unlike lacquers, two-part enamels will retain their gloss for years, even without waxing.

Disadvantages—The first two-part enamels were difficult to touch up or respray. If a problem occurred during painting, a car might have to wait days to be resprayed. Some paints couldn't be resprayed until they dried for months. However, today's two-part enamels have largely solved these

problems. Check the information sheets of the individual paint to see the recommendations for recoating.

The main drawback is price. Two-part enamels are costly. Just the cost of the basic materials, including the paint, primer, reducers, catalysts and special additives can run over $500 for some cars.

Equipment & Application—Two-part paints have become much easier to use, but their application requires special breathing apparatus for the painter. At the very least, experienced painters will use a face mask with new charcoal elements. However, a fresh air system (a pump delivering fresh air to the painter's hood by means of a hose) is strongly recommended, particularly when spraying paints which contain isocyanates, one of a number of toxic chemicals a painter will encounter. Always make sure the spray area is properly ventilated with fire-safe

exhaust fans for your health and to improve vision.

COMPONENTS OF AUTOMOTIVE PAINT

Binders, solvents, additives and pigments are the four major components of automotive paint. Lacquers, enamels and two-part enamels represent the major types of the binder, the main ingredient composing the paint. Lacquers can be nitrocellulose or acrylic (plastic) based. One-part enamels are alkyd or acrylic, and two-part enamels can be epoxy or polyurethane or acrylic urethane, among others. The binder is made of a resin (melamine is common in OEM paints), a drying oil (such as linseed oil in house paints) or a plastic (polyurethane or polyvinyl chloride, for example).

Even though the binder is the major component, you don't really see it. Even the best painters can't tell which kind of paint it is by looking at it, at least not on a high quality paint job!

MILESTONES IN AUTOMOTIVE PAINTING

1924: First spray painting of cars began with nitrocellulose lacquer.

1926: Nitrocellulose lacquer became used on all GM cars.

1929: Alkyd enamel introduced. It provided a tough finish, and no compounding was needed.

1920's & 1930's: Chrysler and Ford used either enamels or lacquers on their cars at various times during these two decades.

1940's: Chrysler and Ford changed over exclusively to enamels.

1948: Reynolds introduced a coarse non-leafing aluminum flake.

Mid-50's: Reynolds, Alcoa and others introduced better non-leafing aluminum flakes. This, along with improvements in re-sins, began an era of beautiful metallic automotive finishes.

1956: Acrylic lacquer was introduced. It improved finish and durability.

1957-1960: GM changed from nitrocellulose lacquer to acrylic lacquer.

1960's: Auto paints were mostly low solids mixtures and had chromates, lead, and other hard chemicals. Such chemicals are not used now but they did help produce durable paints in that era.

Late 60's: Governmental regulations on atmospheric emissions began to force changes at auto manufacturers. GM switched from solution lacquers to dispersion lacquer system which used high solids paints. Ford and Chrysler switched to acrylic enamels.

1970: Aftermarket polyurethane enamel introduced. These were extremely durable and had a high gloss. DuPont's Imron was one of the first well known polyurethane brand names.

1970's: First waterborne enamel introduced by Inmont (before becoming part of BASF). It was the first automotive coating to use water instead of solvent to get paint from gun to the surface.

Late '70's: High solids acrylic enamel became the first choice of paint by the auto manufacturers.

1980: Clear coat/base coat on US car on Lincoln Versailles with metallic colors.

1982: First clear coat/base coat factory paint jobs as standard equipment on the Corvette.

1982: Some of the first factory mica-based pearlescent colors appeared on Corvettes.

1987: Factory tri-coat pearl paints appeared on Cadillac Allante.

1987: Water-borne primers introduced on new cars at GM's European plants.

1989: Water-borne base coat paints used by GM and Ford at various plants.

1989: First written repaint warranties for consumers offered by major paint manufacturers.

1990: Strict auto repainting laws go into effect in California.

1992: Stringent air pollution laws regulating spraying of automotive paints take effect in the Los Angeles district.

1993: Chrysler applies the industry's first full-body anti-chip primer to LH model lines and uses it on others.

1994-1996: Manufacturers introduce lifetime paint warranties to consumers when their best products are applied by certified shops.

1996: GM extensively tests refinish paint system performance and requires that only GM4901 approved paints be used by dealerships for warranty work.

1997: Ford evaluates refinish paints according to the same rigorous tests used for OEM paints and displays some of the differences in performance at the NACE trade show.

1997: Chrysler applies the industry's first full-body anti-chip primers to a number of model lines.

You don't see the next two components, the solvents or the additives, either. The solvents are used to make the paint thinner (more watery) so that it can be sprayed more easily.

The solvents used to thin lacquer are called thinners, and the solvents used to reduce the viscosity or thickness of enamels are called reducers.

Additives, if used at all, comprise only a small portion of the paint and are added to promote special properties such as faster curing or greater gloss.

1981 Corvettes with metallic colors were among the first American cars to come standard with clear-coat paint jobs. By the 1982 model year, all Corvettes, regardless of the top coat finish, came from the factory with clear-coat paint. Now all GM cars and light trucks made in North America have clear coat.

Pigments

The component of paint that is seen by everyone is the pigment or color. Not only is it the most visible component of paint, it is sometimes the most expensive, accounting for 20% to 80% of the cost of automotive paints. One particular purple is the most costly pigment now but, in general, reds are among the most expensive. I recently paid about $40 for just a pint of a red metallic base coat. A number of yellows are in the very pricey category also. The least expensive pigments are the whites and silvers. Pigments can be separated into three main categories in terms of their appearance: solids, metallics and tri-coats.

Solids—Of these three, the solid colors were the first colors used on cars, and they are still common today. Solid colors have no metallic or pearl particles added to the pigment to change the appearance of the color when it is viewed from different angles. Solid colors look the same when viewed up close or from any angle. The most popular basic colors, like white, red, black and yellow, are usually solids. Solid colors can also come in any shade.

Metallics—These colors differ from solids because they contain very fine glittering metallic or mica particles which can easily be seen upon close examination of the paint. The metallic particles make the paint sparkle and look somewhat grainy. Metallics became popular in the sixties and are very popular today.

Metallics are a little more difficult for an inexperienced painter to apply properly because the metal particles can lay down at different angles and thereby reflect light differently. Also, if the paint is applied too thickly and too wet, the metallic particles can settle out or fall, causing non-uniform patterns, often described by paint professionals as a blotchy appearance.

Spot repainting and respraying small areas can also be a little trickier, because in addition to matching the tint or color, the quantity and appearance of the metallic content has to match. Although metallic paints come premixed with the particles in solution, just the way a painter sprays them on can change the effect.

Metal-flake paints are like metallic paints on steroids: the size of the metal-flakes are much larger, and often different colors of flakes are mixed together. Metal-flake paints are primarily used for custom paint jobs. Metal-flake paints require coverage with a clear coat because the particles are so big they can actually stick out from the surface.

Tri-Coats—Sometimes called pearls, these pigments were once only seen on custom paint jobs, but they are becoming more popular on factory cars. True pearl paint jobs are called tri-coats because their finish has three separate layers: a color coat, a pearl coat and a clear coat. The pearl coat is a transparent paint with fine mica chips mixed in. Cadillac's Allante was one of the first production cars to offer a pearl tri-coat.

Pearl paints show subtle highlights of different colors when viewed at certain angles. For example, a white car with a blue pearl tri-coat will show a hint of gold along its curves or top body panels when viewed from one direction. Also, if you look closely, you'll see a very fine grain pattern in pearl paints, finer than most metallics.

Pearls require even more experience to apply properly and to blend than metallic paints. For spot repainting, first a proper color match must be obtained. Then a let-down (test) panel needs to be prepared to see how many coats of the pearl paint are needed to match the surrounding paint.

Pearlescent—Some manufacturers blend mica into their color coat

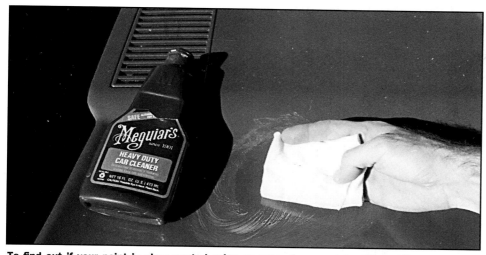

To find out if your paint is clear coated, wipe an area of your paint with a white rag and car cleaner or wax. If color comes off on the rag, the car is not clear coated. Tip: Use a dark rag to test white paint.

instead of having a separate pearl coat over the color coat. Chrysler vehicles, for example, have a number of colors which are called "pearl," but they do not have a separate pearl coat. The effect of the pearlescent color is not as pronounced as a tri-coat but, on the other hand, it isn't as expensive or as hard to repair.

The first three mica-based pearlescent colors were introduced on the 1982 Corvette, and they have grown tremendously in popularity. The color changing effects of pearlescent colors and true pearl tri-coats is enhanced on darker colors. The combination of a black dye and a red oxide coated mica flake became the best-selling color, Black Cherry. It debuted on the 1984 Cadillac and was then offered on the Buick and Oldsmobile lines the next year. By the beginning of the nineties there were over 200 mica-metallic pearlescent colors in automotive use. In fact, over half the metallic colors now employ mica flakes.

If you're repainting your car and are faced with having to choose a new color or "pigment," then there are some general guidelines you may wish to consider.

CLEAR COATS

Automotive paint jobs today also differ in whether they have a transparent (clear) coat of paint applied for protection over the color (base) coats. Like pearl paint jobs, this is another type of "glamour" paint job which has made its way from the custom paint shop to the factory production line.

One of the first popular production cars with clear coat was the Sun Bug—the Volkswagen Beetle which had this extra cost paint option. One of the first American production cars which had base coat/clear coat as standard was the 1981 Corvette, starting first with the metallic colors. By 1982, all Corvettes were painted with a base coat/clear coat system. And by 1996, all U.S. made GM cars and light trucks were painted with base coat/clear coat systems.

Clear Coat Benefits

Most painters feel that applying a clear coat over the color gives the car a wetter look, and makes the paint look "deeper." This was the original reason for its use, but now there are also several functional reasons why clear coat is used almost exclusively.

Protection—A clear coat adds an extra degree of protection from the sun. The ultraviolet rays can fade and destroy the pigments in automotive paint, just like these rays can damage your skin. In fact, sunscreens, transparent chemicals which absorb ultraviolet light, are added to all high quality clear coats to protect the paint, just like similar sunscreens can block the sun's burning rays from your skin.

Repair—Clear coat has another advantage: shallow surface defects

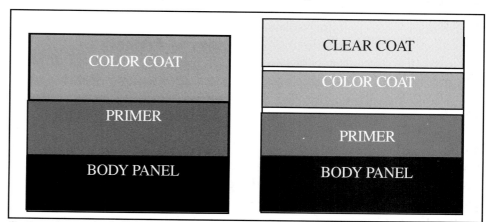

Contrary to popular belief, clear-coated cars do not necessarily have more paint. Even though clear coat adds an additional layer, the total paint thickness is about the same because the color coat applied on clear-coated cars is much thinner. In addition to giving a "wetter" look, the clear-coat layer filters the sun's ultraviolet rays to protect the color from fading.

Primer is a dull-appearing paint applied before the final glossy top coats of paint. It helps to smooth the body panel's surface and also helps adhesion of the final top coat.

can often be sanded and buffed out (called finessing) without changing the appearance of the paint. Defects such as spotting from acid rain or harsh water can be removed. If there is no clear coat, removal of surface defects is riskier, especially with metallic paints, because the appearance of the paint can change as you sand down into the layers of color.

Environmental—Another reason for clear coats is environmental. Although paint manufacturers haven't yet come up with a tough top coat which doesn't use polluting solvents, they have produced excellent color coats which are waterborne. However, these paints must currently have a clear coat for protection. But by separating the top coat into a color coat and a clear coat, they can reduce using solvents in at least part of the painting process.

PRIMERS

All automotive paints, be they lacquer or enamel, solid or metallic, with or without clear coat, have one thing in common: primer. Primer is a dull-looking paint which is applied to the bare body of the car.

Primer is necessary because the paint which you see as the top coat doesn't stick well to bare metal. The top coat has to be formulated to be hard, hold a shine and stand up to the sun and rain. Plus, it is full of pigments (colors) to make it look good. Fortunately, the top coats do stick well to their ugly brother, the primer, which is formulated to firmly adhere to the car body.

Types of Primers

There are a number of different types of primers. Some special primers are called *etching primers* because they chemically etch into the metal to provide an exceptionally strong bond. At the factory, it is now common practice to dip bare steel parts into tanks and use an electric current to help deposit the primer into every crevice and fold of the metal. These are electrocoated or electro-deposited primers, often called E-coats.

Another type of primer is formulated to make a thick layer to cover surface flaws. Body panels of cars and trucks always have small surface irregularities such as scratches, or high and low points. Primer can be used to fill in shallow imperfections and "build up" a surface to be sanded off level and smooth. Although this could be done with other types of paint, primers are easier to work with and easier to sand. Sometimes specialized primers called high-build or sanding primers are used for this step.

Undercoating—To the painter, the primers and sealers (described in more detail in Chapter 2) are called undercoats, which is not to be confused with undercoating. Undercoating is a thick black or brownish sticky material which is sprayed on the underside of the car and into auto body cavities, such as the inside of doors, to protect the metal from corrosion.

However, both undercoats and undercoating are designed to stick well to the body panels and become a layer of corrosion protection, but good undercoating never completely hardens. By staying somewhat sticky, undercoating resists chipping and peeling. You wouldn't have much luck painting over it!

Now that you've become familiar with the basic types of paint and their related components, let's go to the next chapter and get "deeper" into paint technology.

This 1923 photo shows Charles Jeffrey, an instructor at Master Motor Coach Refinishing of Detroit, using the latest technology in automotive refinishing—paint brushes. Cars were sanded with gasoline between brush-painted coats and then finally polished with emery cloth. The slow drying of the cottonseed or linseed oil-based paints meant cars took about a week to paint, and the final paint job was lucky to last one year out in the sun. But in 1924, all that changed with a breakthrough in auto refinishing—the spray painting of nitrocellulose lacquers. Photo courtesy John Jeffrey of PPG.

Chapter 1 gave a brief overview of the categories of paint and their primary components and also introduced some of the various top coats and undercoats widely used today. In this chapter, I'll be discussing the current technology employed by the automotive manufacturer, followed by a detailed discussion of top coats, base coats, undercoats, and waterborne paints.

FACTORY PAINTS AND PAINTING

The paint sprayed on your car at the factory is different than the paints you or your body shop can buy. Likewise, the paint a new car dealership uses to fix up the common bumps and scrapes that occur to a new car during shipment is different in composition than the factory paint it is covering. In fact, even the paint the factory applies off the assembly line, when repair work and touch-up needs to be done at the factory, is different than that which was sprayed in the assembly line spray booth.

Factory paints are different, partly due to the requirements of mass production. Although a neighborhood body shop can wait an hour or two for paint to dry before moving a car out of its paint booth, a factory which needs to make 1000 cars a day cannot. It would need over 100 paint booths and sprayers operating on two shifts. The costs to the car manufacturer to prepare buildings and buy equipment and air purification systems on that scale would be prohibitive. As it is now, the cost of the painting facility at a major car manufacturer can be $400 million. It is one of the most expensive phases of car manufacturing today.

By the nineties, the vast majority of cars were painted at the factory by robots. Both the method of application and the composition of automotive paint has changed radically. Photo courtesy Chevrolet.

How the Factory Cures Paint

The solution for the factory is to speed up the curing time of the paint. Most chemical processes speed up at higher temperatures, and the curing of auto paint is not an exception. Increasing the temperature of the paint after it is sprayed onto the car is accomplished by running the car (bodies) through an oven. Drying times can be cut down to under 30 minutes.

You might think the factory "baking" of paint is the same as done by paint shops which have heated booths or infrared lights to bake enamel. Yet it is literally different in degrees, because the factory can use much higher temperatures to cure or "kick" the chemical reaction in the paint. On the assembly line, the body and its components are painted before the glass, rubber weatherstripping, wiring, electronics, interior, and other plastic parts are installed.

This permits use of high temperatures, from 250 to 450 degrees Fahrenheit, which would damage many car parts. Another reason the body parts are painted before assembly is that it is much faster and easier to paint hard-to-reach areas such as seams and door jams. Also, it eliminates the need for hours of masking, to prevent unwanted paint overspray on parts.

Factory Paint

How are factory paints different than the paints your body shop applies? For one thing, factory paints are thermoset enamels whose molecules cross-link at higher temperatures. Factory-applied top coats contain resins such as melamine for toughness and these require temperatures over 250 degrees Fahrenheit to cure. However, does this make the original factory paints more durable? Paint experts say the best urethane aftermarket paints are nearly as durable as the factory applied paints in most respects, with the notable exception of chip resistance.

Paint Repairs—Repainting and touch-up is often necessary at factories. After the parts are painted, the cars still have most of their assembly to be completed. During assembly, scrapes, dings, and dents can occur. Also flaws in the paint, such as poor coverage, might not be noticed until the car has moved farther down the assembly line. If a paint defect is noticed after assembly has started, the car is tagged and it will receive paint repairs after its assembly is completed.

Because the interior, glass, rubber, and plastic parts are now assembled into the car, the repainting can't undergo the high heat used for curing the original thermoset paint. Therefore, the paint used for repairs must be somewhat different than the original paint. In most cases, the factory tries to make the paint as chemically identical as possible. With some paints, a catalyst is added to enable the "repair" paint to cure faster at lower temperatures. Some of these "doctored" factory paints are then heat-cured with an infrared light at about 180 degrees Fahrenheit.

Dealership Repairs—Repairs done at the dealership are a different story. They are limited to use of conventional aftermarket paints which are even more different in chemistry than the original factory paint and some factory-applied "repair" paints. The paints available to dealerships are no different than those available to you or your body shop.

TOP COATS

Now, let's take an in-depth look at some of the current top coats in use today, both at the factory and, in some cases, at your local body shop.

FACTORY PAINT METHODS

Galvanizing: The use of thinner sheet metal and the use of unibody construction have increased the need to protect body sheet metal from rusting. Galvanized steel parts have been plated with a thin layer of zinc. The zinc is chemically more active than the steel, and when corrosive elements are around, they tend to feed upon the zinc first. The zinc is in effect a sacrificial barrier to prevent rusting of the underlying steel part. The same principle is commonly used on outboard motor drives on boats; a piece of zinc is bolted to the metal case of the drive so that the zinc will corrode instead of the more expensive boat parts.

Pretreatment: This involves as many as eight stages including such steps as degreasing, rinsing, air or temperature drying, phosphate treatment, and again rinsing and drying. The cleaning and phosphate treatment are used to help the primer bond to the metal.

E-Coat: This is the electrocoating of primer, which involves dipping the metal parts in a tank and passing an electric current through the part and the liquid paint solution. The electrocoating method not only enables the primer to get into places a spray gun wouldn't reach, it also helps the primer bond to the metal and helps produce a uniform thickness for the coating. After E-coat, the parts are typically cured at a temperature of about 350 degrees, although some plants use oven temperatures as high as 450 degrees. Some new epoxy-based urethanes can cure at around 300 degrees. Traditional E-coats are about 1.2 mils thick, but new formulations may allow that to be reduced to a .7 to .8 mil thickness. The E-coat is usually called ELPO (for electrophoretic) on General Motors cars.

Anti-Chip Coatings: These are sometimes applied to lower body panel areas and the underneath of the body. The anti-chip coatings can be powders which are applied after the E-coat has been preheated to drive out its moisture, but before the E-coat is baked. The Chrysler truck plant uses high-intensity infrared heaters to increase the temperature of the lower panels to about 260 degrees for a few minutes to dry the E-coat. The powder coating is sprayed on to a thickness of 10 mils at the bottom and tapers off to about 3 mils before being blended into the E-coat. The powder coating allows such a thick film to be applied; on vertical panels, waterborne or solvent-borne paints would run before a thickness of 10 mils could be reached. Some cars, the BMW 3251 being one example, also receive a flexible PVC coating on the door sills and the underbody. By the '90's, Chrysler had began use of full-body anti-chip primers on a number of models.

Primer-Surfacers: These are a second stage of primer applied on top of the E-coat primer. Although this step has not always been used in the past, the trend seems to be that it is becoming more widely used. Primer-surfacers are used by refinishers to fill and smooth out surface irregularities, but they also they help make the paint resistant to stone chips and they help promote adhesion of the top coat to the E-coat. Poor adhesion of the top coat to the E-coat is blamed for the delamination (peeling) of hundreds of thousands of new cars in the early nineties. Primer surfacers may be either solvent-borne or waterborne. General Motors began using waterborne primer-surfacers in the late eighties in their European plants and later converted all of these plants to waterborne primer surfacers.

Base Coats: Factories are frequently using waterborne base coats today. The base coat is the color coat, and like, the primer-surface, it is sprayed on. Most automotive plants use pre-programmed robotic arms for spraying applications. A waterborne base coat is usually applied to a thickness from .5 to 1.2 mils. Some colors must be applied thicker for good coverage. Solvent-borne base coats are applied to a slightly greater thickness than waterborne base coats. Infrared heat is then used to increase the temperature of the waterborne base coats to about 160 degrees Fahrenheit to get rid of most of the water. The clear coat is applied while the base coat is still somewhat wet and both are baked at the same time.

Clear Coats: These are currently still solvent-borne but much research is being carried out to develop a waterborne clear coat which is sufficiently durable and can be used in automotive applications. The Harley-Davidson motorcycle painting facility initially used powder coatings for many of their clear coats, and in Europe, BMW began use of non-solvent-borne clear coat at one plant in 1997. Automotive clear coats are applied to a thickness of about 2 mils and then baked.

GM was the first major manufacturer to apply waterborne paints on the assembly line in the late seventies on Camaros and Firebirds built in California. However, GM discontinued use of these early waterborne paints because of problems such as difficulties with repainting in body shops.

Waterborne Paints

Waterborne paints should have the accent placed on the word "borne." They are not water paints like you used as a kid, or like the watercolor paints an artist uses. Waterborne paints don't dissolve in water, and if you remember carrying your prized kindergarten painting home in the rain, you'll understand why that is desirable.

Water is simply used as a liquid medium to help transfer the paint from the can onto the car. In this task, it performs the same function that thinner does for lacquer and what reducer does for enamel. Yet water has one important advantage: it doesn't pollute the atmosphere. You might think cost is a second advantage. Although there's no doubt that water costs less than thinners or reducers, the costs of modifying auto paints to be compatible with water outweigh those savings at the present time.

The first automotive uses of waterborne paints at the factory were in the eighties on Camaros and Firebirds. After a few years this was discontinued because of a number of problems including difficulties encountered by body shops with repainting.

Waterborne paint technology made a strong comeback at the OEM level in 1989 at both a Ford and a GM plant. And in 1990, waterborne base coats were used exclusively at the Saturn plants. Pollution considerations were again the major factor for giving waterborne paints another chance. GM's Saturn division and the paint manufacturer BASF worked together to make automotive applications of waterborne paints a success on these cars.

High Solids Paint

High solids paints are basically paints with a higher content of the materials that solidify after spraying, such as resins and pigments, and less of the liquid thinners or reducers which evaporate. A high solids color coat has a proportionately large percentage of the pigments so that it will take application of fewer coats to get good coverage.

The main reason for increasing the solid content in automotive paints was to reduce the amount of air pollution during spray application. However, high solids can be a benefit in ways other than reducing air pollution. High solids base (color) coats, as mentioned above, can cover in fewer coats and with less material thickness. Chemists

By 1990 GM was using waterborne paints extensively again, this time for the base coats on all Saturn cars. However, a solvent-borne clear coat is applied over the waterborne base coat for durability. For details on Saturn's procedure, see the sidebar on p. 15.

have said that the flow and setting properties of high solids base coats can help metallic particles self-orient or align with one another to produce a brighter look when viewed head on.

The term high solids has been a buzz word in the paint industry for over a decade, however, there has been no exact definition of what high solids means. The most commonly accepted definitions are that high solids finishes average 50% or greater levels of pigment, medium solids are in the neighborhood of 40% pigment, and low solids refer to around 30% or less. For more technical details on the development of waterborne paints, see Chapter 3, page 24.

Pearl Tri-Coats

As discussed in Chapter 1, automotive paints using pearls can be separated into two categories. In most cases today, pearl effects are found in factory paint jobs when mica particles are blended into a color. Such paints will be referred to as pearlescent colors throughout this book. In the past, pearl paint jobs have been produced by applying a separate translucent pearl layer over the color coat. These are referred to as true pearl paint jobs or pearl tri-coats.

Pearl tri-coats have made their way from custom car shows to the showrooms of new car dealerships. The first U.S. car with factory pearl paint was the Cadillac Allante in 1987. The Japanese were quick to follow in the introduction of pearl tri-coats. By 1991, Mitsubishi had pearl paints available on their twin-turbo 3000 GT VR4 sports car and the Galant performance sedans.

Pearl paints have very fine grain mica particles which separate light into complementary colors. Many of

The Saturn Method
by Bob Hiser, Body Service Engineer, Saturn Corporation

GM's Saturn subsidiary took advantage of their "start from scratch" opportunity to employ new painting techniques and technologies. Developing an all new manufacturing plant in Spring Hill, Tennessee and all new "stand alone" national retail dealer network has introduced some real opportunities for breakthroughs in the way their vehicles are painted at their plant and repaired in their dealerships.

All of the latest technology has been used in developing the Spring Hill painting facilities. Space-frame assemblies are submerged in several phosphate wash tanks before being submerged into an ELPO primer (short for Electrophoretic Deposition of Polymers) which is electostatically applied to the space frame while the space frame is submerged. A low gloss black paint is then applied to the areas of the space frame that will be exposed to sunlight (door frame areas, specifically).

Exterior panels are primed and painted off of the car on a panel "buck" which supports and separates the parts, allowing for easier and better coverage during painting. The vertical plastic panels are mounted to support castings which allows them to keep their exact shape during the baking process. The panel set is first primed and baked followed by application of the waterborne base coat color, which is used for all colors on the Saturn cars. After color is applied, the a two-component urethane type clear coat paint is applied to the base coat color that cures during the next baking cycle. This clear coat represents the majority of the paint film thickness and affords the paint its luster and durability. These panel set are then stored in giant racks until production schedules call for them.

As the ELPO primed space frame is assembled in the General Assembly section of the Spring Hill facility, the panels are assembled to the car at different locations. The roof panel is first to be attached to the space frame by a urethane adhesive and bolts. The remaining panels are some of the last components to be assembled in final assembly. These are but a few of the many high tech methods that are employed at the Saturn plant to achieve a high tech paint job.

the earliest pearl paints actually had additives ground from sea shells or fish scales, but today they contain mica.

Light entering the pearl layer is either reflected back by one of the surfaces of a mica flake or it goes through the mica particles before being reflected. Pearl paints alter the reflected light so that different colors or hues show up when the paint is viewed at certain angles.

Mitsubishi was one of the first foreign car manufacturers to offer tri-coat pearl paint on models such as this white 3000 GT VR4.

The effect pearl paint creates depends on the viewing angle. This motorcycle cover plate appears to be completely black on some areas, but when viewed from another angle, patterns emerge that were painted in pearl.

Today's factory-applied pearl paint jobs are also called tri-coats because three layers of top coat paint are used. The first of the top coats to be applied is the color (or base) coat. Because light must pass through the mica and be reflected back out, pearls can't be mixed in with an opaque paint and still produce the full effect, although they can be applied on top of an opaque paint, even on top of black. The second coat is a clear paint with the pearl particles or flakes in it. The third coat is the clear coat. Pearl paints are, after all, a glamour finish and the owners want the deepest, wettest look possible.

Pearls alter the appearance of the underlying paint, however. They reflect light, so if more pearl is applied over a dark color, the lighter the color will look. This is similar to the effect of metallics in paints. If more metallic is on the surface, more light is reflected and the paint appears lighter in color.

Pearl tri-coats are beautiful and exotic. This comes at a price however. First, they are more expensive. Second, they are harder to make uniform in appearance. Third, they are much more difficult to repair and

blend. If you have a pearl tri-coat paint job that needs some spot repainting, make certain the painter has a lot of experience, or else his experience will be gained at your expense. To find a qualified shop, call your dealership and ask for the name of a painter who has experience matching pearls, or talk to owners of other cars that have pearl paint.

UNDERCOATS

All top coats, be they high solids, metallic or pearl tri-coats, all have at least one or more undercoats. The top coats are designed for appearance and durability. They have to excel in such cosmetic qualities as color retention (fade resistance), surface hardness, and the ability to retain gloss. They also need to protect, which calls for chip resistance and resistance to environmental chemicals such as acid rain, spilled gasoline, road salt, bird droppings, etc.

That's a lot to ask of one type of paint. Chemists haven't found any paints that have all the above properties plus the ability to adhere to the underlying body panels. That's where the undercoats or primers come

into play. Today there are many different types of primers, each formulated to excel at a specific application such as maximum adhesion to body panels, corrosion protection, or filling surface defects. To help make their differences more clear, we'll separate them into categories of prep coats (used to prepare a bare, unprotected surface) and intermediate coats (used between prep coats and the top coats).

Prep Coats

The primer must bond securely to the body panel or all the painting that follows is wasted. And body panels made from steel must be free from the most minute particles of surface rust. In the past, cleaning and chemical preparation of bare steel to promote paint adhesion was often accomplished by an acid etch. An acid was wiped or brushed on to the bare metal to etch into the smooth surface of the steel and give the primer something more to hold on to.

Metal Conditioners—These are used in some paint systems as the first

When body parts are welded, the area is composed of two or three different steels. This can accelerate the rusting process. The weld-through primers used in repairing are zinc-rich paints applied to the body parts where they will be welded. During welding, heat causes some of the zinc to melt into the area, which prevents rusting. Some of these primers should be sandblasted off prior to repainting, so be sure to check the paint manufacturer's instructions. Saturn frames receive over 4000 separate spot-welds during their trip down the assembly line. Courtesy Saturn Corp.

stage of preparation of bare steel parts. The metal conditioner is usually mixed with water and rubbed onto the steel parts with a rag. It is used to remove surface rust and etch the metal to aid adhesion of the following coats. While still wet, the metal conditioner should be wiped off with a clean dry cloth.

Conversion Coatings—These are often applied after metal conditioners. Conversion coatings chemically alter the surface (a color change occurs on the metal's surface after application of some conversion coatings) to promote corrosion resistance and also improve adhesion of the primer. Some conversion coatings are applied with a brush or abrasive pad and then left on the surface for a few minutes. After that, they are sponged or rinsed off and the surface is wiped dry. The mess of applying and rinsing the acid, and the potential problems caused by water and acid remaining in cracks and seams, have made other types of prep coats popular.

Self-Etching Primers—These primers are now available and they replace the need for metal conditioners and conversion coatings. Some of these self-etching primers offer far greater corrosion protection and adhesion than has ever been possible before. Self-etching primers "bite" into the surface of the steel and provide a strong bond to the metal. Some self-etching primers can be used over steel and aluminum.

Epoxy Primers—Another type of primer, waterproof epoxy primers, have become popular. Two-component epoxy primers cure chemically instead of by evaporation of solvents, so they tend to shrink less than other primers, such as lacquer-based primers. Less shrinkage means that areas filled with primers, such as feather-edges and sand scratches, are less likely to sink and become visible later. Waterproof primers also have the advantage of preventing the steel surface from rusting in cases where the top coats aren't applied for days or weeks after priming. This type of surface rust is difficult to see and can eventually result in blistering or bubbling of the paint. Other primers, such as lacquer primers, are somewhat porous and don't give the same degree of corrosion protection. This is particularly important when a car must be left outside after priming or during restoration that takes several months (or years!).

Weld-Through Primers—Nearly all of today's cars are of unibody construction, in which the body is composed of many thin pieces of metal spot-welded together. Saturn's space frame, for example, has over 4,000 separate spot welds. During repair, new sections have to be welded in place of the older collision-damaged or rust-damaged sections. The heat of the welding can burn off primers in areas which can't be reprimed.

These areas are particularly

PREPARATION AND UNDERCOAT PAINT MATERIALS

LOW VOC SURFACE CLEANERS

Akzo Nobel	Sikkens Autoclean Degreaser
BASF	909 Water Base Final Wipe
DuPont	3949S Kwick Clean
ICI Autocolor	Waterborne Pre-Cleaner, P980-251
PPG	Deltron DX393 Low VOC Cleaner
Martin-Senour	6388 Kleanz Easy II
Sherwin-Williams	Aqua-mate W4K157
Spies Hecker	Permahyd Silcone Remover 7090
Standox	Standohyd Low VOC Remover

PRETREATMENTS
Self-Etching Primers & Metal Conditioners

Akzo Nobel	Sikkens Washprimer Cr
BASF	Glasurit Etching Primer 283-150
DuPont	615S Variprime Self-Etching Primer
ICI	Long Life Etch, P565-597
PPG	Deltron DX1791/1792 Wash Primer
Martin-Senour	6877 Triple Etch
Sherwin-Williams	GBP Etching Primer E2G983
Spies Hecker	Priomat Primer 3255
Standox	Etching Adhesion Primer

PRECOATS
Epoxy Primers & Zinc Phosphate Primers

Akzo Nobel	Sikkens Washprimer EM
BASF	DE15 Diamond Epoxy Primer
Dupont	2740S Low-VOC Prime 'N Seal
ICI Autocolor	Epoxy Primer Surfacer, P565-896
PPG	Deltron DPLF Lead-Free Epoxy Primer
Martin-Senour	5120 4.6 Epoxy Primer
Sherwin-Williams	Prime-Shield 4.6 Epoxy Primer PSE4600
Spies Hecker	Permacron Precoat Primer 4031
Standox	Standohyd 2K WP Primers

LOW VOC PRIMER-SURFACERS

Akzo Nobel	Sikkens Colorbuild LV 2.1/2.8
BASF	DP 210 Low VOC Primer-Surfacer
DuPont	2220S Waterborne Primer-Surfacer
ICI Autocolor	Extrafiller, P565-761
PPG	Deltron DPW1842 Low VOC Primer Surface
Martin-Senour	5005 Waterborne Primer-Surfacer
Sherwin-Williams	Aqua-Fill Waterborne Primer-Surfacer W7A2250
Spies Hecker	Permasolid 2:1 VHS Surfacer 5150
Standox	Standohyd 2K EP Sandin

susceptible to rust. After welding, the repaired area has two or three different steels (the two separate panels and the welding rod, if one is used) which are electrically joined together and that create a battery-like effect that can accelerate the rusting process. Additionally, the overlapping body panel creates pockets where moisture can collect, and greatly accelerate the development of rust.

Weld-through primers are zinc-rich paints applied to the body parts where they will be welded. During welding, the heat causes some of the zinc to melt into the welded area. Like galvanizing, the zinc helps prevent rusting of these steel parts in overlapping or inaccessible areas. The use of weld-through primers during such repairs is recommended by a number of car manufacturers to preserve the car's rust- through warranty. Read the paint manufacturer's information sheets to see if the weld-through primer should be removed from the exposed areas before painting. Some of these primers have poor adhesion and should be sand-blasted off the exposed welded areas.

Anti-Chipping—These primers or coatings are sometimes applied to the lower exterior body panels to help cushion the top coat and prevent chipping by stones or gravel thrown up during driving. Some anti-chip primers, such as BASF's Glassohyd Stone Chip Protector can be applied over either bare steel or certain other primers. Some types of anti-chip coatings, however, are not designed for application over bare metal and should only be applied over primer or over other paints.

Plastic Primers—Some of the new plastics used for making autobody

Lower rocker panels and front air dams, such as those shown hugging the ground on this Z28 Camaro, are often coated with a clear coat which has a flex agent to help prevent chipping and cracking.

Many body parts used today are composed of a plastic called TPO (thermoplastic polyolefin). Manufacturers are now stamping a plastic identification code onto the back of the panel. Why? One reason is so that anyone repainting the panel will know what primers to use. Adhesion promoters are generally specified by manufacturers as the first coat, or prep coat, over a bare TPO part. To help identify plastic parts, see the chart on page 20.

The Chevrolet Corvette was one of the first mass-produced cars with fiberglass panels. In the early eighties, Corvette switched over to body panels made of SMC, sheet-molded composites, which are used on this 1992 model. SMC uses glass fibers to reinforce a partially cured resin. The material is then compressed in a heated mold to produce a dense panel of uniform thickness that is smooth on both sides. Some of the types of primer used on steel-bodied cars are not compatible with SMC body panels. Courtesy DuPont.

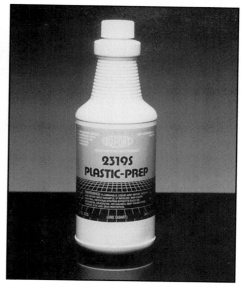

Cleaning of plastic parts often requires use of special cleaners to remove mold release agents, silicone, and static charges prior to painting. Courtesy DuPont.

parts don't adhere well to conventional primers, so a special primer had to be developed. However, even the primers designed for use on plastics won't work on all plastics. It is very important for a painter to find out what type of plastic is being painted. To help identify what type of plastic a body part is composed of, manufacturers are beginning to mold an identification code into plastic parts. After finding out what type of plastic the part is made of, check the technical information sheets on the primer you will be using to learn what the manufacturer's recommendations are. For details on determining plastic components, see the chart on p. 20.

Adhesion Promoters—These are specified by some manufacturers for use on certain types of plastic such as TPO (thermoplastic polyolefin) instead of primer. In this application, the adhesion promoter would be used as the first coat, or prep coat, over the

19

COMMON AUTOMOTIVE PLASTICS

SYMBOL	TRADE NAME	MAIN USE
ABS	ABS, Cycolac, Absafil, Cadon Lustran, Novadur, Teluran	Instrument clusters, consoles consoles, steering columns, grilles
ABS+PC	PULSE	Doors, rocker panels
PC	Lexan, Calibre, Merlon, Macrolon	Bumper covers, interior trim valence panels
PC+PBT	Xenoy, Valox, Macroblend	Bumper covers, interior trim, valence panels
PPE +PA	GTX-910	Quarter panels, fenders
UP	BMC, SMC, XMC, Derakene Fiberglass	Fender extensions, roofs, deck lids, air scoops, air spoilers
—	Bexloy V, Bexloy K550	Fascias
PUR	Rim, RRIM, Adiprance, Bayflex	Bumper covers, filler panels, front and rear
TPU	Pellethane, Bayflex, Texan Estane	Soft bumper covers, gravel deflectors filler panels
PP	Azdel, Daplen, Profax, Oleflo Tenite, Marlex	Door, kick, deflector & cowl panels, wheel & bumper covers, air dams, valence panels, inner fenders
TPO	Ferroflex, Moplen, Telcar Polytrope, Vistaflex, TPR Himont ETA 3055, ETA 3061	Bumper covers, valence panels, fascias, air dams
EPDM	Nordel	Headlamp doors, exterior panels
AES	Rovel	Headlamp doors, exterior panels
PVC	PVC (soft) vinyly	Headrests, dashboards, trim moldings

Courtesy DuPont

bare TPO plastic part. Adhesion promoters are also widely used as an intermediate coat when repainting is being done on existing clear-coated finishes whose surfaces are smooth and less porous than other painted surfaces.

Zinc Chromate Primers—These primers are often used for preparing other types of bare metal. They can be used on aluminum panels and on applications where aluminum and steel are combined, such as on lightweight trailers. They are also used as an insulation between two different kinds of metal, and they have excellent rust-preventing properties.

If the bare metal surface is very smooth, a prep coat is all that is needed. Most prep coats don't have to be sanded, but they can be lightly sanded if it's necessary to remove any surface dirt before application of the top coats. However, if the surface has noticeable nicks, scratches, or other surface defects, a primer-surfacer, or intermediate coat should be applied before the top coats are applied.

Intermediate Coats

A primer-surfacer is designed to fill in scratches and nicks so that a smooth surface can be made for the top coat. It is designed so that it can be built up into a thick layer and fill in the low points. It then must be sanded smooth, so ease of sanding is another desirable characteristic. A third, valuable trait for a primer-surfacer is a quick drying time, so that the painter won't have to wait long to begin sanding after spraying it on.

Some new primers can be tinted to more closely match the color which will be applied over them. Although you can't see it in this black and white photo, the primer-surfacer of the author's car was tinted red to match the final color coat, which ended up being Guard's Red.

Primer-surfacers are used wherever scratches and nicks need to be covered. They are often applied over etching primers or over old paint jobs. They also can be applied to bare metal and will provide enough adhesion and corrosion protection for many applications.

Primer-surfacers are available in nitrocellulose lacquer base, alkyd, acrylic, and urethane. Lacquer primer-surfacer has been popular with painters because it dries quickly and it is easy to sand. However, its adhesion to bare metal is not the best, and I recommend using other types of primers where large portions of bare metal need to be covered. Also, many paint manufacturers warn against applying coatings other than lacquer over lacquer primers.

Primer-Sealers—These primers do not have the filling qualities of primer-surfacers. Their main function is to seal off the coat beneath them and not necessarily to turn a rough surface into a smooth surface. Primer-sealers and sealers are recommended

when the top coat has to go over several different kinds of paint. This situation is common in spot repairs and in complete repaints when all the old paint is not stripped off. Primer-sealers can also be used to provide a uniform color background for the top coat. Like primer-surfacers, primer-sealers also can be used over bare metal, but they don't have to be sanded before application of the top coat. Some primer-sealers are epoxy based and have very high chemical and corrosion resistance.

Tintable Primers—These help provide good color coverage for the new, relatively thin base coats used today. The optimum thickness of automotive paint is about 4-6 mils (thousandths-of-an-inch). The color coat on clear coat/base coat cars has become so thin that a problem often develops with the underlying primers showing through the color. One solution is to tint the primer to match the color coat so that thin coverage won't be noticeable.

A second advantage is that some

chips won't be as noticeable. If you've seen a white car that has numerous chips down to its black primer, you'll appreciate the value of tinted primers. A third advantage is that the tinted primers are much cheaper than the more expensive color (base) coats.

Many paint manufacturers have introduced tintable primers. In some paint systems, the same tints used in coloring the top coats are added to the primer.

Sealers—These are not to be confused with *primer-sealers,* which can be used on bare metal. Plain sealers are only used over other paint such as primers or old top coats. Unlike primers, they are not recommended on bare metal. Sealers also differ from primers in that some are clear or semi-transparent.

Sealers are designed to prevent the solvents in the new top coat from seeping into the various paints below. The sealer acts as a protective barrier and holds the new paint (and its solvents) out of the paint and primer it's being applied over. This quality is called *hold-out.* Freshly applied wet paint will sink into the different underlying materials to different degrees. For example, paint usually will sink deeper into porous areas. By preventing these tiny sinking spots, sealers help provide uniformity and gloss for the surface finish.

Sealers are designed for two other purposes in addition to sealing off the lower layers of paint. One purpose is to make a uniform color background for the top coat to go over. They share this function with primer-sealers. However, the other purpose is to increase the adhesion between the new top coat and the old paint. Sealers are particularly good at this and are strongly recommended when alkyd enamels are being painted on a lacquer base.

Like prep coats and primer-sealers, sealers can be lightly sanded to remove dirt particles, but sanding is not mandatory with most sealers.

ADDITIVES

There are a number of chemicals that can be added in small quantities to automotive paint to provide special qualities. These additives have become increasingly popular, and their use has eliminated a number of defects that used to plague paint surfaces.

Flex Agents—A flex agent is added to promote a greater degree of flexibility in the paint before cracking occurs. It is typically added to the paint which is sprayed on soft bumper covers and other flexible fascia parts. Painters usually separate the flexible parts and paint them separately, away from the car. Some manufacturers will recommend adding the flex agent to the primers and clear coat on soft plastic parts but not to the color (base) coat.

It is difficult to get a paint which is flexible yet still retains a high gloss. Very hard surfaces, such as diamonds and glass, have no problem holding their shine, but they're brittle. Softer, more flexible materials, like Plexiglas™, lose their gloss easier. When the 5 mph impact bumpers first came out, their flexible body-colored parts often became dull within a few years. Unfortunately, this still can happen; the difference is most noticeable between the areas painted with the flex agent and adjoining body panels.

One "solution" is not to add flex agent to the paint used on the flexible

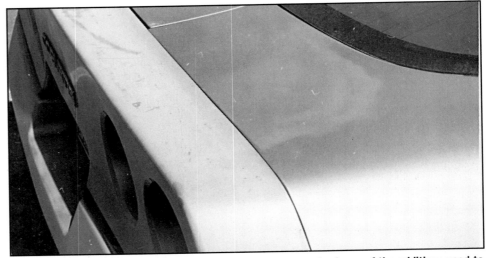

It is not uncommon to see faded paint on flexible bumper parts. Some of the additives used to help make paint flexible can cause the finish to dull prematurely.

bumper parts and just hope that nobody bumps into the bumpers. Another solution is to use a somewhat more flexible paint for the whole car. Some paint manufacturers, such as DuPont, offer more flexible paints which can be used on the entire car, including the flexible components, without the addition of flex agents.

Fish-Eye Eliminator—This additive tries to help prevent certain defects during the application of paint. If minute particles of silicone, oil, or water get into the paint, or onto the surface being painted, they can cause the wet paint to pull back from the contaminant. This creates small circles, called fish eyes. Painters sometimes add a few drops of fish-eye eliminator to their paint just before spraying to reduce the chance of fish eyes developing on the paint surface.

It is important that the fish-eye eliminator is formulated for the type of paint it will be used with. They also should be used in moderation. Some painters have reported that over-use of this additive caused a slippery surface on the color coat which eventually led to delamination, or peeling, of the clear coat.

Drying Additives—Other additives also assist in the application of automotive paint. Hardeners or initiators speed up drying times or improve gloss. Retarders slow down drying times. In hot, humid weather, retarders can reduce blushing and improve the flow-out and gloss.

Flattening Agents—These reduce the paint's gloss. Although gloss is usually a highly sought-after characteristic in a paint job, in some applications such as dashboards and many other interior parts, it is desirable to tone down the gloss. Flattening agents are also used by restorers who are often fanatical about matching the gloss of black paints on frames, inner fenders, fan shrouds, and suspension components to exactly the same finish these parts had when they left the factory.

More information on the use of primer-sealers and additives can be found in the step-by-step procedures in Chapter 6, *Small Paint Repairs* and Chapter 7, *The Complete Paint Job*.

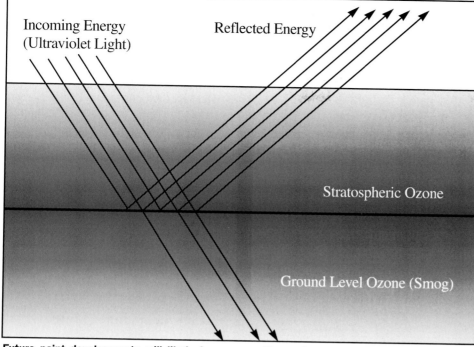

Future paint developments will likely focus on making paints and painting environmentally safe. Solvents and overspray either rise up into the stratosphere and deplete the protective ozone which filters out harmful UV radiation or remain at ground level and create too much ozone, resulting in smog. Photo courtesy I-CAR.

Today's automotive paints actually fulfill their main functions—to look good and to protect—so well that future developments will concentrate on other areas. Improvements and indeed, dramatic changes, will continue to be propelled by the increasing global awareness about protecting our environment. The application of automotive paint is a field of concern because of the amount of air pollution it creates. This wouldn't be as much of a problem if automotive paint was applied by brush or roller, but thinning paint down so that it can be sprayed in a fine mist allows a great deal of harmful solvents to evaporate into the air.

Solvents—Because of the type of spray gun used most frequently (see page 32), paint must be relatively thin like water, not thick and viscous like molasses. If you've tried to suck a thick milkshake up through a straw,

you understand the principle. Solvents must be added to make the paint thin. After the paint is sprayed, the solvents must evaporate so that the paint can dry and solidify.

Unfortunately, the types of solvents used in automotive paints are composed of volatile organic compounds or VOCs. Volatile means that these chemicals easily evaporate into the air. Organic compounds contain molecules made of carbon and hydrogen atoms, and the types of organic compounds in traditional auto paint solvents react with other molecules in the air to create smog, and that increases the greenhouse effect.

Lacquer paints are the worst polluters. When they are thinned down for spraying, less than 15% of the mixture ends up as paint on the car which means as much as up to 85% of the thinned paint mixture ends up evaporating into the atmosphere. That's a transfer efficiency (TE) of under 15%. By comparison, many

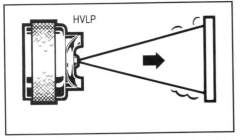

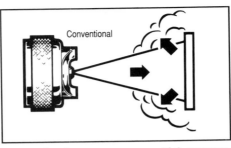

Many HVLP guns look similar to standard guns but some have a small hose connected to pressurize the paint cup. Other designs have the paint cup on top of the gun so that gravity helps feed the paint into the air stream. The most striking improvement that first-time users of HVLP equipment see is the reduction in overspray and bounce back. For details on HVLP and LVLP paint guns, go to Chapter 4. Courtesy ITW DeVilbiss.

Conventional spray guns use a high pressure air stream to suck the paint mixture up from the cup. A high proportion of VOC solvents must be used to make the paint thin. The higher velocities of paint particles coming from conventional guns ricochet much of the paint back at the painter and into the air making a lot of wasted, air-polluting overspray. Courtesy ITW DeVilbiss.

The world's first waterborne clear was introduced by Standox, the first completely waterborne paint system: from primer to basecoat to clearcoat. The milky appearance disappears upon application. If waterborne clears become popular in the refinish market, VOC pollution would be reduced. Courtesy American Standox

paint manufacturers now offer enamels with paint solids at over 65%, which means less than 35% of the thinned paint mixture is VOC released into the atmosphere.

Waterborne Paints

As mentioned in Chapter 2, waterborne paints are not new. However, they are still not widely used for a variety of reasons, although they are more environmentally friendly. Using water to transfer the paint through the gun onto the car reduces the need for solvents that contain VOCs.

Problems—Durability remains a problem. As of this writing, paint manufacturers are working hard to develop an automotive paint that can be mixed with water for spraying and that has the durability needed for the final top coat. Many of today's cars, have a waterborne color coat, but it is covered with a solvent-borne enamel clear coat for durability.

Waterborne paints have another problem, which is sensitivity to humidity during application. Humidity-controlled (air conditioned) booths had to be used and they had to be very carefully controlled when spraying the first waterborne paints.

The first cars manufactured with waterborne paints created some difficulties for refinishers when repainting had to be done. Advances in the chemistry of waterborne automotive paints have largely eliminated those problems, and they'll be increasingly used in the regions where the toughest environmental laws are enacted.

Advances—Waterborne paints have been used extensively by car manufacturers for the color base coat. In the future, the number of assembly plants which use waterborne primers and primer-surfacers is likely to increase. By the mid-nineties, General Motors was already using them in all of their European plants. One of the reasons it takes time to switch plants to waterborne technology is the enormous cost involved. Because water is corrosive, all lines, tanks and equipment must be replaced with stainless steel, which can cost millions of dollars.

Changes are also being explored in the chemistry of waterborne primer-surfacers. Most are now based on polyester-melamine but work is being done on polyurethane waterborne primer-surfacers for OEM factory appli-cations.

Chemists are working toward the

Paints On New Vehicles

	Chrysler	Ford	GM
Undercoat (on steel)	E-coat	E-coat	E-coat
Primer-surfacer	anti-chip powder	solvent-borne	powder, solvent- or waterborne
Base coat	waterborne	water- or solvent-borne	water- or solvent-borne
Clear coat	solvent-borne	solvent-borne	solvent-borne

More than one type of paint is listed in some categories because different plants use different systems. The trend in the paints being applied at the factory continues toward "greener" systems such as waterborne and powder. Powder has the least VOC's but has the most technological challenges in its application. Ford, Chrysler and GM are working together in reasearch and devlopment of powder paints. In particular, powder clear coat would significantly reduce VOC's and it is already being used on some Mercedes and BMW models.

development of durable waterborne clear coat systems as well. Research is making progress in another area: the combination of powder and waterborne technologies in an aqueous powder system.

Several of the more expensive Japanese cars, for example, Mazda and Infinity, have a urethane clear coat with the addition of fluorine. Mazda says that the addition of fluorine helps filter out the sun's ultraviolet rays and thereby gives greater protection from weathering. The manufacturer says that the gloss and luster of the fluorine clear coat remains virtually the same for at least five years whether it is waxed or not.

Another difference is the use of multiple clear coats with a small degree of color tint. The manufacturer says that this enhances the color and produces a deeper luster than conventional clear coats. Repair and repainting of these clear coats requires forced drying in down-draft or cross-flow baking paint booths. Air drying is reported not to work.

Powder

What has even less VOC's than waterborne paint? Powder. And it has at least three other very desirable features: improved durability, greatly reduced clean-up of overspray and almost no waste or disposal costs. All these advantages make power very desirable for automotive paint use but there have been technological challenges in its application. In the US in the early nineties, Harley-Davidson made a pioneering effort in the use powder for some of their clear coats, and in Europe BMW has begun use of a powder clear coat at one plant. The Big Three are working together in a consortium at the Ford Wixom plant to develop materials and methods for use on assembly lines. A breakthrough in powder paints promises to deliver significant improvement in two areas which have proved difficult to achieve simultaneously: durability and lower pollution.

Although powder may be the next

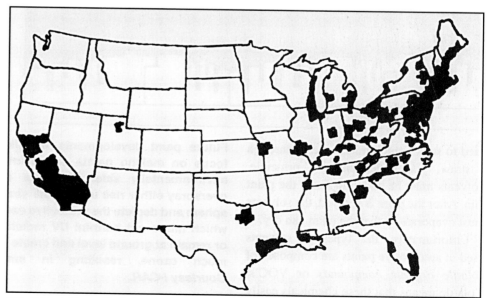

The federal Clean Air Act amendments listed regions of the country which have not attained acceptable ozone levels. These "non-attainment" areas must reduce emissions according to a schedule based on the severity of their current air pollution. Photo courtesy I-CAR.

NEW APPLICATION TECHNIQUES

As new paints are developed, so are the methods to apply them. What follows are some of the new techniques that are currently employed to apply paint or will be in the near future. Most of these developments are in response to environmental concerns.

SUPERCRITICAL CO$_2$: When carbon dioxide is under supercritical pressure or temperature, it can have the properties of a liquid and can be used in place of much of the solvent in fluid spray application of paint. It is already being used for application of nitrocellulose lacquers in furniture manufacturing and is being studied by automotive manufacturers also. It can reduce emissions by up to 80% by itself, and in conjunction with incineration and solvent recovery, total emissions can be reduced by as much as 95%. Recycled byproduct carbon dioxide is used and therefore no new carbon dioxide is vented into the atmosphere.

ELECTROSTATIC APPLICATION OF WATERBORNE PAINT: The use of electricity to draw paint to a surface is very efficient and is often used with dip tanks for solvent-borne primers and airborne powder coatings. However water is conductive and creates a few challenges for electrostatic applications, one being the need for electrically insulated spray equipment, lines and tanks. New methods of application are close to being ready for use in automotive manufacturing. The waterborne paints help reduce atmospheric pollution, and the electrostatic method draws more of the paint to the painted part so that material savings are also gained.

Methods to reduce of tank temperatures, solvent content and heavy metals (such as lead) are all being developed to make the E-coat process of priming more efficient, safer and less polluting. At the same time, it has been shown that E-coat applied to stainless steel or stainless steel clad aluminum trim moldings greatly improves the adhesion of paint or powder coatings. Such moldings have been in common use since the eighties, but they were not E-coated and delamination of the paint or powder has been noted as a problem.

POWDER COATINGS: Powder coatings not only reduce atmospheric pollution by solvents to nearly zero, they also have a great advantage in material savings through reclamation of powder. Automotive uses of powder coatings already include anti-chip coatings on lower body panels. Consideration is being given to such chip resistant powder coatings over the entire car, and these coatings may also be tinted to the body color in the future. Powder clear coats are already used on a number of manufactured items, and Harley Davidson implemented a state-of-the-art paint shop which powder coated their metal motorcycle parts. Although powder coating for metallic base coats seems unlikely at this time because of limited control of the flakes or mica, other automotive applications of powder coatings aren't far away, and researchers are hoping for widespread use of powder clear coats in car manufacturing soon.

ASSEMBLY LINE: Improvements in the equipment used on automotive paint lines at factories range from simple-to-understand concepts to new filtering and waste recycling systems which require a chemistry degree to appreciate. To reduce the amount of dust and dirt falling onto freshly painted parts, factories are changing from overhead conveyors to floor systems to transport the parts. Below the floor, paint overspray is picked up by water traps. Improvements in the chemical processes and filtering have reduced the amount of sludge which has to be disposed of by as much as 90%. And in Europe, because some regions charge car manufacturers dearly for any polluted waste water they dispose of, they have cut such wastes to nearly zero.

IMPROVED CLEAR COATS: Rapid advances have been made in the field of solvent-borne clear coats, both in lowering the VOC pollutants and in durability. Research continues on isocyanate two-component polyurethane clears and non-isocyanate two component epoxy clears. These are already being used on a number of the pricier cars. Buick, Oldsmobile and Cadillac began using a polyurethane clear coat in 1989. Saturn was one of the low to mid priced cars which also came with a polyurethane clear coat.

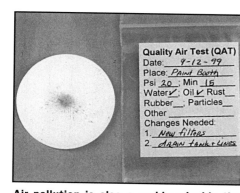

Air pollution is also a problem inside the compressed air lines. This Quality of Air test (QAT) filter shows contamination withich would have entered a spray gun and mixed with the paint. Minuscule amounts of oil, silicone, water, rust, or other dirt can ruin a paint job. Placing the filter in a bag and recording the date and location of the test provides a means of comparison for later tests. Comparisons can show when a system begins to degrade and thereby alert you to problems before they cause wasteful repainting.

revolution in automotive paint at the factory, it is not likely to be used by body shops or restorers because of the very expensive equipment, tightly controlled application conditions, and high temperature baking it requires.

The Near Future

Over the next several years, changes in factory methods of painting will continue along with advances in chemistry (see sidebar p. 26). It is likely that refined electrodeposition in dipping tanks of solvent-borne first primer coats will be followed by spray application of waterborne primer-surfacers. Waterborne or solvent-borne color coats would then be sprayed on, and the final coat would be a spray application of high solids solvent-borne clear coats.

Paint Films—One way to virtually eliminate air pollution is to eliminate the use of liquid paints and spraying procedures altogether. Researchers are now working on the application of heat-shrinkable films which would be laid on and bonded to bare body panels. This technique would eliminate the time-consuming paint line at a factory, and it would reduce emissions to almost zero. Some of these films can take a lot of stretching and therefore could even be applied to the flat sheet metal before it is stamped or formed in a die. Perhaps in the future, you'll repaint your car like you apply vinyl decals or stripes: with a squeegee and a hair dryer!

Molded-In Color—The Plymouth Pronto design car featured use of plastic exterior body panels which had the color molded in. If this goes into production, it would eliminate the need for a paint shop at that plant and virtually eliminate paint VOC's at assembly.

ENVIRONMENTAL LAWS

Prior to the nineties, there were few pollution laws that affected the application of automotive finishes at body shops in the United States. Although car manufacturers and large industrial concerns that applied coatings had air regulations to contend with, local body shops and DIYers did not. Some counties had regulations regarding the disposal of hazardous wastes, but these laws were more concerned with the water supply than the atmosphere. Consequently, tons of polluting VOC's were going into the air each day.

Rapid Changes

Changes that radically alter how body shops can paint cars are occurring rapidly. The first strict air pollution laws regulating automotive aftermarket painting were passed in certain districts in California. You may remember that California legislators forced automakers to

Chances are you haven't seen a work station like this Pro-Prep model before, but it is likely you will soon. It is increasingly important that the sanding dust and spot-priming overspray associated with prep work be removed from the air in the body shop. The work stations can have both overhead and floor mounted filters and options such as light fixtures and pneumatic lifts. Courtesy ITW DeVilbiss.

install pollution control equipment on cars sold in their state several years prior to the federally mandated standards for automotive emissions.

The Clean Air Act Amendments of 1990

The nation's first Clean Air Act was passed in 1963, and the EPA was created in 1970. The 1990 amendments to the Clean Air Act were the catalyst for many regional and state regulations. These amendments, which were signed into law on November 15, 1990 by President George Bush, were the most extensive environmental laws ever passed by Congress. They created new federal regulations, tightened up some regulations which had already been passed, set deadlines for action by the EPA, and put some power into enforcement of these laws. The U.S. Congress appears to be serious about this subject; the amendments passed the Senate by a vote of 89 to 11 and

A separate and fully enclosed paint mixing room was seldom seen in body shops prior to the nineties, but it is now required to meet fire, safety, and environmental regulations in most parts of the United States. Courtesy ITW DeVilbiss.

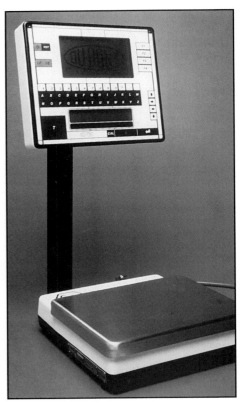

Computerized mixing room scales, such as this Intellinet model from DuPont, are used to mix colors and can monitor material use and track VOC emissions. If a painter accidentally pours too much of one color, the system can automatically adjust and display how much of the other components need to be added. Courtesy DuPont.

passed the House by a margin 401 to 21. This legislation is to be fully implemented by 2005 and is expected to cost approximately $25 billion per year by that time.

The amendments are grouped under eight titles. Title II deals with pollution by vehicles, Title IV deals with acid rain, and Title VIII covers miscellaneous subjects. The remaining titles directly affect the auto paint industry.

Title I—Ozone Standards. Compliance deadlines were established for non-attainment regions of the country—those regions which had ozone levels of more than 0.12 PPM (parts per million), which is the national standard for safe ozone levels. There are 96 non-attainment areas, and approximately 80% of the U.S. population lives in these areas.

Categories were established depending on how high the ozone pollution currently is, and the worst category, "extreme," refers to levels over .28 PPM and includes only Los Angeles.

Baltimore, Chicago, Houston, New York, Philadelphia, and San Diego are in the "severe" category with more than .18 PPM, and levels in excess of .16 PPM earned the category "serious" for Atlanta, Boston, and Washington DC. These categories must reduce VOC generation by 3% until attainment is reached. In addition, the EPA established deadlines for the adoption of control techniques guidelines, CTGs, for a number of industries.

Title III—Hazardous Chemicals. Included in the list of 189 hazardous chemicals are many solvents and pigments used by the paint industry.

The EPA is directed to set standards for use of these chemicals by industry, and the EPA must also name 30 chemicals which pose the most threat to urban areas. After being named, those source emissions must be reduced by 90%.

Title V—Mandatory State Permit Program. All states need a program in which all businesses or sources of industrial pollution must submit permit applications which specify emission limitations, compliance schedules, and reporting requirements.

Title VI—Phasing Out Certain Solvents. The solvents in question are specified chlorinated and fluorinated solvents which were classified as

Air quality inside the bodyshop is greatly improved by a new type of equipment, the extraction system. These are vacuum systems which capture sanding dust and other air-borne particles at the source to create a non-toxic dust-free workplace. Such systems are becoming more common in shops, and in some regions they are necessary to comply with workplace air quality standards. Extractors are available as permanent, semi-permanent or mobile systems, like the Herkules Exidust shown with a power sander attached. Courtesy Herkules.

ozone depleters. These solvents are rapidly being phased out because they were found to cause serious damage to the ozone layer. In the auto repair field specifically, it is chlorofluorocarbon 12 (more often known as CFC-12, R-12, or Freon) which is used in air conditioning systems. Regulations included the certification of technicians and the use of equipment to capture and recycle Freon at body shops and repair shops.

Title VII—Federal Enforcement. This authorizes the EPA to issue field citations with penalties of $5,000 per day. Deliberate violators face criminal sanctions including felony conviction, imprisonment up to two years, and fines up to $250,000 per day. In addition, the EPA can pay up to $10,000 for information leading to a conviction or penalty. Knowingly endangering the public can lead to fines of $1,000,000 per day, and citizens can seek additional civil penalties.

Other Potential Changes—EPA guidelines for states may eventually require that all auto body shops have afterburners on their paint booths to reduce airborne contaminants. Another suggested method of limiting VOC levels is to ban the sale of automotive paint refinishing products to businesses that don't have an EPA number. This, of course, would prevent backyard painters, private car owners, and unlicensed shops from painting vehicles legally.

The National Rule—The EPA has been working on a nationwide rule which would limit the VOC content on automotive paints made by manufacturers. The VOC limits in the Federal rule can be achieved by today's solvent-borne paint and therefore it does not requires the use of waterborne paints.. Furthermore, it does not have regulations for plastic or surface cleaners nor does it regulate the body shops directly or their equipment, such as HVLP spray equipment, enclosed gun cleaners, or new types of spray booths. Although the Federal Rule does not regulate cleaners and equipment, state and local laws often do—and body shops will still have to comply with the stricter state or local regulations.

State & Regional Laws

Many states and regions took the initiative to pass their own laws before the Federal Rule come in effect. In 1998, Fred Wissemann, project manager for DuPont VOC-Compliant systems, reported that VOC regulations have been implemented in 17 states: California (which has by far the most stringent regulations), Delaware, Illinois, Indiana, Maryland, Massachusetts, New Jersey, Pennsylvania, Rhode Island, Tennessee, Texas, Wisconsin, and parts of Arizona, Kentucky, Oregon and Washington, and the metropolitan New York City area.

Los Angeles—Rule 1151. The strictest environmental laws on auto refinishing come from the South Coast Air Quality Management District (SCAQMD). The regulations specified emissions so much lower than those of available automotive paints that manufacturers had to hastily try to invent products to meet the emissions requirements. One good effect of Rule 1151 is possibly that it spurred activity in the laboratories of paint manufacturers to come up with ultra-low VOC paints sooner than would have been the case. Regulations in the LA area are not limited to just paint fumes—petroleum-based cleaning solvents are also banned from use in body shops.

San Francisco—Rule 45. The San Francisco Bay Area Air Quality Control District's are known as "Rule 45". These regulations gave the paint companies a little more time to work on the development of ultra-low VOC paints than did Rule 1151, but they have other differences some experts think will ultimately have a greater impact on reducing emissions. Paint manufacturers worked closely with the Bay Area district to form the Rule 45 regulations and a number of other regions based their regulation upon Rule 45.. In some regions, body shops and other refinishers are required to keep records on the paint materials they purchase, use, and dispose of.

Dallas/Ft. Worth—State regulations went into effect in 1990. Among other regulations, body shops in the

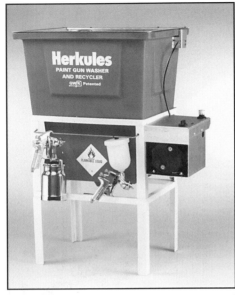

Air pollution regulations mandate the use of another new piece of body shop equipment in some regions. Enclosed automatic paint gun cleaning systems permit the necessary daily cleaning of paint guns while cutting down on the amount of VOCs getting into the air during the process. Courtesy Herkules.

Dallas/Ft. Worth area are must have enclosed equipment for cleaning paint guns and closed containers for paint storage.

New York City—In 1988, regulations for auto refinishing were introduced which impose penalties of up to $25,000 per day on businesses that do not comply.

New Jersey—Regulations on VOC's went into effect in 1990. The regulations only apply to larger body shops, and they set some limits which couldn't be attained with available paint technologies.

Pennsylvania—In 1997, a group appointed by the governor recommended that automotive paint products containing VOC's be sold only to autobody repair shops which use HVLP guns and approved gun cleaning equipment.

Illinois—The state legislature approved a bill in 1991 that banned the bulk sale of industrial paints, including automotive finishes, to

customers who do not have a state registration number as a hazardous waste generator. This is intended to eliminate pollution by unlicensed shops. Unregistered individuals, such as do-it-yourselfers or hobbyists, are limited to the purchase of two gallons of automotive paint per year.

Alaska—Since 1990, it has been illegal for anyone to paint a car without a license. Called the Alaska Hazardous Paint Handler Certificate, the license has the painter's photo and description and must be nearby during painting. Fines for painting without a license are $250 for an individual and as much as $1000 per day for an employer. The law is enforced by a team which visits shops and checks anyone who is painting.

Seattle—In 1992, the Puget Sound began implementing environmental regulations that affect many businesses, including auto refinishers.

Florida—Broward County Ordinance No. 9112 in 1992 was one of the first in the Southeast to set extensive requirements for body shop licensing. This included certification of paint and repair technicians and minimum equipment standards such as possession of MIG welders, lift equipment, anchoring systems, and power tools for straightening bodies, lifting equipment, and body measuring devices. Shops must also have electronic or printed crash manuals and sources of dimensions for body and suspension part measurements. The management must show active participation in I-CAR (Inter-Industry Conference Auto Collision Repair) training programs, and technicians must be certified by ASE (National Institute Automotive Service Excellence).

Environment Friendly Equipment

The move from highly polluting lacquer paints to high solids enamels is not the only way to reduce pollution at body shops. New types of paint equipment make a significant difference too. New generation paint guns transfer a much higher proportion of the paint materials onto the car than into the atmosphere, and are described in Chapter 4. The paint gun cleaner is a relatively new piece of equipment which benefits the environment although it was initially designed just to save money.

After each use, a paint gun needs to be cleaned with thinner. In the past, frequently used paints such as lacquer primers could be left in a gun. However, if not cleaned out soon after use, today's catalyzed paints will solidify inside the gun's passages and render it useless. Manual cleaning of guns involves repeated rinsing of the cup with fresh thinner and then spraying it through the passages. This not only takes 10 minutes or more, it creates fumes, and uses a lot of thinner which needs to be disposed of.

Closed automatic gun cleaners can cut the painter's cleaning time down to under a minute, nearly eliminate the associated air pollution, and enable repeated re-use of the thinner. This results in a considerable cost-savings to a busy body shop. Another advantage is that the painter's hands don't get immersed in thinner several times a day. Thinner is rough on the condition of your skin, and it gets into your bloodstream remarkably fast. The automatic spray gun cleaner is one example of new equipment which is environmentally friendly, saves shops money, and improves the life of the painter too.

FEDERAL & LOCAL VOC LIMITS

California has initiated some of the most stringent laws governing the emissions from automotive painting. "Rule 45" concerns San Francisco Bay area and Rule 1151 concerns the Los Angeles area. The numbers indicate the amount of VOC's in pounds per gallon that are acceptable. The year listed was the date those limits were effective. Courtesy Auto Body Repair News.

REGULATION 8 RULE 45
San Francisco Bay Area (1995)

Pretreat wash primer	6.5
Precoat	5.0
Primer/primer-surfacer	2.1
Primer-sealer	3.5
Topcoat, single stage	3.8
Topcoat, base/clear coat	4.5

CALIFORNIA RULE 1151
Southern California (1995)

Pretreatment	6.5
Primer	2.1
Topcoat, single stage	3.5
Topcoat, base/clear coat	3.5

NATIONAL RULE
(1998)

Pretreatment wash primer	6.5
Primer/primer-surfacer	4.8
Primer-sealer	4.6
Single stage topcoats	5.0
Base coat/clearcoat	5.0
Specialty coatings	7.0

Proper disposal of used paint materials has become very expensive. Use of paint gun cleaners greatly reduces the amount of waste thinner for a shop but going another step can cut it still further. A tip is to drain the old thinner from the paint gun cleaner and place it in a 55-gallon drum for a couple months. A good percentage of the paint solids will fall to the bottom of the drum, enabling the thinner on the top to be reused for general cleaning or as part of the solution in the gun cleaner.

New Environmental Products

Water-based aerosol spray paints have been marketed by PlastiKote. Their new generation of paint is called "Premium Water Based Enamel."

Soluble filters may help solve the problem of disposing of paint booth filters. After use, the filters can be dissolved in the shop's waste thinner and then handled by the service used for removal of the used paint thinner (some of which is recycled).

Brake friction linings with no asbestos content are the norm today. The first stage of the phase-out of asbestos friction products began in 1992; the final year for use of asbestos was 1997.

Substitutes for the CFC's used in automotive air conditioning systems are already being introduced and refined. Several car manufacturers, including BMW, already use them. The goal was to have no new CFC's produced after the year 2000.

Lead-free paints are the norm now

Tempo's new Manual Paint Filler enables a paint store to make custom-color aerosol paints on the spot. The custom-blended color is poured into the reservoir, a Universal Blend can is placed in the bottom, and the paint is manually pumped in. On the spot mixing can reduce aerosol paint inventories and waste. Courtesy Plasti-Kote.

after being phased out in stages. In the early nineties, the lead content of paint was limited to 3%. Lead was originally used because it was so effective at helping pigments such as yellow and red hold their color through long-term exposure to sunlight.

The automotive paint industry underwent dramatic changes in paint and equipment during the 1990's. The result was a truly significant decrease in pollution.

4

PAINT EQUIPMENT

The new generation HVLP paint guns are the first truly new designs in almost 50 years. The OMX gun has a disposable liner for fast clean ups which only require one ounce of thinner. Plus the sealed liners enable this gun to be sprayed up side down. Other features include a second top trigger to comfortably maintain a 90-degree angle over horizontal surfaces. The plastic body is very light weight and can be outfitted with LVLP air heads for low air consumption such as from a 2 hp compressor. Courtesy ITW DeVilbiss.

There's much that's new and exciting in the field of paint equipment. In just the 5 years since the release of the first edition of the Automotive Paint Handbook, there's been almost a revolution in paint tools and instruments. New generation HVLP guns are the first really new paint gun designs seen in almost half a century. Affordable equipment now exists to measure paint thickness, quality of paint finishes and color itself. These new measuring tools will permit the first-ever national standards for the automobile refinishing and help lift the industry into a new level of professionalism. And an impressive amount of innovation has also occurred with hand tools.

This equipment section has many more photos than the first edition— and nearly all are of entirely new products. That's a big change for an industry which was relatively sleepy for decades. This chapter will focus mainly on tools used in the preparation and application of paint. Chapter 12, *Inspecting Paint & Body*, will focus on the tools used for inspecting and evaluating paint on the vehicle.

SPRAY EQUIPMENT

The two most essential items needed to spray paint are the paint gun and compressor used to deliver air pressure.

Spray Guns

The type of spray gun used for the past 60 years utilizes a fast-moving stream of air to create a vacuum which sucks the paint up out of the cup and into the air stream where it is atomized. The first sprayers using this principle were made by DeVilbiss in 1890. Back then, two of the most

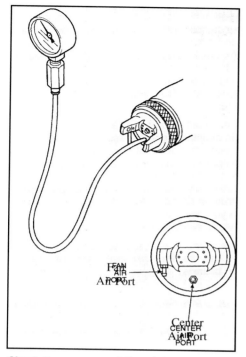

Check the pressure at the air head on HVLP guns to make sure they have sufficient air flow to operate properly. Problems in using new HVLP guns are often caused by poor air flow due to conditions such as small hoses or restrictive quick-disconnect couplings. Courtesy ITW DeVilbiss.

DeVilbiss created sprayers for perfume and misting water back in 1890 and the principles they developed then were later applied to paint spray guns. Their JGA-HVLP model spray gun features a high performance air cap, producing excellent atomization while complying with environmental codes, using suction feed technology. The gun also has stainless steel fluid passages, which are essential when using the new waterborne paints. Photo courtesy ITW-DeVilbiss.

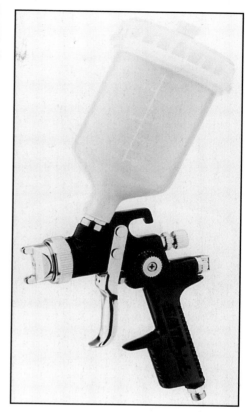

The paint cup is on the top of a gravity feed gun but is on the bottom of a siphon feed gun. The siphon feed design has always been the most popular in the U.S. but gravity feed guns have become common in part due to increased use of the thicker, less-polluting paints. Sata says their HVLP95 series gun delivers over 65% transfer efficiency and uses only 13.5 cfm—which is close to same volume of air that some older non-HVLP guns use. In addition to gravity feed guns, Sata also offers siphon and pressure tank systems. Courtesy Sata.

popular uses were for spraying perfumes and for misting water. In these earlier sprayers, the air stream was created by manually squeezing a rubber bulb.

In today's siphon-feed paint spray gun, the air stream comes from a high pressure air line attached to the back of the gun. When the trigger is pulled, air rushes over the air passage of a tube that reaches down into the paint cup. The liquid paint is drawn up by the vacuum the air stream creates. To create sufficient vacuum, the air stream has to be moving very fast, which requires a relatively high air pressure, typically 30 to 60 pounds per square inch (psi), and relatively thin paint, usually thinned or reduced with solvent. Although there are a variety of professional paint gun types that use large separate paint tanks pressurized to deliver the paint to the

gun (used for high-volume, commercial work), the most common gun used for automotive painting has been the siphon-feed type described above.

HVLP Paint Guns—A method which cuts down the amount of solvents used in the application of automotive paint is to spray thicker paint. This can be achieved by pressurizing the paint cup to help get the thicker paints up into the air stream. The other major change is in the air stream used to deliver the paint to the car. The air pressure is considerably reduced and the volume

of air is increased. High Volume, Low Pressure (HVLP) is the name given to this type of spray gun.

Development of HVLP guns has progressed remarkably fast. The first HVLP guns were tricky to use, and they often splattered and spurted paint on cars. However, the latest HVLP guns are an entirely new generation, designed from a blank sheet of paper instead of the first generation, which was often only a modification of older designs.

Selecting an HVLP Gun—Be very careful in your selection of an HVLP

New Paint Tools Enable Measurable National Standards

A profound change is coming in automobile painting. The quality of a paint job has always been just a subjective evaluation by the painter, car owner or body shop owner. An opinion. The problem with opinions is that everyone has a different one, and they even change from day to day. It is necessary to have objective, measurable parameters to set and maintain standards and to turn automobile painting into a modern, efficient, quality-driven industry. This profound change is at hand because technology has now advanced to the point that affordable means are available to measure the most important paint quality parameters: thickness, finish and color.

Thickness: The measurable paint parameter most critical to durability is thickness, plus it provides the best information about a paint's preparation and past history. A paint thickness gauge can tell if paint has been buffed too thin, whether it was repainted, and whether it has too much paint. The ETG electronic thickness gauge is accurate to better than 1%, comes with memory to store readings, measures to .1 mil or 1 micron, and is available in models which read on steel, aluminum or both.

Finish: For the first time, there is an affordable instrument which can measure the quality of a paint's surface finish. The battery powered QFM enables painters, dealerships, detailers and manufacturers to set and monitor the quality of the finish on cars, match repaint to factory finishes, or show the quality of work to customers.

Color: Spectrophotometer is the ten-dollar word for a complex (read expensive) instrument which measures color. They have been essential in other industries for years but are now making their way into local paint suppliers and even some larger body shops. Hue (color), chroma (the color's intensity) and value (lightness) are each measured at from three to five different angles depending on the model. That data is then compared to a paint manu-facturer's database to correlate with one of their formulas or to suggest how a formula should be changed to make a better match. The ability of the spectro-photometers and their database to produce blendable matches on the first try is continually improving. This very much anticipated by painters because matching color on partial repaints is one of their most difficult tasks. Courtesy PPG.

gun, because there is a wide variation among manufacturers. Don't put all your faith in magazine articles or in what salespeople say. If you are interested in a particular gun, talk to several people who use that brand of gun or that system on a daily basis. Then test the gun to see how it performs spraying different consistencies of paint such as primers, base coats, and clear coats.

Compressor

The compressor you choose must be able to produce sufficient pressure and deliver it with consistency to the gun. Air pressure is expressed in pounds per square inch (psi) and volume in cubic feet per minute (cfm). The pressure is needed to atomize the paint, and volume is needed to distribute it evenly.

There are several different types of compressors available today: piston, diaphragm, and blower driven. Of the piston-type, there are single- and two-stage types.

Single-Stage—A single-stage, 1-1/2 hp, 12 cfm compressor that produces 100 psi is the smallest you should consider for simple painting projects. This capacity develops enough volume and pressure to spray primers,

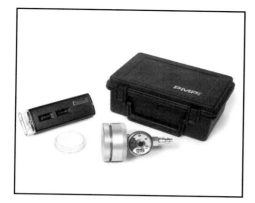

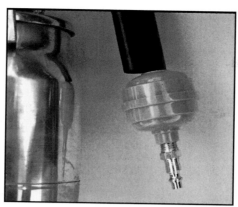

When you consider how much hard work and money goes into properly preparing a vehicle for painting, it's amazing that so few people check the cleanliness of the air which goes into the paint gun. The QAT Quality of Air Test system enables you to check the air at the gun or anywhere in the air supply. The compressed air is blown over a filter so fine that it traps particles as small as 8 millionths of an inch. The 30x illuminated microscope magnifier and illustrated instructions help determine the cause of contamination.

One of the least expensive filters is the most effective, and it's really worthwhile. Motor Guard's canister filter contains a filter which is inexpensive and easy to change. Plus a roll of toilet paper can be substituted for the filter if desired. Some painters wisely put a new filter in before each new paint job.

A filter on the spray gun is the cheapest insurance there is. This Motor Guard filter traps particles as small as .01 micron which is so small that if you blow cigarette smoke in one end, it won't come out the other. Change these little filters often.

Air going to the gun isn't the only source of problems. Non-incendiary smoke sticks quickly show air sneaking past the booth filters, through seams, or past the door seals. They also point out isolated turbulence in booths which can obscure visibility or blow dirt onto freshly applied paint. After cracking the swab end with pliers, they produce smoke for about 10 minutes.

Multistage filter-dryers just before the paint gun are very desirable but they should be inspected and maintained regularly. Don't assume it's removing all contamination; test it upon installation and periodically thereafter. Courtesy Motor Guard

surfacers, and lacquers on small areas. On a cool day, it can provide enough air to spray a full car with lacquer.

Two-Stage—The smallest two-stage compressor will serve your painting needs better than the largest single-stage compressor. Two-stage compressors range from 1-1/2 hp, 110V, 12 cubic-foot units to huge industrial types. Generally, the pressure of a two-stage compressor will be able to "stay ahead" of the painter.

In most cases, if you're looking for a compressor, buy the largest you can afford. Base your decision on the amount of cfm consumed by the equipment and length of time you'll be using it. A difficult paint job becomes more difficult if the compressor keeps cutting out or overheats and shuts off. Having too much air is better than not having enough.

Hoses & Couplers—The standard air hose inside diameters (ID) are 1/4, 5/16, and 3/8 inch. The larger the hose, the less air pressure drop there will be between the compressor and the gun. Most paint shops use a 5/16-inch hose because a 3/8-inch is too heavy and bulky, while a 1/4-inch hose is not sufficient for most professional paint jobs. But if you're using a 1/4-inch hose, it shouldn't be longer than 12 feet.

Tips—Hoses can deteriorate on the inside and contaminate the air, and this can occur after the filters. Also, High Volume, Low Pressure (HVLP) guns need plenty of air. Small hoses, long pipes and restrictive quick-disconnect couplings can choke the air volume.

Filters & Traps—Moisture and dirt are a painter's worst nightmare. Because air is compressed inside the compressor, it contains more moisture, which gradually condenses inside the tank. To prevent this water from reaching the paint, you must trap the water so it can be drained. Make sure you purchase a moisture trap compatible with your compressor in terms of size, and get the best you can afford. Nothing will ruin a paint job faster than water spots. Air drawn into

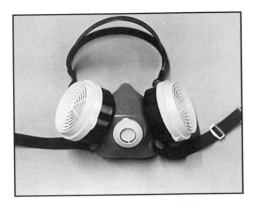

Charcoal-filtered masks should be worn whenever paint is being applied. This is especially important when spraying catalyzed enamels. Paints, in particular those which contain isocyanates, should not be breathed. The mask (and any filters which are no longer in a sealed package) should be kept in an airtight container when not being used.

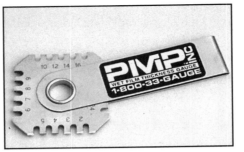

Wet film gauges measure the thickness of a freshly applied paint while it is still wet. Different sides of the gauge are for different thickness ranges. The appropriate side is pressed down into the wet paint and the "finger" with largest number that is touched by paint is the wet film thickness. The thickness of the film will decrease as it hardens but the change is far less with modern 2 component (2K or catalyzed) paints than with solvent drying paints. The gauge is stainless steel so that it can be cleaned after use.

the compressor must be filtered as well. Generally, a filter is positioned just inside the compressor cover. Check this filter periodically to ensure it is in good condition. A multi-stage filter with a dryer is a wise investment. At the very least, use a new filter at the gun and a "toilet paper" style filter on the wall in the paint booth. A QAT kit is also available now which can be used to test the quality of the compressed air in your system and can spot any contamination which would get into your gun or tools.

SAFETY EQUIPMENT

The safety equipment used today is not really new, it's just new to most automotive painters. The air filtration system is a good example. Fifteen years ago most professional painters wouldn't be seen with a charcoal filter face mask. Such masks were deemed uncomfortable and awkward, and they made a person look like an alien or a mutated insect. A painter who used this kind of equipment would be looked upon by his peers as a safety nut. Today, however, that idea has changed. Most paint professionals would think a painter is just plain stupid if he didn't wear at least a charcoal mask when painting, especially with catalyzed enamels.

One of the reasons for the growing use of face masks and fresh air systems is the change in the chemistry of the paint. The new catalyzed paints are downright nasty to breathe. The immediate result of not wearing a charcoal mask while spraying catalyzed paints can be a severe headache or nausea. The long-term effects are thought to be much worse. That's where the second reason for

SANDING EQUIPMENT

A good DA (dual action) or orbital air-powered sander is essential for all practical purposes when repainting an entire car. Used equipment and tools are often found at pawn shops at prices as low as 25 cents on the dollar but be careful when buying used air-powered tools. Make sure to test them out as soon as possible and ask if you can return them if they are defective. Note that most of the DA's made by well known manufacturers are rebuildable. That's important because some parts wear (the disc bearing for example) and can be easily changed on a rebuildable tool.

A power sanding board is a favorite of many painters and body men. It can help keep long body panels flat when they are being sanded. A sanding board isn't essential, however, for a complete paint job. Some painters never bother with them.

When purchasing an air-powered tool, check the amount of high pressure air (measured in cfm—cubic feet per minute) needed for it. As a rule you'll need at least a 5 horsepower compressor to keep a DA running continuously.

For hand sanding, a small hard rubber sanding block and a flat rubber sanding block are both useful. The new flexible rubber sanding block which has a spring steel core helps prevent finger ruts in high quality jobs. During wet sanding a small soft rubber squeegee is very useful for wiping the surface to check for any remaining orange peel.

As for sandpaper, you'll need an assortment from 80 grit to 240 grit for sanding body fillers, 400 to 600 grit for sanding primers, and from 1000 to 2000 grit depending on the method you choose for finish sanding before buffing or finessing.

A new type of sanding block has been designed to produce the flattest finishes. The Pro Block has a spring steel core which distributes pressure evenly and thereby eliminates the finger groves common to other flexible sanding blocks. A thumb tab gives better control when sanding, and helps keep it from slipping out of your hand when wet sanding. It's available from Pro Motorcar, 813/726-9225.

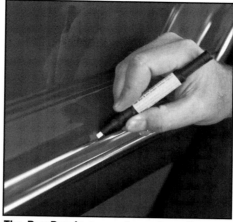

The PrepPen is a new type of sanding tool which has a bundle of fiberglass bristles to permit sanding in areas where sandpaper can't reach. It's useful for getting in to degloss paint near glass or moldings and it won't scratch the glass. Again, the PrepPen is available from Pro Motorcar, 813/726-9225.

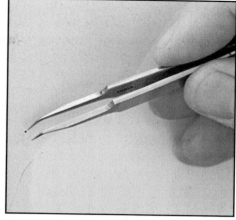

Every painter has had the heart break of seeing a piece of dirt (or bug or hair or lint) fall appear in the middle of a perfectly painted panel. ProPick is a light spring force tool whose tips are ground to ten thousandths of an inch to enable you to lift any unwanted debris out of freshly applied wet paint.

the increased use of safety equipment comes in: increased awareness of what some of the automotive paint materials can do to your body over the long run.

Today, many painters would choose to wear a hood with face shield and external fresh air system if it were available. A fresh air system takes air from outside the booth and pumps it through a hose to the hood. Such a system is recommended when spraying isocyanate enamels.

It is also becoming common practice for painters to protect their hands with gloves, and even to cover their entire bodies with disposable suits. Not long ago, painters, body men, and other workers such as helpers and mechanics would think nothing of cleaning their hands a few times a day by rinsing or wiping off with paint thinner. Now we know that many of the chemicals in automotive

paint are absorbed into the skin, and then are picked up by the blood-stream.

Paint manufacturers today have made safety a very prominent part of their training programs. For example, at most paint certification training seminars, the first thing instructors talk about is safety, not their company's product line. The safety instruction they provide is both convincing and in-depth. In addition, some provide new charcoal masks and filters, safety eye protection, and gloves to each attendee. These items of safety equipment are required to be used by the participants during the hands-on painting portions of the course, and they are given without charge to the painters to use at their shops.

MEASURING TOOLS AND ACCESSORIES

Painting automobiles has evolved to the point where the professional needs more than just a paint gun, paint, and a place to spray it. The desire for paint

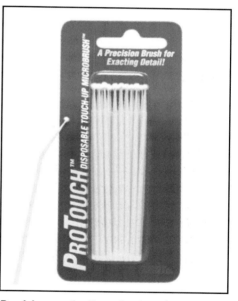

Precision application of paint or solvents is made possible by the tiny ProTouch brush. The non-absorbent fibers can either apply or remove paint, cleaners or lubricants. The shaft can be bent for difficult to reach locations and can be used for precision cleaning of such delicate places as the air head and passages of spray guns.

surface perfection has led to the development of a variety of special tools and accessories.

Paint Gauges

There are only a few aspects of

The ProTemp infrared thermometer enables paint temperature to be measured while it is in the can or gun cup. Paint temperature is much more critical with today's thicker low VOC paints and it is essential to check temperature before using a Zahn cup. This non-contact thermometer can also be aimed at body panels to check their temperature before during and after paint application.

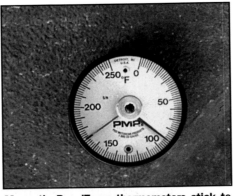

Magnetic PanelTemp thermometers stick to the back of steel body panels to enable a painter to see the temperature of the substrate being painted. Ancillary hands record the highest or lowest temperature and thereby help in adjusting heat lamps or in calibrating infrared sensors.

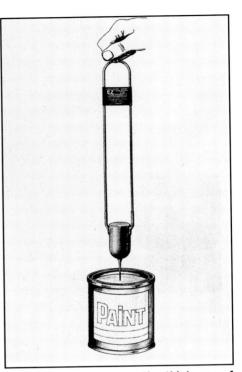

Viscosity Cups measure the thickness of paint. Proper viscosity is essential for the efficient application of modern paints. Viscosity cups are easy to use: just dip it into the paint can, lift it out and use a stopwatch to time the number of seconds until the paint coming though the hole in the bottom of the cup changes from a stream into drips. Be aware there are different sizes (#2, #3 etc.) and kinds (Zahn, Signature, EZ, Ford, etc.) of viscosity cups. The paint must be at the proper temperature or the test is worthless. Courtesy Paul N. Gardner Co.

automotive paint that can be measured. Fortunately, one of the most critical paint parameters can be measured easily: the film thickness. Gauges that measure film thickness are called a number of different names: coating thickness gauges, mil gauges, or simply, paint measuring gauges.

Thickness—Coating thickness can tell you a lot about the past, present, and future of a paint job. The readings can tell if repainting has been done, and they tell you if a car was stripped before repainting or restoration. A paint gauge also tells if the paint is so thin that buffing may go through into the color, reduce the effectiveness of the clear coat, or if the paint is so thick that the paint will soon crack, dull, or peel. Details on paint thickness and its effects are covered in detail in Chapter 5 and Chapter 12.

Finish Quality—For the first time since paint has been on cars, there's an affordable instrument called a QFM (Quality of Finish) instrument, which can measure the quality of the surface finish, available to painters. The unit helps match the original paint finish when spot repainting, and will enable national standards to be set for refinishing and reconditioning.

Color—Spectrophotometers can help in measuring and matching automotive colors. They're becoming more common but are typically found at only the largest body shops or paint suppliers.

Accessories—Painters today have a lot more equipment to contend with when they're in the paint booth. They often have to handle bigger HVLP guns or hoses, and possibly an HVLP regulator or a fresh air hose. During spraying, a painter's attention is so focused on watching the spray pattern and the wetness of the paint, that it is easy to bump into wet paint or touch it with a hose. A chest harness helps keep all this hardware out of the way. Quick disconnect snaps make attachment and removal of each hose, well, a snap.

Nib Cutters—Increased use of enamels and HVLP techniques make a couple of common spraying problems a little more common: runs and sags. An inexpensive tool, called a nib cutter, helps trim down the high points, sags, runs, or particles stuck on the paint. The tool is a small square piece of grooved steel that looks like a very sharp file. It is usually encased in a piece of plastic to make it more convenient to hold. Carefully sliding the tool over the problem area slices off the high spot, like a wood plane trims down wood. It is a useful item for any professional painter to have.

Black is the paint color that puts a detailer or painter to the test with buffing and polishing. On a black car, every scratch, pit, and wave is apparent upon close examination.

How does the word "finesse" apply to caring for today's automotive paints? A dictionary definition of finesse is "skill in handling a highly sensitive situation," and that meaning applies well to the procedure of finessing car paint. It is the process of very carefully sanding and polishing the top surface of automotive paint to remove surface defects without having to do any repainting.

Finessing must be done with great care because it is easy to remove too much paint—which will create new problems that are worse than the original. It takes skill because you have to know which defects are too deep to remove without heavy repair, whether or not there is enough paint to remove the defect, what procedures and materials will work safely, and when to stop.

Why Finessing?

The increase in finessing is primarily due to the increase in paint problems, and the increase in people who are picky about their car's appearance. The environment that auto paint has to endure has become harsher at the same time evolutionary changes in paint were mandated by law. The chemistry and application of automotive paint has had to change drastically. As with any major change in technology, there has been (and will continue to be) new problems to solve in the application and manufacture of automotive paint.

If this weren't enough change, many car owners have become more conscious and concerned about the appearance of their cars than ever before. This is substantiated by the increase in car care product sales, detailing shops, and by the increase in customers wanting expensive, glamorous paint jobs such as pearl and tri-coats. Another reason is that since cars have become so expensive, people are hanging on to them longer. The cost of repainting a car has also gone ballistic. These two factors alone are reasons why body shops, detailers, and car owners want to take the time

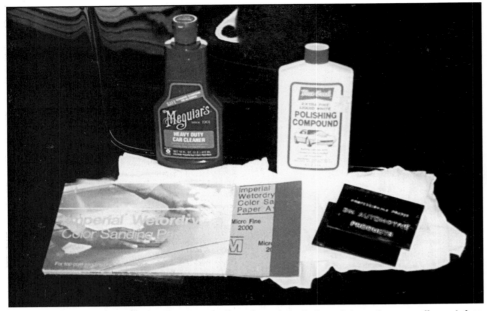

Finessing is the new technique for removing surface defects in paint, such as small scratches and water spots. Most light surface defects can be finessed by hand, using two polishes, a few sheets of fine sand paper, two inexpensive rubber sanding blocks, and clean rags.

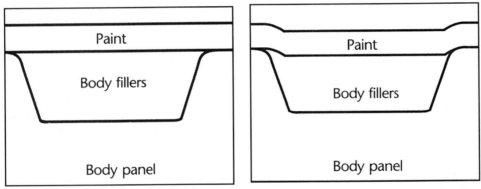

"Sink Marks" are common on cars that have had bodywork. They often appear over bonding strips, repaired areas, and filled holes. When the bodywork was first done, the surface was sanded smooth. Yet over a period of time the underlying plastic body filler, or mixed fiberglass, shrank either from solvents slowly evaporating or from curing. If there is sufficient paint thickness, these surface blemishes can be block sanded out. Photo courtesy Corvette Fever Magazine.

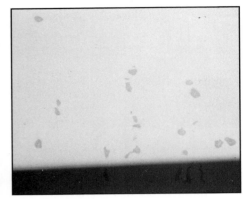

These surface spots caused by bugs are typical of the type of defect that can be finessed out if the paint is thick enough.

to finesse a car's paint. Finessing is an inexpensive method to remove the defects and damage in the paint while keeping it beautiful for a longer period of time.

Problems Not Solved by Finessing

The process of finessing eliminates paint defects by carefully removing a portion of the top layer of paint. Problems which lie under the top surface can't be repaired by finessing. Examples of these include: blistering, peeling, bubbling, and, for the most part, cracking, or poor color matching.

Cracks—Cracking or crazing of the paint, although it appears to be only on the surface, is a symptom of an underlying problem. Common causes of cracking are too many paint jobs (paint that is too thick) and substrate problems (plastic panels or bodywork which is deteriorating). Even if the cracks are very shallow and can be easily sanded out, they are likely to return. One exception is a car that is always garaged. When a car is protected from the elements, years can be added to an ailing paint job.

Color-Matching—Color-match problems can seldom be solved by finessing. The exception is when the difference in color or appearance between two body panels, such as a fender and door, is caused by a difference in the surface finish. For example, if a door was resprayed in lacquer (lacquer was commonly used in panel repairs), the paint may have dulled down over a period of months. Paint loses its gloss when the surface becomes rough or uneven. Reflected light is scattered more by such surfaces, and the color can look lighter on that panel.

This effect can be noticed during the process of finessing. Rub a portion of a very glossy panel with a fine polishing compound and then compare how it looks with the area not rubbed. If the color was dark red for example, the rubbed area will not be as deep in color—it will look a milkier, lighter red.

If there is a big difference in color or shade between two panels, finessing won't help. However, if the

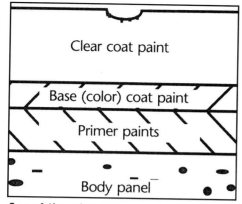

One of the advantages of clear coat paint jobs is the ability to finesse out surface blemishes. A good factory paint job is at least 4 mils thick, and the clear top coat should be nearly 2 mils of this. Photo courtesy Corvette Fever Magazine.

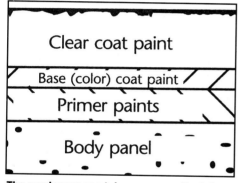

The sandpaper scratches are smoothed down by a polishing compound. Actually, this technique is used in all types of polishing, going to successively finer polishes to smooth the surface. You could start with the fine polishes, but it takes forever to remove the initial material. It is quicker to sand first, then polish. Photo courtesy Corvette Fever Magazine.

difference is only slight, it is worth trying to finesse the lighter colored panel if it has the poorer finish of the two. Try the fine polishes (specific brands are recommended later in this chapter) on the lighter panel and then compare the color match again. It is worth taking the time to try this because the only other solution to fixing a color match is repainting, and sometimes a good color match can be extremely difficult for even the best painter to achieve.

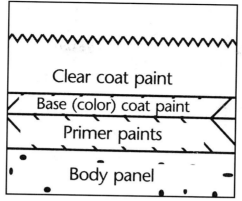

Most surface blemishes are a small faction of a mil thick and therefore can be safely removed. A finer grit paper is used to sand the paint down to remove the blemish. The surface scratches left by the modern "color sanding" papers such as 2000-grit are remarkably shallow. Photo courtesy Corvette Fever Magazine.

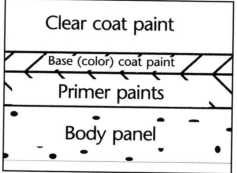

The scratches left by the polishing compounds are almost too small to see; the surface just looks slightly cloudy or lighter in color from the reflected light. The final step is to use a polish that cuts very little and removes almost no paint. The gloss and shine are dramatically increased. This is the step needed to remove "swirl" marks left by a buffer which was used with polishes a little too gritty for the final phase. Photo courtesy Corvette Fever Magazine.

Problems Solved by Finessing

The types of paint problems that can usually be fixed by finessing are: water spots from hard water such as used in sprinkler systems; etched areas from bird droppings and bugs; acid rain spots; and small scratches, abrasions, and rub marks.

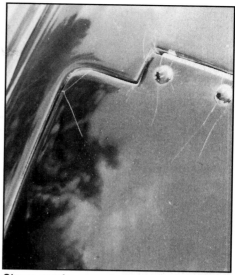

Stress cracks around corners and fasteners cannot be finessed out. This is a sign that the paint has become brittle or the panels are poorly supported.

BUFFING & FINESSING EQUIPMENT

Finessing and buffing requires some specialized equipment. Here's a brief rundown on some of the items you'll need. Some are mandatory, others are nice of have if you can afford them.

Rotary Buffers

A large electric rotary buffer, a wool pad and a can of rubbing compound were the primary tools and supplies used to buff automotive paint for many years. The heat generated by the buffer and pads was actually desirable and helped some earlier paints to flow out. However, it also it commonly burnt and smeared the paint on high spots, or if the speed increased too much, or if the compund dried out.

Variable speed buffers which can be switched to a few different speeds or which have infinitely variable speed controls are an improvement over single-speed models. Better yet is the electronic speed control buffer which allows the user to dial in a specific

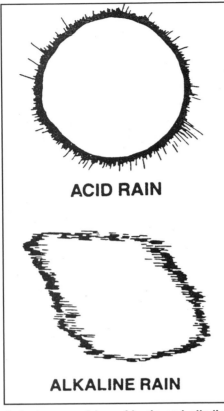

ACID RAIN

ALKALINE RAIN

Defects caused by acid rain and alkaline water spots can often be finessed out.

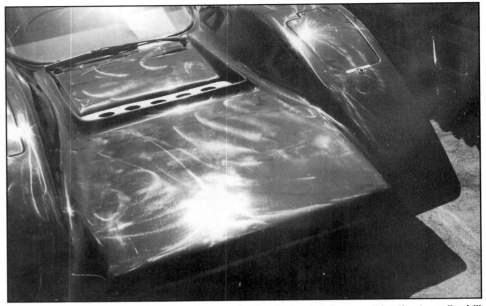

The patterns of reflected light on this car clearly show what is meant by the term "swirl" marks. Swirl marks are actually very fine scratches which usually result from a power buffer, hence their circular or curved pattern. The last compound or cleaner used on the paint was just a little too coarse. The swirl marks can be removed by use of a cleaner with finer abrasives or they can be temporarily filled and hidden by some types of waxes or polishes.

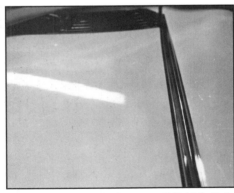

The reflection of the fluorescent light bulb in this car's finish shows a very slight wave pattern. This can be caused by finger pressure when a sanding block isn't used.

rpm. This is a considerable advantge because the other buffers slow down as they are pressed down toward the paint, and then speed upbuffers. These surfaces act softer and this property increases as the temperature is elevated. In fact, cooling the paint down below freezing helps make the surface rigid and makes buffing faster

and easier.

Removal of scratches by buffing alone is now dangerous on these finishes. During conventional buffing, scratches have been shown to propogate further down into the paint. Scratches which were only .1 mil deep were not eliminated until .7 to .8 mil of paint was removed by buffing. The amount of paint buffed off is seven to eight times the depth of the original scratch and this is far more paint that any manufacturer allows to be removed. Repainting would be needed. The best procedure to use on these surfaces is to finesse and sand out the scratches before buffing and to keep the temperature down while buffing.

Orbital Polishers

Rotary buffers create scratch patterns in large sweeping arcs due to the rotation of the buffing pad. By comparison, orbital polishers have a much smaller oscillating motion

which creates smaller, more random patterns which are more difficult to perceive at a distance. Because of this, they are effective at removing the swirl marks created by buffers and their use has become popular as a step following buffing.

Orbital polishers are very safe to use, even for novices, and are good for applying fine polishes, fine cleaners and waxes. The cotton, terry cloth bonnets of many orbital polishers can be washed and reused. Two-handed electric models are common and relatively inexpensive. Air power models are also available.

Pads

Wool pads are the most aggressive in removing paint and should be avoided by beginners. However, in spite of the many types of new foam pads, wool pads remain the favorite cutting pad of many professionals (see sidebar p. 48) who maintain that no other type of pad can cut as fast or

The three most common ways paint is damaged by buffing are burning, buffing through edges and excessive thickness reduction. Burning can be prevented by measuring paint temperature with a non-contact thermometer, which is particularly helpful during training or when using new products. The foam pad and automatic speed controlled buffer showm here also reduce the likelihood of burning.

Air power also works well for cleaning and buffing. One advantage is that air powered tools are lighter in weight than most electric buffers. For details, see the sidebar nearby.

effectively. A variety of wool pads and different blends of material are available today.

Foam pads also come in many models and materials. The pads can screw directly onto the buffer or be attached with a Velcro backing. Often manufacturers colorcode the pads for their respective applications. The last polishing step of finessing or buffing is commonly carried out with a foam pad.

HOW TO FINESSE PAINT

The first step is to determine whether or not the defect can be finessed out, and this is mainly decided by how deep the defect is. In most cases, you won't be able to finesse out defects unless they are only a few 10 thousandths-of-an-inch in depth. In most cases, it is risky to try to finesse out a defect more than five ten-thousandths deep (one-half mil). The reason is not because it is too difficult to remove that much paint, in fact, the opposite is true.

In the case of a paint job that is not clear coated, the risk is that you will remove so much paint that the underlying primer will begin to show through. If the color coat is simply made too thin in spots, the color will look blotchy or show different hues in those areas. In either case, by the time you see the primer, it's too late. The damage is done to the paint job, and it is irreversible. Repainting is the only solution.

The risk to a clear-coated car is that the clear will be so thin after the finessing that it provides insufficient protection for the lower layer (the color coat). The clear coat contains sun screens to filter out ultraviolet rays. The more of the clear surface paint that is sanded or buffed off, the more UV light gets through to deteriorate the underlying color coat of paint.

Determine Paint Thickness

It is critical that you measure the thickness of your paint before you begin any sanding and buffing to make sure there is sufficient paint. Paint surfaces can be measured with a paint measuring gauge, such as the one offered by Pro Motorcar Products. The top panels and the horizontal surfaces such as the hood,

Meguiar's has a color-coded system to label their pads, and others have similar systems. From left to right is a wool bonnet for aggressive buffing, a red polyfoam cutting pad (less aggressive than the wool pad) used on the orbital buffer, the yellow pad for polishing, tan for finishing and the small yellow again for polishing but used on a small orbital polisher.

roof, and trunk lid experience much more damage from UV rays than do the sides of cars. It only makes sense that thickness is more critical on the hood than on the doors.

When measuring paint thickness, be concerned about your new car warranties or paint guarantees. In these cases, you have to go by what the car or paint manufacturer specifies if you want to preserve your warranty. You'll find some differences between the specifications of different manufacturers, too. Ask the service manager or body shop manager at

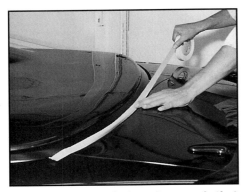

I can't recommend strongly enough that edges and high spots should be masked with tape before buffing. The pressure and heat at these points is much higher; you can buff down into the primer in seconds. When that happens, it's costly in time and money to fix these mistakes.

your car dealer for information about what the manufacturer specifies. In the case of repainting, ask the painter or paint supply store for information on what the paint manufacturer specifies.

Thickness Guidelines—If you can't locate information specific to your paint or your car, the following general guidelines can be of use. If the total paint thickness is 4 to 5 mils (undercoats, base coats, and clear coat combined), it is likely that an experienced and careful person can finesse out shallow defects without the paint becoming too thin. If the car is clear coated and the thickness is already under 4 mils, finessing may take the paint down farther than the manufacturer recommends and may cause problems later. Use caution, particularly on top panels. If the paint is less than 3 mils thick, don't risk sanding. In fact, abrasive car polishes or buffing alone may cause the primer to show through.

If the paint is more than 6 mils, there is a possibility that the car has been repainted over old paint. That may be the case even if you owned the car since new. Some cars are repainted at the factory. Many more

SAFE BUFFING SPECIFICATIONS

Measurement of paint thickness before and after any buffing or finesse sanding is now required by all car manufacturers.

Why? Because the clear coat protects the underlying paints, but no one can see how thick it is or how much is being removed by buffing. If a person polishes off too much paint, its life is cut short even though the finish looks great. In a few seasons, the paint can begin cracking, flaking or peeling (delamination), especially on the hood, roof and trunk.

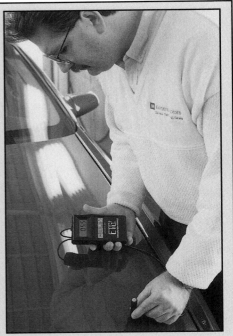

How much is too much? If as little as .0003 of an inch (.3 mils) of a monocoat or .0005 of a clearcoat is removed, repainting may be necessary. To give you an idea of how little this is, it's about 1/10 the thickness of this page—or less than the thickness of the clear wrapper on a cigarette pack.

What's needed? Electronic thickness gauges which measure to 1/10 of a mil help make sure that clearcoat thickness is not reduced too much. If the person buffing your car doesn't use this type of gauge, then they don't know how much paint they are removing.

Maximum Allowable Paint Thickness Reduction Specifications

	Monocoat	Clearcoat
Chrysler	.3 mils	.5 mils
Ford	.3 mils	.3 mils
GM	.3 mils	.5 mils

Note: The above amounts are the total allowable reductions in paint thickness before repainting is required. In other words, .3 mils cannot be removed each time if the vehicle is buffed or finessed more than once. Specifications by other auto manufacturers are similar; check technical service bulletins for updates.

are repainted at the dealership before the customer ever sees them.

Cleaning & Inspection

An overall cleaning and inspection of the paint is the first step. It doesn't make sense to spend hours finessing the front end of the car, only to discover later that the car needs a repaint anyway because the rear portion has defects that can't be finessed out.

First, thoroughly wash and rinse the car, and then wipe it down with towels

Most professionals recommend that you squirt the cleaners, polishes, or even waxes on the cloth and not directly on the paint.

A good technique is to rub only in one direction. When you go to the next stage, rub in another direction. That way, you'll be able to tell at what stage any scratches appear.

or chamois to prevent water spots. Move the car to a place that has especially good lighting. If you are inspecting for color-matching, an outside location that is not in shadows or directly in sunlight is the best choice. An outside location can also be good for inspection before finessing, but the best lighting situation for finessing is inside under fluorescent tubes.

Visually examine the car, panel-by-panel. If defects in the paint look like they could be on the surface, try rubbing them off with a solvent such as a bug and tar remover. 3M's *General Purpose Adhesive Cleaner* is also an excellent solvent. It's always a good idea to first try the solvent on a hidden, painted spot, such as a door jamb or inside the trunk or hood lip, to make sure it doesn't hurt the paint.

If the solvent fails, try some polish on a rag. If the area is crusty or appears corroded (such as acid rain spots often do), Pat Wilson, Meguiar's Southwest Field Training Manager, suggests cleaning the area with the PrepPen brush. The brush has a point composed of a bundle of thin glass fibers. The glass fibers are even strong enough to scrub off surface rust, but they won't scrape or gouge the underlying paint.

Another use for the PrepPen brush is removal of rust specks. If a defect looks like a tiny brown dot, it may be that a tiny bit of steel or iron is embedded in the paint. It's wise to try to brush it off before sanding or buffing because if it gets dislodged and trapped under the sandpaper or buffing pad, it can do a lot of damage scratching up the surrounding paint.

After cleaning the paint defect, take a few measurements with a thickness gauge inside the damaged area. Record these readings and then take several readings on the surrounding paint. If the defect is only a few tenths of a mil deep and if the surrounding paint is thick enough, give finessing a try.

If a few of the spots are deep but most of the other spots are fairly shallow, you still may want to try finessing the car. However, you may not want to try taking the worst spots all the way out.

The deeper defects will probably look even better if the surrounding paint is taken down only a few tenths. If the defects are small in diameter, you can try cleaning and filling them in with touch-up paint. This type of spot repair is shown in detail in Chapter 6, *Small Paint Repairs.*

Sanding

"Sanding" might be too strong a term for the next step because the new types of sandpaper used in finessing are really more like "polishing papers." The finest grit available used to be 600-grit, but now grits of 1000, 1500, and 2000 (often called microfine and ultrafine) are common. It is best to use the finest paper possible that will still remove the defect. Start with 2000-grit paper, especially if you are a beginner. If that doesn't remove the defect, then move up to 1500-grit and so on.

The 1500- and 2000-grit papers are so fine and they remove paint so slowly that you can actually remove paint faster with a buffer using a wool pad and polishing compound. Then why use them? Control. Less than a thousandth of an inch can make the difference between saving a paint job and having to pay for a new one. By using microfine sandpapers with a sanding block, you can remove paint steadily and uniformly. If a power buffer is being used for polishing, professionals will sand with a coarser paper, from 1000- to 1200-grit. However, if you haven't had much experience, be very careful using 1000-grit or a buffer. Both can remove a lot of paint very quickly.

True Grits—The higher the number, the finer the grit, right? Well not always. In my tests, 3M's 2000 grit made less deep sanding scratches then the 2000-grit marketed by Meguiar's. 3M's did seem to wear down faster, however, and when it wore down it became a virtual polishing paper. Also some manufacturers, including Norton, use the micron grading system in which larger numbers mean larger grit size. Norton's 10 micron

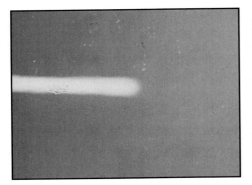

1. You'll be surprised at how easily the smallest surface irregularities will be visible under the proper lighting. The reflection of overhead fluorescent tubes is best for spotting small details. This pot-marked area, visible in the light's reflection, looks pretty bad up close but is only about two ten thousandths-of-an-inch in depth.

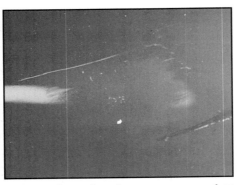

2. Clean the surface to remove any sand or dirt. Then splash on some water and lightly sand with 2000-grit paper. Squeegee the water off with a soft pliable rubber block to check your progress. Move around to find the best angle for viewing the area. Any remaining low points will be quite visible as shiny dots.

3. After less than a minute of sanding only a few low points remain. If you polish this area now, it will look much better than before but the remaining points will be visible under close examination in the proper light. It's a judgment call about how far to sand because you never know when you will break through the clear coat, or color coat. If the rest of your car is not show car perfect it may be wise to stop while you're ahead.

paper in use appears closely matched to 3M's 1500-grit.

If you're finessing by hand the finest grits are important because it takes some effort to get the sanding scratches out. However people who use a power buffer usually sand with a coarser grit to get the job done more quickly.

Dry sanding cars with a DA before buffing has become popular due to the availability of very fine grit papers for them. Using a DA to remove orange peel on a fresh paint job is much faster than sanding by hand, although some hand sanding will always be necessary in tight spots.

Sanding Block—Fold the paper around a thin, flexible rubber sanding block. If a sanding block is not used, the pressure of your fingers will create ruts in the paint. Even though these ruts are very shallow, they can show up in reflected light and produce a wavy, patchy appearance on the paint's finish.

It is best to use a sanding block during finessing but there are cases where it can be omitted. For example, if there is one particularly deep defect, such as a sunken or pitted spot, and

you don't want to risk sanding the surrounding paint down too far, use just one finger to sand that spot.

Wet-Sanding—Wet-sanding helps the paper last longer and helps it cut through the paint better. Keep the paper and the paint wet during sanding to prevent the paper from getting clogged up with the removed paint. Thoroughly clean out a bucket to remove any sand or grit and then fill it halfway with water. Add a few drops of dish detergent to help keep the paper from gumming up.

Rinse the paper and surface frequently while sanding. I can't stress the importance of this too much because if a speck of grit or accumulated paint builds up, the scratches it will leave will be far deeper than those of the sandpaper. The problem is that such deep scratches won't be noticed until the polishing stage is done; and then the paint will have to be sanded again, resulting in the removal of more paint. To prevent these scratches, frequently check the surface of the sandpaper for any buildup or traces of grit.

It's a good idea to continually bathe the areas you are sanding with a small

stream of water from a garden hose. If the hose has a metal connector on its end, cover the metal part with tape to prevent it from chipping or scratching the paint.

Sand in one direction, polish in another direction (typically at right angles). By doing this, any remaining scratches can be identified to see which step is creating the problem.

If you want to remove very small defects or pits, mark the spot with tape or other means. When you are working in the middle of a panel, it's easy to get off base an inch or two. By marking the spot, you also save time when you try to find and inspect the spot as it becomes smaller and smaller.

Use a second rubber block as a squeegee, and wipe the area every minute or so. When the water is wiped off, the remaining small pits show up as shiny spots and this makes them much more visible.

Remember that sandpapers tend to become finer as they wear down. A well-worn piece of 600-grit paper can become finer than a new sheet of 2000. The difference isn't just in how

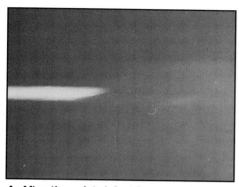

4. After the paint defect is removed to your satisfaction, wipe the area clean. Placing a piece of tape in line with the defect at the start helps make it easier to inspect that area during the process. As you sand, the area you're covering typically gets bigger and bigger, and sometimes it's hard to remember exactly where the defect was located.

5. Use a clean soft cotton cloth and fine polishing compound to remove the tiny sanding scratches left from the 2000-grit paper. A fresh unused section of the paper removes paint relatively quickly and leaves deeper scratches. After it has been used a little while, it becomes duller. A worn piece "cuts" slower but it leaves only very minute sand scratches. If you have a well-worn piece available, use it to do the final sanding. After using the polishing compound the reflection will return but it's still a little hazy from scratches left by the very fine abrasives.

6. Polish the area with a separate soft cloth using Meguiar's Heavy Duty Car Cleaner. The photo doesn't do justice to the increase in gloss and brilliance this last step accomplishes. If the last sanding was done with a sufficiently worn piece of 2000-grit paper, try skipping the polishing compound and go right to the cleaner. Finish with a wax if you desire.

fast the paper removes the paint, it also is noticeable in how deep the resultant sanding scratches are.

For this reason, worn sandpaper can be useful in finessing, particularly when the job is done by hand. Use fresh pieces of paper to sand out the defects; then clean the surface and go over it with a well-worn piece of sandpaper. Such paper is so fine that it acts like a fine polishing compound, and it can even leave a bit of a gloss to the paint. Worn paper removes the deeper scratches left by the fresh paper, and using it can sometimes save one intermediary step in the polishing process.

Polishing

After the surface defects are sanded out, the next step is polishing. The goals of polishing are to bring the gloss back to the paint and to remove any sanding scratches. If the final paper you used in sanding was a well-worn piece of 2000-grit paper, you might be able to get by with using only one type of polishing compound or cleaner.

Dark colors, especially black, often need a little more attention because

fine scratches and swirl marks show up so well. Hand-polishing also requires more effort because you have to use grittier compounds to make progress in a reasonable amount of time. Machines that spin their pads at many revolutions per minute can use finer compounds because they make many more passes in a minute.

If you are doing the polishing by hand, and if you are picky and have a dark color, two stages may be required. First, use a fine polishing compound to remove the sandpaper scratches; then use a cleaner with even finer abrasives to remove the scratches or haze left by the polish.

Choose your polishing cloths carefully. Anything which is clean, soft, and 100% cotton is a good bet. Such things as nylon threads, buttons, or any type of dirt contamination in a polishing cloth can create problems. Look in Chapter 9 for more information on choosing a polishing cloth.

Be aware that it is particularly risky to do the polishing outside. Sand or grit is likely to blow on the area you

are polishing at some time, unless you are doing it under a carport in the rain. Even one particle of sand can create many nasty scratches.

Recommendations—There are many polishing compounds and polishes to choose from. For hand polishing, Blue Coral's *Liquid Fine Polishing Compound* followed by Meguiar's *Heavy Duty Car Cleaner Wax* has worked for me. There's a chance that these products might not be readily available in your area or that the manufacturer may change these formulations at some time, so general information on how to select a polish is in order.

Selecting a polish would be much easier if the manufacturers agreed on a grading system and then labeled their polishes and compounds appropriately. Unfortunately, that's not the case. First try reading the labels. The labels may be of some help, but often they were written by marketing people who say the product is good for just about all applications.

After reading the labels, it comes down to trial and error. Select and try a very fine polishing compound (not rubbing compound, which is usually

Abrasive blocks as fine as 2000-grit are available from Meguiar's. They are good for sanding small defects in a paint's finish, and they last almost forever.

PRODUCING FANTASTIC FINISHES

There are so many products to choose from at every stage in sanding and buffing a top coat, where does someone new to this start? Here's one shop's procedure and I'll bet most have never tried the first step which can be a real time-saver. Final Finish in Branford, Connecticut specializes in high-end restorations (if you consider cars like supercharged Bugatti roadsters high end) and refinishes many of the custom Calloway supercars. This is a five-step process which owner David SeCaur, pictured at right, is first to point out is far more than is needed for most refinish work.

1. Wet-sand all orange peel out with 500-grit (Norton) paper after waiting 2 or 3 days. The waiting period is very important because once the topcoat fully cures sanding and buffing is MUCH more difficult. Even though the paint manufacturer says wait 24 hours, Dave has found that no matter what the air temperature, it's still too soft after only one day. He is careful to schedule the final clearcoating so that time is available 2 or 3 days later for the sanding and buffing.
2. Wet-sand the 500-grit sand-scratches out with 1500-grit (Norton) paper. At both sanding stages, he uses a sanding block with spring steel core. The very last sanding involves going lightly over the entire surface with 1500 paper without the block.
3. Buff with a 1.5 inch thick wool pad (Schlegel 875C) and 3M 06021.
4. Buff with lambs wool pad (Schlegel 904) and 3M 05992.
5. Polish with a foam pad (3M 05725) and 3M 05996 Polish Glaze.
Most people won't strive for this level of finish quality and therefore they can use combinations of other papers, pads, and polishes to streamline the topcoat sanding process to a four step or even a three step process.

more coarse) as the first step. If the last paper you sanded with was a well-worn piece of 2000-grit paper, it is unlikely that any sand scratches will be visible after polishing.

If the finish is still a little dull or cloudy after polishing, try a cleaner, or cleaner polish, or cleaner wax that has very fine abrasives. Use the same inspection as above to see if it works well to remove the fine scratches left behind by the polishing. In other words, if the product doesn't remove the scratches, you'll have to find a cleaner which contains coarser abrasives. If it leaves new scratches, you need to find a cleaner with finer abrasive.

Power Buffers—Power buffers should not be used unless you have some experience or you are going to be very careful. For the inexperienced, there are some new, safer alternatives. Foam pads are a more forgiving addition to rotary buffers. They tend not to cut as aggressively as the older wool pads and therefore are a safer choice for beginners. In either case, it is wise to tape any edges—because it is so easy to buff through there.

Less expensive orbital polishers with terry cloth boots are also fairly safe to use. They can even be used to clear scuff marks from the plastic rear window on convertibles. If the marks are light enough, they can be removed by hand with a fine polish or a cleaner-wax. Turtle Wax works well for this.

If you are interested in having your car sanded and buffed by someone else, then be very careful about who you have do it. A custom paint job can be worth $5,000 to $10,000 on some cars, and careless buffing can ruin it in seconds. Find someone who will take their time and measure the paint thickness wherever possible to make certain the amount of paint they

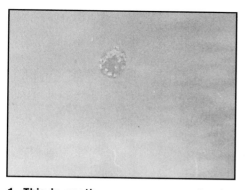

1. This is another common example of a surface defect that can be helped by finessing. This spot was caused by acid rain. When you find a rough spot on your paint which you suspect to be an acid rain spot, it's best to examine and clean the area as soon as possible.

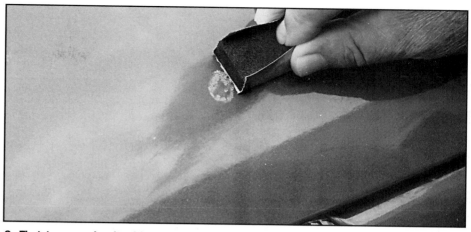

2. First try removing it with a bug and tar Remover or similar cleaner. If that has no effect, cautiously try block-sanding it with 2000-grit paper. Use plenty of water to flush any hard particles that may break off.

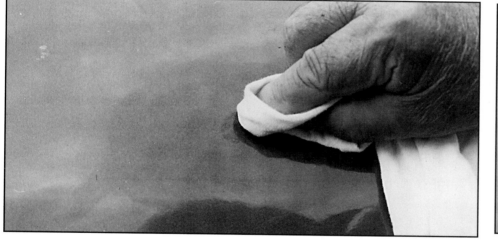

3. The sanding will very quickly tell you whether the crust is only on the surface of the paint or if it has etched down into the paint. In this case, the etching was deep and completely sanding it out would have risked taking off too much paint. Use a fine polish to bring back the paint's gloss.

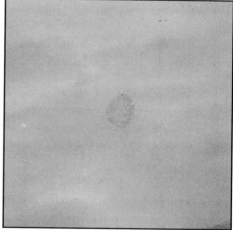

4. Although the blemish is not entirely removed, it is a lot less noticeable. The sanding and cleaning also removed any remaining traces of the chemicals which caused the damage and thereby ensured that the etching and damage to the paint wouldn't continue.

are removing is minimal. To carefully sand and buff a medium-sized car can take eight hours or more, while a quickie buff with relatively coarse compounds can be done in a couple of hours. Therefore, there is a large economic incentive for the person doing the work to hurry the job. It's critically important to choose a shop that won't rush the process or take off too much paint.

If possible, have the shop show you the paint thickness before and after the job. The shop will not have a gauge that measures paint on plastic panels, but they certainly should have one for measuring paint thickness on metal panels. The reason why you and the shop should know the paint thickness is because the clear coat can be sanded too thin and you won't know by looking at it. Although you

won't see anything wrong with the paint (in fact, it could look terrific), if the top coat of paint is buffed too thin, you could be faced with a very expensive paint failure in the future, such as delamination (peeling).

CHEMICAL SPOTTING

by Bud Abraham, Detail Plus Systems

By definition, chemical spotting is the discoloration or disfigurement of a painted surface due to the action of chemical contaminants that have fallen on the surface of the paint from air borne mists and/or dusts. In general, these contaminants are either acidic or alkaline in nature. For example, what we call acid rain is a solution of a gas such as sulfur dioxide in water that acts just like sulfuric acid on the painted surface. Or, cement dust when mixed with water is alkaline, forming a material which acts like caustic potash on the paint finish

Acid Rain—Acid rain is created when sulfur dioxide or nitrogen oxides combine with smog and water to form sulfuric and nitric acids. The etched areas on the paint can often be seen as a white ring around dulled paint. The size of the spots can vary from very small to larger than a nickel. Acid rain spots are generally rounder and more uniform than alkaline rain spots.

Alkaline Spots—Alkaline spotting occurs when minerals or chemicals in water are left behind on the finish as the water dries. The gloss can be dulled in the spots and appear with a white film resembling salt deposits. If the deposits aren't cleaned off, the condition can deteriorate with later stages showing rough or jagged edges. A common cause of alkaline spotting is harsh water from sprinkler systems. When such described contaminants settle on the paint finish, two things can occur: First, the pigment of the paint is attacked by the contaminant causing all or some area of the colors in the paint to be changed. For example, a red color (made from yellow and maroon) will increase in maroon color leaving purple, or deep red spots (if the contaminant attacks the yellow part of the red pigment.)

Second, some contaminants will mark or disfigure the resin part of the paint which results in milky or dull spotting in the form of lighter or white spots or dull patchy low gloss spots.

Without exception, all paint finishes can be affected by airborne contam-inants; however, some are more resistant than others. In general, the most resistant paints used today are the polyurethane clear coats whose resin system is more resistant to these contaminants. Air-dried paint finishes are more susceptible to attack than baked finishes, especially when the paint finish is new and not cured. The older an air dry finish, the more resistant it becomes to chemical attack. However, neither air dry nor baked finishes are totally impervious to contaminants and the longer the contaminant remains on the surface, the greater the chance for marking, discoloration, and spotting.

In general, metallic colors are the most susceptible to attack from airborne contaminants. This is due to the aluminum flake used which is a reactive material when exposed to acids or alkali. Some solid colors are also very sensitive to contaminants, and depending on the type, concentration, and the length of time it remains on the surface, these solid non-metallic colors can spot or damage also.

Chemical fallout will come from industrial sources such as effluent from the smoke stacks of manu-facturing and processing facilities and oil or coal fired power plants. The source of the contaminant can be very close to the paint finish or very far away because contaminants are wind borne, and can be released into the atmosphere where they are dissolved by moisture and returned in the form of rain on the vehicle surface.

The most logical protection against chemical spotting is to keep the car finish clean. This means regular washing of the car. This is important because it is impossible to notice contaminants on the paint finish. It is therefore recommended to wash the car weekly.

Keep in mind that new paint finishes are far more susceptible to chemical spotting than older ones. For the first two to three months a new paint finish should be regularly hosed off to remove any accumulation of chemical contaminants. Thorough routine waxing of the paint finish will go a long way to help reduce chemical spotting, but it will not guarantee freedom from chemical attack. It depends largely on the type of chemical, its concentration, and the length of time it is on the finish.

Auto manufacturers claim that the new clear coat paint finishes will provide significant protection against chemical spotting by protecting the pigment. This may be true, but clear coats also present other problems. The clear coat itself is also subject to attack by chemical contaminants, which tend to leave dull or milky spots on the finish, as well as pitting and etching. Polyurethane enamels tend to be the most resistant to chemical attack.

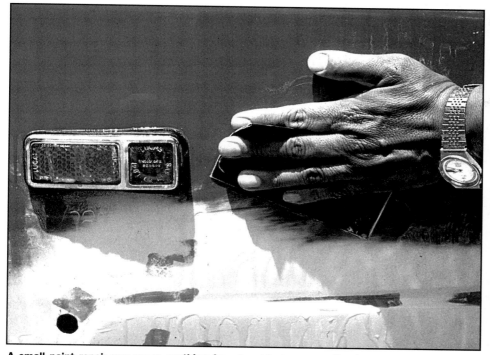

A small paint repair can mean anything from touching up a small paint chip to repainting an entire panel. Color-matching, feather-edging, and blending are the keys to successful spot repair. The left rear quarter panel of this Jeep Cherokee has been feather-edged and soon will be sprayed with paint. If the painter does his job properly, the new paint should blend with the old, and the area that was repaired should be impossible to detect without gauges. Photo by Michael Lutfy.

6

PAINT REPAIRS

There are a number of auto paint problems and surface defects that can be repaired without major repainting. Many of them can be handled by car owners who have no previous experience in auto repainting. Even if you don't do the repair yourself, you should learn what's involved to help protect both your automotive investment and your checkbook.

In this chapter, we will discuss how to repair the inevitable paint chip. Inevitable because, no matter how carefully you park your car or take steps to protect it, sooner or later it will have a chip in the paint (unless it's a museum car, and even then, it's possible). The repair methods shown on the following pages are quick, easy, and of professional caliber. Furthermore, the tools and materials you need are inexpensive and easily procured.

Another common surface defect is the "scuff and scrape." With drive-in windows, toll booths, and pylons everywhere these days, an occasional scuff or rub mark is a common sight on today's cars. Add to this the increased use of painted body parts which are just begging to be hit, such as wide mirrors, impact or aero-styled bumpers, front air dams, and pavement-hugging ground effects kits, and you'll find scuff marks to be a paint problem many car owners experience. Again the methods of repair are fast, easy, and could save the expense of extensive repainting.

However, some paint problems can only be fixed by repainting. When they are limited to a small area or a single body panel such as a door or fender, they are called spot repairs. A body shop or paint booth isn't needed to handle most spot repairs, if you want to do them yourself. If spot repairs have to be made, then color-matching becomes important. The

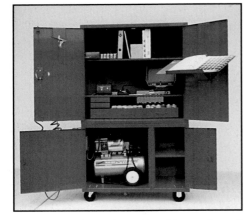

An option for repairing paint chips and small scratches is to take the car to a shop that has a touch-up paint system such as Paint Plus. This self-contained unit has a small compressor and air brush equipment, plus tints to mix small containers to match thousands of factory colors. An addition system repairs buff marks and scrapes on bumpers. Courtesy Detail Plus.

Ground-effects parts such as spoilers, rocker panels, and air dams, plus two-tone paint schemes make spot repainting easier by providing breaks in body panels where masking can easily be done. Photo courtesy Nina Pfanstiehl.

Before repainting, chips, scratches, or other lower areas in the bare metal should be filled with glazing putty. The putty is worked into the low areas and smoothed off with a plastic spreader. After it hardens, it is block-sanded flush with the panel.

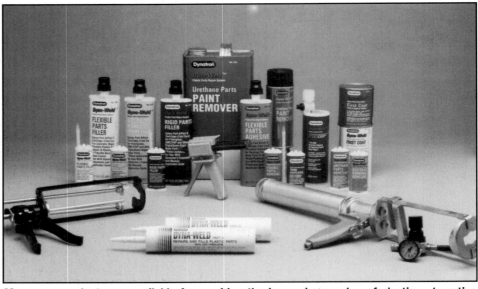

Many new products are available for repairing the increasing number of plastic automotive parts. Dynatron makes a line of repair materials, including two-part adhesives mixed during application by the gun shown in the foreground. Photo courtesy Bondo/Mar Hyde Corporation.

basics of color-matching are explained along with tips on how to blend together the freshly painted areas and the surrounding older paint. Again, this is valuable information for car owners, whether they do the work themselves or not. With well over 10,000,000 cars reported in accidents each year, and countless millions more cars involved in small unreported fender benders and scrapes, there's a pretty good chance that you will be faced with the possibility of spot repainting portions of your car at some point in time.

PAINT CHIP REPAIR

Although there is spirited disagreement about the need for waxes and sealants, there is no debate about the need for paint chips to be repaired. Here's an area of car maintenance, like keeping sufficient oil in your engine or sufficient air in your tires, where a little care prevents costly future damage. Car enthusiasts will want to fix chips to keep their finish looking great but there's also a strong functional and economic reason to repair paint chips.

A chip in automotive paint frequently goes down to the bare metal of the car's body. Even if it only goes

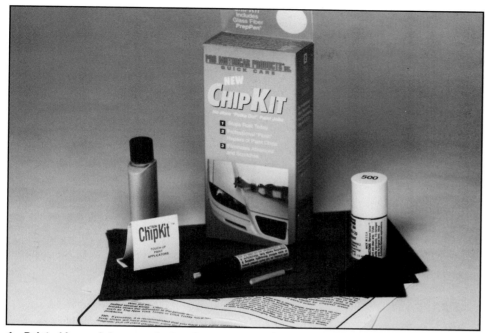

1. Paint chip repair is convenient and easy with this all-in-one kit from Pro Motorcar Products. The ChipKit tm contains the PrepPen, clear coat paint, sanding block, applicators, microfine sanding papers, and a fine polishing compound selected to match the papers. All you need to do is get the proper color touch-up paint for your vehicle. It's available at GM dealers and direct from Pro Motorcar at 813-726-9225. By the way, the PrepPen brush also works well for many detailing tasks such as cleaning aluminum parts and hard to get at areas.

2. Begin by thoroughly brushing the chip with firm pressure. The glass fibers in the brush won't scratch or scrape the surrounding paint but they will degloss it. This prepares the surface so the touch-up paint will stick. TIP: Wait a few days between successive applications of touch-up paint, and then lightly brush the area to clean and prep it before applying the new coats of paint.

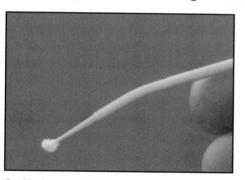

3. Shake or stir the touch-up paint for a minute, or longer in the case of metallic colors. ProTouch is a micro-sized brush which has non-absorbent fibers at the end to precisely apply small quantities of paint, or remove it if too much is applied. You can also use the trimmed end of a paper match which works much better than the cheap brush that comes with touch-up paint.

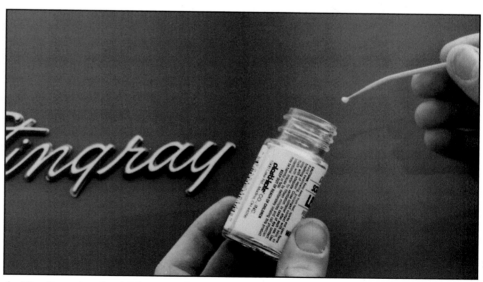

4. After the colored paint has completely dried, apply a coat of clear paint. Build it up higher than the surrounding finish, so several applications will probably be necessary. The paint will shrink down as the solvents evaporate. TIP: Store your touch-up paint or left-over paint upside down. If there's a small air leak at the cap, the paint will seal it and the remaining paint won't dry out.

down to the primer, the primer is usually not a thick enough barrier to prevent rusting. The primer promotes adhesion of the paint to the body panels; the color coat (of base coat/clear coat paint) is for purely cosmetic reasons, and it is up to the top coat to provide protection from

the elements. When there's a break in the armor of the top coat, the underlying paint and body panels are prone to deterioration.

The corrosion and damage can

progress to become much larger than the original chip. Check your car's rust-through warranty. It may stipulate that all paint chips must be repaired or the warranty is void. Even if your car

5. Allow the paint to dry for a day or more. If the touch-up paint has remained higher than the surrounding paint over the entire area of the chip, it's time to block-sand the repair. Use plenty of water to clean the paper and surface after every few strokes. Check to make sure the paint isn't balling up on the sandpaper.

6. Use ultra-fine polishing compound on a soft cloth to bring back the shine. If you can still see very fine scratches or swirl marks, next try using a car cleaner-polish that has even finer abrasives. Some cleaner-waxes will also work well.

7. If there are a number of scratches still noticeable after polishing, you'll probably have to go back a step and lightly sand them out. Dirt may have blown onto your polishing cloth, or the paint may have formed little balls or rolls on the paper during sanding. TIP: Do each step with strokes only in one direction and change to another direction for the next step. If you discover deep scratches, then you can find out in which step the problem lies.

8. The end result will be a smooth repair that is hard to see, if the touch-up color was a close match. By making the repair flush with the surrounding finish, there are no edges to interrupt and distort the reflections on your paint.

doesn't have a rust-through warranty, the meaning should be clear—it is important to fix paint chips. Today's cars use thinner sheet metal than ever before to decrease weight and increase fuel economy. On modern cars, it doesn't take long for a paint chip to rust completely through a body panel.

There are a number of other reasons to repair chips or nicks in the surface paint. For example, some bumpers and fascia parts are constructed of a flexible material that can be damaged by constant exposure to ultraviolet radiation from the sun. Even if the entire part is stripped and repainted at a later date, the exposed areas may become more brittle and deteriorate more rapidly.

Most paint chips can be repaired without repainting the entire panel. Repainting panels can present some problems, which will be discussed shortly, and therefore should only be done as a last resort. The original factory paint is usually very durable and therefore should be repaired and preserved when the damage is simply small chips or nicks. The photo sequence on p. 53-54 illustrates the step-by-step procedure.

Touch-Up Paint

Whenever your car is being repainted, remember to think ahead. Make sure to get a bottle of touch-up paint from the same batch used to paint your car, if at all possible, to use for paint chip repair because matching paint is more difficult than it used to be.

But if you're like most car owners, you will not have touch-up paint on hand from a recent paint job, nor are you likely to have some from the factory. Therefore, you will have to hunt down the proper color touch-up paint to repair paint chips and scratches. New car dealerships are a good place to look, not because the paint is any better, but because they should have the color in stock.

Buying touch-up paint at a dealership does not guarantee the paint will be a perfect match, however. As mentioned before, the touch-up paint you buy, whether it be a one-ounce bottle or a quart can, is different than the paint the factory sprayed on your car. Furthermore, it is likely the manufacturer of the touch-up paint is not the same manufacturer of the factory paint.

And, in the case of cars with base coat/clear coat paint, you wouldn't want the original paint anyway. The color coat (base coat) applied at the factory was specifically formulated to

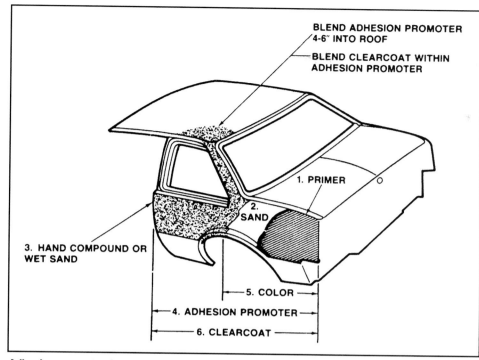

BLEND ADHESION PROMOTER
4-6" INTO ROOF

BLEND CLEARCOAT WITHIN
ADHESION PROMOTER

1. PRIMER

2. SAND

3. HAND COMPOUND OR
WET SAND

5. COLOR

4. ADHESION PROMOTER

6. CLEARCOAT

Adhesion promoter is often used when blending spot repainting into the surrounding older finish, particularly when the older finish is a clear coat. The diagram shows how the color coat, clear coat, and adhesion promoter would overlap when repainting a spot on the rear of a fender. Courtesy I-CAR.

Masking is made a lot faster and easier with a tape machine that applies the masking tape to the paper as it is pulled off the roll. A portable unit like this provides several different widths of masking paper widths. For masking tips, go to Chapter 7, p. 74. Photo courtesy Composite.

add the color and cover the underlying primers. It is not weather-resistant by itself and is often dull in finish. Most base coat paints need a clear coat for protection and to provide gloss. Many base coats today are water-borne paints which are then covered with an additional urethane clear paint. However, touch-up paint is usually a lacquer-based paint to permit easy application and fast drying with only one step.

There are so many automotive colors today that before driving to a dealership it is wise to call the parts department to see if they have the right color on hand. It costs a lot to keep a large inventory of paint, so don't be surprised if a dealership or parts store doesn't have your color on the shelf. The counter person may know immediately which paint you need if you tell them the model and year of the car and describe the color,

for example, "dark blue metallic."

Paint Codes—The paint code is a number assigned by the car manufacturer to a particular color. This is often needed to locate the proper color paint. The paint code is written on a tag located on the car's body. To find the location of the tag, look for a book attached to a store display rack of touch-up paints. Inside will be diagrams showing where to look for the code on the various models of cars, and then there will be a table to cross-reference the car manufacturer's code with the number on the bottle so that you can select the closest color.

Unfortunately, you'll find that some factory paint codes today list four or more variances—different looking mixtures from which you have to choose the best match. The variation in color in some factory paint codes is one reason why buying touch-up paint

from the car dealership or getting "factory packs" of premixed-mixed paint is no assurance of getting a close match. Therefore, always check the match of the paint before driving away. Shake the paint very thoroughly because the metallics and even the color pigment can settle to the bottom of the bottle after being on the shelf for several months. Apply a little touch-up paint on a clean area of the car to check for color match. If there is no area on the outside of the car where you wish to test the color match, open the trunk or hood or try the door jams. Check the color match after it has dried.

Tools

Although the touch-up paint you buy today is not much different than touch-up paint made 10 years ago, there are new methods of preparing the chipped area before application of the paint. It is critical to get into the chipped area and clean out any wax,

These before (top) and after photos illustrate how paintless dent repair (PDR) works. Done properly, it is a much faster and less expensive method of repair. And, because there is no filler involved, the integrity of the original panel is left intact. Courtesy It's Dents or Us!

dirt, or road film so that the touch-up paint can adhere and seal off the chip. It is equally important to clean out any loose surface rust because it traps air and moisture and allows the rusting to continue even after it is covered up by paint.

A new tool which is remarkably effective at both cleaning out rust and wax, silicones, or road grime is the PrepPen Brush, as mentioned in Chapter 5. The tip is composed of a bundle of fiberglass bristles each smaller in diameter than a human hair. The bristles permit a strong, almost pinpoint cleaning and scrubbing of a paint chip or scratch. The fiberglass is strong enough to scrub off surface rust yet it doesn't chip or scratch the surrounding paint. However, it does scuff the original paint to promote adhesion of the touch-up paint.

A different type of tool is 3M's *Rust Avenger*, which is a chemical that converts surface rust into something better to paint over. It doesn't remove rust scale or any accumulations of wax, salt, or films. And obviously it is not for use on non-metal panels such as aluminum, plastic, fiberglass, or rubber body parts.

Cleaning a small chip or scratch

with sandpaper is better than no preparation at all, but be careful not to sand down the surrounding paint too far while trying to get at the edges of the chip or scratch. Also be careful if you use a pointed tool such a screwdriver or ice pick to scrape out a chip because it is easy to slip and create a deeper scratch or scrape next to the chip. A step-by-step demonstration on repairing paint chips is on pages 53 and 54.

PAINTLESS DENT REPAIR

The past few years has seen a dramatic increase in the use of Paintless Dent Removal (PDR), a process whereby small dents are massaged out from behind without the need for body fillers and repainting. Spoon-like hand tools are used to apply pressure to the metal and slowly reform it back to its original shape.

PDR has largely been a trade secret for the past few decades, carried out by a small number of experienced "dingmen" at the assembly plants. More recently the craft has become common at dealerships, carried out by mobile PDR specialists who visit when called in to repair a new or used

car. Now franchisees are being formed and some shops specialize in PDR, often along with touch-ups or bumper repairs. If you don't have a PDR shop around, call dealerships to ask who they use.

The beauty of PDR is that, done properly, the repair is faster, less expensive and better than if the dent was filled with body putty and repainted. The problem is not so much with the body filler, these can be very good and produce an excellent repair. The problem is with spot painting. It is always difficult to match colors and finishes. Plus repaints can fade differently so that even if the repair looks good when you pick the vehicle up, it may look terrible a year later. And in some cases, the value of the vehicle is reduced if repaint or bodywork is found by the buyer.

PDR has its limits, however. Although some fairly large dents can be successfully removed by PDR if the metal is not too stretched, generally only small dents or dings can be removed. If paint damage is deep or if the paint is brittle, PDR is not the answer. The flexibility of paint varies from model to model, but it generally gets more brittle with age, so that some PDR technicians avoid cars over three years old.

What should a car owner look for in PDR? It's Dents Or Us!, the company that trains the PDR people at many US assembly plants, provided the following cautions:

1. Holes should not be drilled in body panels to provide access to the rear of the dent. Although this method is faster, it can void your manufacturer's rust-through warranties, even if silicone or a sealer is placed around the plug which is later installed in the hole.

HOW TO PERFORM A SPOT REPAIR

The Sherwin Williams Automotive Finishes Trouble-shooting Guide provided the following photos. It is one of the best guides in the industry and is an example of the specific information for painters which is available today from the paint manufacturers.

1. DETERGENT WASH Before any sanding is started, completely wash the vehicle with hot water and soap to remove water soluble contamination such as dirt, road grime, fresh tree sap, bird droppings, etc. Washing before sanding is needed because the sanding process does not remove surface contamination; instead, contaminants are pushed below the surface, into the sand scratches, making their removal (by surface cleaners or detergents) difficult or impractical.

2. DETERGENT SCUFF If a "High Tech" wax or paint sealant: may have been used on the paint, an additional cleaning step is recommended. (1) Use a 1 to 1 mixture of household all purpose detergent such as Mr. Clean or Janitor in a Drum and hot water. (2) Scrub the surface using fine water proof sandpaper or a gray nylon scuff pad. (3) Rinse well and dry.

2. The tools should be designed, and the technicians trained, so that they do not exert too much pressure and thereby fracture or scrape the coatings (such as the galvanizing or e-coat) on the inside of the dented panel.

3. The repair should be done entirely by reforming the metal and not finished off by sanding/buffing the paint

REPAIRING SCUFFS & SCRAPES

Scuffs, dings, and scrapes are almost as inevitable as paint chips on today's low-slung cars. And just like paint chips, there are easy, inexpensive ways to fix a lot of the damage without having to resort to the expense and the problems associated with repainting.

In many cases the damage looks much worse than it is. I've seen people drive around with ugly black scuff marks on their car because they were sure they had to take their car into the body shop for repainting. However, all that was needed was a little wet-sanding and hand-polishing to totally eliminate the blemish.

The amount of actual paint damage in a scuff or scrape can be deceptive. The transfer of paint or rubber from whatever hit your car can make it appear that there is damage to the underlying layers of paint or primer. Look at the scraped area closely to try to determine if the mark is on top of the surface of your paint or if it is underneath it. Try applying a little rubbing compound or polishing compound on the edges to see if that reduces the problem.

If it does, try wet sanding the area cautiously with microfine sandpapers such as 1500- or 2000-grit (10 or 8 microns). If the problem appears to be getting worse, the color coat was scraped through, and you'll need repainting to produce a complete cosmetic repair of the paint.

The procedure for cleaning scrapes and scuff marks uses the same materials as those mentioned in the last steps of the paint chip repair, and it can be done by hand without any special tools. If there are areas that need further work, refer to Chapter 5, Finessing, to learn about the power buffing equipment and procedures that will make the job go faster.

SPOT REPAIRS

In some cases, body panels have to be repainted to restore the car's appearance or to protect the car's body. Repainting needs to be done

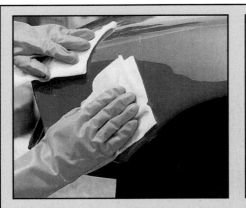

3. SOLVENT CLEAN Solvent clean with appropriate surface cleaners to remove solvent soluble contaminants such as wax, oil, grease, tar, or silicone. TIP: To work effectively, surface cleaners must be used liberally. Contaminants are broken loose by the cleaner and then float on top of the wet film. Contaminants are then removed by drying the surface with a clean lint-free wiping cloth while panel is still wet. DO NOT use thinner or reducer as a surface cleaner.

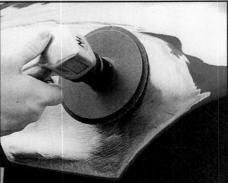

4. GRINDING Remove the old finish from damaged area using 24 to 36 grit grinding disc. Safety glasses are recommended at all stages of refinishing but are particularly important during grinding.

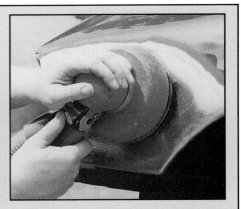

5. ROUGH FEATHEREDGING Sand old paint film along the edge of the damaged area utilizing a random orbital sander and 80 grit paper. Gradually taper (feather) the edge away from the damage until a minimum of 1/4 inch of each layer of undercoat, colorcoat, and clearcoat is exposed.

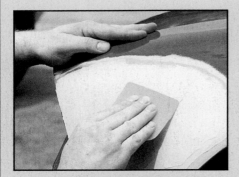

6. BODY FILLER APPLICATION Apply body filler to damaged area to fill imperfections and restore the contour of the panel. Use a plastic spreader to apply the filler to repair area. Firm pressure should be used to bond the filler to the surface and force out any air pockets. For best results, apply body filler in thin coats no more than 1/8 inch thick with a total thickness not to exceed 1/4 inch. TIP: To minimize the possibility of the body filler staining the topcoat, use stain free body filler when basecoat/clearcoat is to be the

7. ROUGH SANDING BODY FILLER Remove excess body filler with a cheese-grater file, then rough sand to contour using 40 to 80 grit paper. Leave the filler slightly high to allow for finish sanding. TIP: Some painters prefer to work the body filler slightly low then apply a nonstaining polyester glazing putty for the finish sanding step.

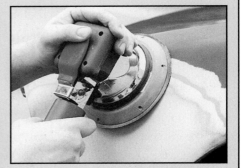

8. FINISH SANDING-FEATHEREDGING Finish sand body filler with 180 or finer grit sandpaper making sure to remove all scratches left by the rough sanding operation. Featheredge the old finish using 180 or finer grit paper. Expose 1/2 inch minimum of each layer of undercoat, colorcoat, and clearcoat to produce a long tapered edge. Sand beyond the featheredge with the same grit sandpaper that will be used for finish sanding. Prepare enough surface to allow priming within the sanded area. Blow off with compressed air, then solvent clean.

when touch-up procedures won't work; but be aware that repainting is not fool-proof. Repainting can cause cosmetic disfigurements ranging from a blotchy metallic layout to color-matching problems, or even more underlying problems such as lifting or sinking. What starts out as a problem the size of a pin can become a problem the size of a panel!

Repainting Problems

As mentioned before, color-matching is a primary problem with partial repainting. It is often difficult (some would say impossible in most cases) to get new paint to match the surrounding older paint. Because of this, it is usually necessary to blend the new paint out onto other panels. In addition to color-matching problems,

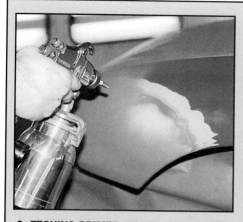

9. ETCHING PRIMER/FILLER APPLICATION Apply an etching primer/filler over body filler, bare metal, and featheredge to provide adhesion and corrosion protection. TIP: To achieve maximum adhesion and corrosion protection, etching filler must be applied in sufficient coats to achieve a minimum of 1 mil (.001 inch) thickness when dry.

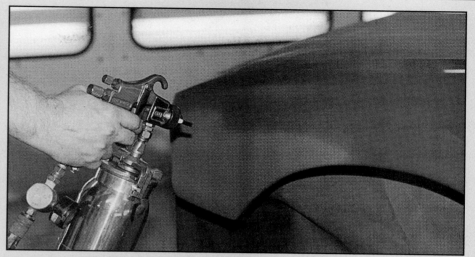

10. PRIMER SURFACER APPLICATION Apply 2-3 medium coats of tintable two-component Acrylic Urethane primer surfacer allowing 5-10 minutes flash between coats. Bring the last coat of surfacer into the fine grit sanded area. (Acrylic Urethane primer surfacer eliminates the need for the use of a sealer to provide gloss holdout, thereby saving a step). Choose a primer surfacer color that closely resembles the topcoat for faster coverage of both basecoats and single stage finishes. TIP: Cure time of primer surfacer can be greatly reduced by force drying with short wave infrared heat or utilizing a baking booth. Temperatures below 60 degrees or applying the paint too thick will make the cure time much longer.

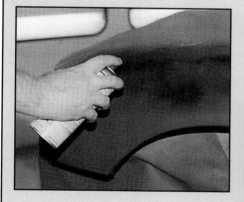

12. BLOCK SANDING Block sand with 320 grit to find low areas. Avoid sanding through the primer, but if you do, lightly sand the guide coat from remaining low areas and reprime. Finish sanding with 400-grit or finer (for best finishes, wet-sand with 600, especially when not applying a sealer). Wipe dust off with a solvent cleaner and then wipe with a tack rag.

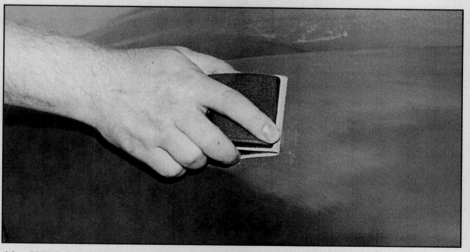

11. GUIDE COATING Spray a light coat of contrasting color lacquer primer surfacer over the Acrylic Urethane primer surfacer. When sanding, this "Guide coat" will highlight imperfections and high/low areas, minimizing total sanding time.

repainting panels also creates the problems of differences in surface finish (such as matching the orange peel) and differences in gloss.

Overspray on nearby glass, rubber, and trim moldings is another problem to be concerned about whenever respraying is done. However, these problems, important as they are to car owners, are only cosmetic. Repainting generally means car owners will end up with thicker paint on their cars, which can lead to problems. Also, the paint used in repainting is chemically different than the original paint. Applying wet, new paint on an older, different type of paint can cause problems such as delamination

13 BASECOAT APPLICATION Use only guns including fluid tips and air caps recommended for basecoat application. Adjust air pressure at the gun to 45 PSI for conventional equipment or approximately 5 PSI at the air cap for HVLP equipment. Apply basecoat in full wet coats, allowing each coat to flash until "hand slick." Spray only until hiding is achieved. Do not spray for gloss. TIP: To help make mica/metallic colors uniform, after hiding is achieved apply a low pressure mist coat. With conventional spray equipment use 25 PSI at a gun distance of 10-12 inches with a 70% overlap. For HVLP, increase the gun distance and spray with a 70% overlap. For HVLP, increase the gun distance and spray with a 70% overlap. The mist coat should have a larger droplet size that stays wet for approximately one minute before flashing off. CAUTION: Do not dry spray the basecoat at any time. To test lightly tack between coats. If the tack cloth catches/drags on the surface or picks up excessive amounts of overspray, the basecoat is being sprayed too dry.

14. CLEAR COATING Allow basecoat to flash before clearcoating. Use a gun, fluid tip and air cap recommended for clearcoat. Spray the clearcoat in medium wet to wet coats, allowing each coat to become "hand slick" before applying the next coat. For proper durability and performance, apply a sufficient number of coats to provide at least 2 mils of clear coat thickness when dry. NOTE: An additional coat is necessary when sanding and buffing to maintain 2 mils dry film thickness. Check with a film thickness gauge if possible to avoid inadequate paint thickness.

(peeling) of the new layers. Sealers are often used to minimize problems with dissimilar layers of paint. Other common problems from repainting are lifting of sand scratches and bleeding through of colors from underlying paint.

Reasons for Spot Repainting

Car owners are often faced with the decision whether to have their cars completely repainted or whether to simply repaint the damaged areas. Some body shops will advise car owners to go with a complete

VARIABLES AFFECTING COLOR

		To Make Color...	
	Variables	**Lighter**	**Darker**
Spray Equipment	Fluid Tip	Use smaller size	Use larger size
	Air Cap	Use air cap with greater number of openings	Use air cap with lesser number of openings
	Fluid Adjustment	Reduce volume of material flow	Increase volume of material flow
	Fan Adjustment	Increase fan width	Decrease fan width
	Air Pressure	Increase air pressure (at the gun)	Decrease air pressure
Spraying Techniques	Gun Distance	Increase distance	Decrease distance
	Gun Speed	Increase speed	Decrease speed
	Flash Time	Allow more flash time	Allow less flash time
Thinner Usage	Type of Thinner	Use faster thinner	Use slower thinner
	Reduction	More thinner	Less thinner
	Use of Retarder	Do not use	Use as recommended
Shop Conditions	Temperature	Increase	Decrease
	Humidity	Decrease	Increase
	Ventilation	Increase	Decrease

Courtesy BASF

repainting because they make more money and they avoid the problems of color-matching. But if the paint on the rest of the car is in good condition and the damage is confined to one or two body panels, then consider spot repainting.

Spot painting is also preferable when replacing single body panels, such as a front fender, or when adding accessory body parts such as air dams and rear spoilers. Spot repainting is also called for when repainting parts that are a different color than the body color, such as blacked-out trim moldings.

Surface Preparation

Care must be taken to properly prepare the body panels or underlying paints or the repainting will be short-lived. If this is a subject you are unfamiliar with, you should consult Chapters 2 and 7. Chapter 2 discusses the differences in the various types of primers and sealers and indicates which application each should be used. Chapter 7 details the actual mechanics of preparing the surface prior to final top coat. If bodywork is needed, you may want to consult HPBooks' *Paint & Body Handbook*, which is largely devoted to body repair and preparation.

Basically, if bare metal is exposed, a primer should definitely be used to ensure adhesion of the top coat. Make certain you choose a primer made for the body panel material. Bare plastic panels generally need a special primer for adhesion.

Before applying the primer, sand the exposed body panel or underlying paint. Scuffing the surface makes it easier for the top coats to grip and

Spot repainting can be difficult, testing any painter's color-matching skills. Shown here is a professional spot repaint. Can you tell which panel was repaired?

bond to the surface. If rust was present, clean it out as thoroughly as possible.

Sand blasting is one of the most effective means of rust removal and surface preparation, but be forewarned that large commercial blasters can warp body panels. Plastic media blasting, on the other hand, is usually safer for the body panel but it may be insufficient in heavily rusted areas. For details on these two procedures, see the sidebars in Chapter 7.

Masking—Masking is most often thought of as a means to prevent overspray from getting on nearby surfaces. However, it has another function in spot painting and this is to prevent accidental damage to adjacent parts while sanding or preparing the surfaces. Even if you are not using power tools, it is wise to tape off surrounding edges, panels, window glass, trim work such as emblems, and chrome or stainless pieces. It is very easy to slip during sanding, and the slightest swipe with sandpaper

leaves indelible scratches on chrome and other surfaces. For more details on masking, turn to Chapter 7, page 74.

Featheredging—Featheredging and color-matching are two particular problem areas that must be handled when trying to blend new paint with old paint. Feather-edging comes into play at the border or edge where the repainted areas join the surrounding paint. Therefore, fetheredging doesn't exist in spot repainting situations where there is no overlapping border with the old paint, such as in the painting of new parts or old parts which have been stripped completely of paint.

In most cases of spot repainting, however, the new paint must overlap the older paint and the trick is to make this boundary as smooth as possible. The edge areas of the surrounding paint are typically sanded with 400- or 600-grit papers until the border is a gradual slope instead of a sharp break. The degree of slope can be seen by

the width of the exposed layers of paint, much like how the rings of a tree become a wider grain pattern as the angle of cut is decreased.

Although fetheredging makes the physical boundary smoother, it creates the potential of other problems as the various layers of old paint are exposed. The solvents in the new primer or top coat paint may soften or wrinkle one of the underlying paint layers. That is one of the primary reasons why sealers are applied over old paint.

To check for the possibility of this problem, soak a rag with the type of thinner or reducer you are using and wipe it on the feather-edged areas. If you are using aerosol paint, spray a portion of the feather-edge area with a fairly wet coat to see what happens. If no wrinkling occurs, wipe it off. If there is a problem with wrinkling, you'll either have to apply a sealer first or try spraying the paint very dry and hope for the best.

Also be aware of the limits of featheredging and the limits of using primer as a filler. If the featheredge extends all the way from the bare body panel through several previous paint jobs, you have a fairly deep hole to fill. It may take six or more heavy coats of primer to fill or build this area back up to the height of the surrounding paint. If the primer was designed for only two to three coats of build, six coats may be pushing its limits. It is not uncommon for such thick paint repairs to contract and sink as the undercoats cure or their solvents continue to evaporate. This happens over a period of time and eventually the outlines of the feather-edged area become visible as a pattern on the paint's surface.

The same effect happens when a

painter tries to fill very deep sanding scratches caused by grinding or uses papers as course as 80-grit. Sand scratches will return and become visible if the preparation and application of the undercoats are rushed.

Color Matching

The advantage of custom mixing paint is of great importance in achieving a color match. The problem of color matching doesn't lie entirely with the manufacturers of touch-up and aerosol paints but instead is often caused by the wide variance in the colors from the factory. Add to that the color changes caused by aging and sunlight (such as fading), and you are asking a lot to get a perfect match from any premixed paint, whether it be from an aerosol can or a touch-up bottle.

If you encounter problems with color matching, most auto body supply stores will custom mix a color for you. You will need to bring a painted part into the store such as a gas lid door or light housing, and there will probably be a minimum amount of paint they'll mix. Some stores will have high-tech color analysis equipment to aid in the mixing, but you'll find that much has to do with the skill, patience, and discrimination of the person doing the mixing.

Variables—Color matching is a lot more involved than just determining if the new paint needs to be a little more blue or a little more red. The color has three interdependent variables which must be examined and matched:

• Intensity: The lightness or darkness of the color.
• Hue: Whether the color is more blue

The Preval spray gun is an option for spraying customized colors when air compressors and professional spray equipment are not available. This system uses disposable aerosol heads that screw onto a glass container. Replacement power heads and containers are available separately. Spray patterns are not adjustable, and you must be careful to mix and strain the paint thoroughly and watch the spray pattern at all times.

or green, for example.
• Saturation: Whether the color is clean and bright or grayish.

Metallics or pearl-effect paints have additional variables to match: the size, color, and intensity of the pearl metallic components. If that isn't more than enough for a painter to have to handle, the gloss and surface finish or orange peel must be matched also.

Color matching is often a very difficult process. I-CAR and the major paint manufacturers have courses and workshops dedicated to just this one subject, and these courses are highly recommended for professional painters. Most courses not only provide theory and hands-on experience, they also give the painter valuable reference books which have comparative color chip samples and

worksheets to use in the shop.

Entire training manual books have been written on the subject of color matches alone, but we'll cover the basic steps here.

Examining—Thoroughly clean the old paint to see its true color; next, look at the colors under color-corrected lights, or preferably, outside; and then look at the color not only straight on but at an angle.

Spray the new paint onto a small test panel and let it dry before comparing it to the original paint. If a clear coat is going to be used, apply it to the test panel before comparing the match. Remember that clear coats tend to darken a color. Also, use the same primer or sealer coat on the test panel that will be used on the repair.

Altering Color by Application—Applying the paint in drier coats can alter its color. This is particularly effective with metallic paint because if the paint is applied in thin, dry coats, the metallic particles can't sink into the paint. The closer to the surface and more exposed the metallic particles are, the more light they reflect and the lighter the color appears. There are a number of ways to put on thinner, drier coats such as higher air pressure, faster strokes, and spraying farther from the surface. Consult the chart on page 61 for other techniques.

The amount of change you can make by altering the application of the paint varies from color to color. Some colors will change little, while the effect of spraying dry coats is almost shocking in others. However, make sure that you look at the color head-on (face) and at an angle (pitch) when lightening a color in this manner. You may find that the head-on view becomes considerably lighter while the view from an angle is much darker.

Altering Color by Mixing—The first step in comparing paint is to make certain the new paint is thoroughly mixed. Sometimes it takes a lot of effort to get the metallics and pigments off the bottom of the can and into suspension again. An automatic agitator that shakes the can is a valuable piece of body shop equipment. Also remember that the color will look darker if clear is applied over it later.

It is important to adjust the darkness of the paint first. Only add one color at a time when correcting for color matching and then respray the test panel. Add tints sparingly: it's easier to intensify a color by mixing than it is to cancel a color out. It is preferable to use the same tinting bases specified in the original mix formula whenever possible.

Only after the darkness level of the paint is correctly matched should you make your modifications to produce the correct hue. Finally, after darkness and hue are matched, add tint bases to produce the matching level of brightness/grayness.

Blending—When the best attempts to match existing paint fall short, there is still another means to achieve an acceptable spot repair and that is by blending. Blending is used quite often because exact color matching takes a lot of time and effort and few people (or insurance companies) are willing to pay for the extra cost.

Blending attempts to have the color gradually change from the older color to the new one. That means the painter must spray farther out onto the surrounding panels as he successively applies less of the new color so the eye doesn't see a sharp line of difference in the shades of paint. This can be accomplished by reducing the amount of paint being applied as the painter goes farther from the repaired area or by spraying diluted mixtures of color farther out on the panels. Another technique is to mix the new color with clear (for example, reduce it by 50%) and apply this in successive overlapping layers going out onto the adjoining panels.

A talented painter can blend colors that would appear distinctly different if they were next to one another. Blending is so effective at fooling the eye that it is used as common practice by many painters. That is why you'll frequently see adjoining panels, such as hoods and doors, that have been resprayed during a spot repaint although the actual damage was confined to just one panel such as a fender.

Getting a perfect match is difficult. In practice, all that most painters hope for is a color mix which can be blended. They don't expect a match that is so close as to allow a panel-to-panel match. As an example, in trying to get the proper color match for a late-model Mercedes, you might find that there are six different variances for a particular white. A color variance is a slightly different mixture of tints and, out of those six different shades, none may be a close enough match to what's on the car to allow a panel-to-panel match.

The trend today is to avoid having to stock thousands of different color mixes of paint and instead to have a mixing station at the body shop or local paint supplier. Premixed "factory packs" are becoming rarer and, with the number of variances in factory paint, even they can't provide assurance of a close match.

Matching Tri-Coats—A painter's color-matching skills are truly put to the test when it comes to spot repainting on tri-coat (pearl effect) colors. Not only do the darkness, hue, and gray level of the paint need to be matched, the effect of the semi-transparent pearl top layer also must be duplicated.

The standard procedure is to prepare a let-down panel after the color itself has been closely matched. The let-down panel is first painted with the color coat and then sprayed with one coat of the pearl effect paint. Then a small part of it is masked and another coat of pearl paint is applied, so that there are two coats of pearl on one area and only one coat in the masked area. More area is masked and more coats applied. After the multiple layers of pearl are applied, the masking tape is removed and the panel is clear coated. When the panel is dry, it is compared to the surrounding paint to see how many coats of pearl should be applied to best duplicate the original paint.

Although this procedure is time-consuming, it is much better than trial-and-error paint matching on the car. If the painter doesn't guess right the first time, the successive coats of color, pearl, and clear would result in having far too much paint on the car.

If you have pearl tri-coat paint on your car and it needs spot repainting, find someone who is experienced and accomplished in this area. At the very least, ask if he makes let-down panels when repairing tri-coat cars; or ask a new car dealer who sells pearl-painted cars who he recommends for paint repairs. For more tips on tri-coat repair, go to pages 66-67.

Also be aware that some paints which are called "pearl" by the manufacturer are not tri-coats. They have pearl-effect mica flakes mixed in with the color and do not have the separate pearl layer. Because they are not tri-coats, they are easier to match and blend for spot repainting.

Although pearl tri-coat paints require a lot of time and talent to match, there are other paints which are still more difficult. Some of the three stage "candy" paints are virtually impossible to blend. Be forewarned that certain types of glamour or custom paint don't lend themselves to easy spot repainting.

But there's more on that in Chapter 8, *Custom Painting*.

Aerosols & Spray Equipment

The do-it-yourselfer has a number of options to choose from when it comes to applying paint. The aerosol can is certainly the most convenient because it is premixed and disposable. Although being premixed means you don't have to buy and blend thinners or paint reducers, it also means you are limited in mixing and modifying the color. If the color in the can doesn't exactly match your paint, there's not a lot you can do about it.

Professional painters will snicker about the use of aerosol spray cans to paint a car, but they use them in certain applications, and some custom painters make extensive use of aerosols. Also, aerosols have the advantage of no contamination of water or oil from air supply lines. This is a serious problem a painter has to continuously consider with commercial compressors and spray equipment.

There's also an option in between professional spraying equipment and aerosol cans, and it shares some of the advantages of each. Cartridge-powered Preval paint sprayers have a self-contained air supply but permit you to use whatever mixture of paint you like. They are relatively inexpensive and work remarkably well. Of course, they don't have the flexibility of adjustable spray patterns

In addition to bottles of touch-up paint, a wide variety of colors are also available in aerosol cans for spot repainting. The manual fill system shown in Chapter 3 enables custom mixes to be put into aerosol spray cans. Courtesy Plasti-Kote.

and pressures like professional equipment, but they do share the ability to choose the paint you want to apply.

At the other end of the spectrum is the professional paint gun. Anyone who has painted with a professional paint gun will tell you there is a vast difference in the degree of control and the rate at which paint can be applied. And new generation HVLP spray guns are even more effective at rapidly applying paint. HVLP guns are covered in more detail in Chapter 4. Spray techniques and how to adjust spray guns are covered in Chapter 7.

Glamorous tri-coat finishes consist of a solid base coat color, an inner pearl luster sandwich layer, and a clear top coat. The pearlescent inner layer, which is made with flakes of translucent mica, is what gives tri-coat colors their opalescent, ever-changing look.

Achieving proper film build in the pearl sandwich layer also is the key to successfully matching tri-coat colors.

And a let-down panel, like the one shown here, is the key to determining how many coats of pearl are necessary for a proper match. (NOTE: Make a separate let-down panel for each tri-coat color.)

Making the let-down panel is the critical first step in the following DuPont system for repairing OEM tri-coat pearl finishes with CHROMABASE, CRONAR or LUCITE.

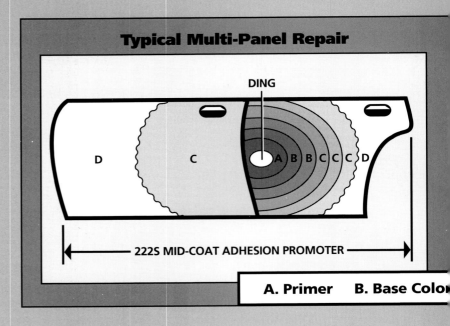

Typical Multi-Panel Repair

DING

222S MID-COAT ADHESION PROMOTER

A. Primer   B. Base Color

#1: Judge the Color

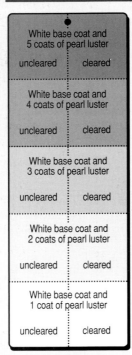

White base coat and
5 coats of pearl luster

| uncleared | cleared |

White base coat and
4 coats of pearl luster

| uncleared | cleared |

White base coat and
3 coats of pearl luster

| uncleared | cleared |

White base coat and
2 coats of pearl luster

| uncleared | cleared |

White base coat and
1 coat of pearl luster

| uncleared | cleared |

Make a let-down panel to help you decide how many coats of pearl it will take to match the original finish. A separate let-down panel should be made for each OEM tri-coat color. To make a let-down panel:

1. Apply base coat color to hiding over the entire panel.

2. Mask the panel in five sections, leaving the first section exposed.

3. Apply a medium-wet coat of pearl and allow to flash.

4. Remove masking from next section.

5. Apply a medium-wet coat of pearl over exposed area of the panel.

6. Repeat steps 4 and 5 until all five sections have been uncovered. Your panel will illustrate the effects of one, two, three, four and five coats of pearl.

7. Once the panel is dry, mask it off lengthwise and apply two coats of clear to the unmasked half. Remove masking paper and let the panel dry.

8. Compare the panel to the car in natural daylight or under color corrected indoor light to determine how many coats of pearl you'll need to apply.

9. Store your let-down panel for future use.

#2: Prepare the Surface

1. CLEAN AND DEGREASE the repair area with 3919S PREP-SOL or 3949S KWIKCLEAN (in VOC regulated areas).

2. UNDERCOAT with either the DuPont Tri-Layer Undercoat Refinishing system or the URO Primer-Filler system.

3. WET SAND the primed area with 400-600 grit sandpaper.

4. SAND all panels to be blended with 1500 grit sandpaper. Tri-coat colors require more area for extended blends than conventional base/clear colors. (See diagrams above.)

5. CLEAN the area with 3939S or 3949S (in VOC regulated areas) to remove primer sludge, fingerprints, etc.

6. SEAL all primers with appropriate sealer. PRIME 'N SEAL 2600S can be tinted to match the topcoat color.

Typical Spot/Partial Repair

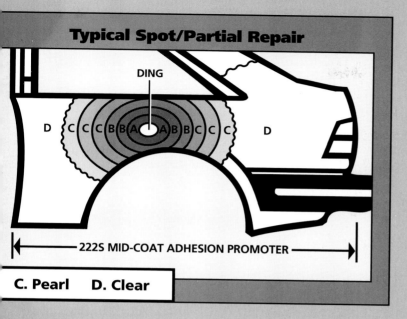

DING

D | C | C | C | B | B | A | A | B | B | C | C | C | D

← 222S MID-COAT ADHESION PROMOTER →

C. Pearl   D. Clear

Helpful Hints

When applying the pearl during both the let-down panel preparation and the repair:
- use an agitator cup to keep the heavy mica flakes in suspension and properly oriented;
- use the same air pressure for both the preparation of the let-down panel and the repair;
- build up the pearl gradually by applying thin, light coats, and
- because of individual variations in technique and equipment, each refinisher should make his or her own let-down panel.

And when doing the actual repair:
- Clean the spray area well. Dirt is a major enemy of successful tri-coat repair.
- Plan on making light blends of the pearl coat into adjacent panels.
- Never rush a tri-coat repair. Always allow sufficient time.

#3: Apply the Color

1. APPLY one coat of Mid-Coat Adhesion Promoter 222S or 9222S over all unsealed panels involved in the repair. This should be applied beyond the areas where the last coat of clear will go in order to help the material adhere to the slick OEM surface. (See diagram above.)

2. APPLY the base coat to full hiding, extending each coat slightly beyond the previous one. Allow adequate flash time between coats.

3. CONSULT the let-down panel to decide how many coats of pearl are needed for a match.

4. APPLY the number of pearl coats indicated by the let-down panel. Be sure to fully cover the base color before tapering the blend edge of each coat of pearl. Blend each coat beyond the next (see diagrams) and allow sufficient flash time between coats.

5. CLEAR all the panels with one of the DuPont clear coats recommended for use with the CHROMABASE, CRONAR or LUCITE base/clear system.

OEM Tri-Coat Colors

DuPont matches for these OEM tri-coat colors are available in CHROMABASE, CRONAR and LUCITE.

Manufacturer	Manufacturer's Code	DuPont Code*	Manufacturer	Manufacturer's Code	DuPont Code*
Audi/VW	LOA9	W8936 G8701	Subaru	075	N9160 N9161
Honda	NH515P	W9285 W8817		267	L9641 L9642
GM	55/9069	D8870 D8722		891	L8802 L8903
	93/8933	B8469 B8609	Toyota/Lexus	042	K8806 K8807
	58/9814	B9215 B9216		049	N9033 L9018
	O4/9818	B9256 B9257		051	L9246 L9247
	84/9976	B9260 B9261		568	L9341 L9342
Mitsubishi	W75	W9277 L9285		046	L9339 L9340
Nissan/Infiniti	234	H8932 L8902		3J7	L9345 L9346
	CHO	W9002 L9098		187	K9342 K9343
	EH7	W9001 N9004			
	KH1	L9294 L9295			
	KH6	W9003 N9010			

* In all cases, the base coat color code is listed first, followed by the pearl luster color code.

7

COMPLETE PAINT JOBS

After many hours of body and surface preparation, it's time to spray the car with paint. But remember, a paint job is only as good as the surface to which it is applied—regardless of the type of paint or how skillfully it is applied.

The complete paint job is the crowning achievement of a fully restored car, and it can also rejuvenate the appearance of the most weather-beaten daily driver. On the highest level, the quality of a paint job can often mean the difference between first and second place in concours competition. Although applying today's paint on any type of car is far more technical than in decades past, you shouldn't let that deter you from doing the job yourself. Car shows have many first-place winners with paint applied by amateur owners with little or no body refinishing experience.

One of the reasons why so many excellent paint jobs are now done by amateurs is due to the greatly increased level of technical information supplied by paint manufacturers. In the past, painters had to rely a lot more on their experience when mixing paints, choosing paint materials, and preparing the surfaces. In the seventies, when I worked at Corvette

Center in Connecticut, no one "measured" materials before mixing paints. Pouring was done by eye, and the mixture was adjusted if spraying or weather conditions dictated change. Today, the same painter religiously uses calibrated mixing sticks.

The level of technical support also has increased dramatically in the area of surface preparation. Professional painters used to have to call various suppliers to determine what primers would work on the various metals found on the car, including brass and aluminum. Today the detailed spec sheets list the substrates the paint can go over, what paints and materials can go on top, what mixing levels to use, which additives can be blended in, what pressure and temperatures to use—everything but what color socks the painter should wear. That is not to imply that a high quality paint job is easy. It requires a great deal of preparation, patience, and plain ol' hard work. First-timers will often tell you it took a lot more time than they figured, and if they knew how much

No matter what type of paint you choose, the mixing of the color is a critical step. A clean, well-stocked mixing room with a computerized weight scale certainly aids the technician, but his skill and patience are equally important.

Using a "paint system" refers to using compatible paints of the same brand for all layers in the paint job: primer, color, and clear. Today's paints are so chemically complex that mixing brands is risky. Courtesy PPG.

time and effort it took, they may not have done it in the first place.

Why Repaint?—Reasons for repainting the entire car can be varied. If you've performed a "ground-up" restoration, then obviously repainting is necessary. Restoring a car to its original factory condition means stripping down to the bare body panels and repainting the car with an original color.

Other reasons for a complete repaint is if the paint is poor all over the car or if there has been collision damage to large areas of the car that would make color-matching difficult. A change of color is another reason for choosing a complete repaint. Cars with good (in this case functionally good) paint are often repainted because the owner just can't stand looking at that color any longer but doesn't want to buy another car.

CHOOSING A PAINT

Chapters 1 and 2 discuss in detail the different types of automotive paint available today. To briefly recap, lacquer is among the easiest of paints to apply, and with the extra work of wet-sanding and buffing, it can produce an excellent-looking finish.

However, it is not one of the most durable paints, and tightening environmental laws may prohibit its use. Quality traditional enamels, including acrylic enamel, are relatively durable and relatively inexpensive. Properly applied, they dry glossy and eliminate the need for buffing. The urethane and other two-part paints are the most durable and the most expensive. They are extremely tough, dry fast and glossy, and can be wet-sanded and buffed for a spectacular appearance.

As mentioned previously, today's automotive paint jobs can get pretty complicated. A paint job can have etching primers, followed by sanding primers, then covered by color coats (and then maybe pearl coats), and topped off with clear coats. Modern paint jobs often have many layers of very different types of paint stacked up on top of one another.

There's good cause for concern

because each layer is sprayed on wet over the other and a bad reaction is possible if they aren't compatible. There's also danger of delamination (peeling off of the paint) if any layer doesn't tightly bond and chemically link-up with its adjacent layer. This has happened to hundreds of thousands of factory paint jobs. Although the car owner doesn't notice anything wrong at first, delamination typically becomes a problem after the car has been subjected to the sun and other environmental stresses for a few years.

Paint Systems

Using a paint system means using one paint manufacturer's recommended products for all the various layers and coats of paint, from the first primer put on the body to the last coat of paint sprayed. Each major paint supplier has extensive product descriptions telling how and when

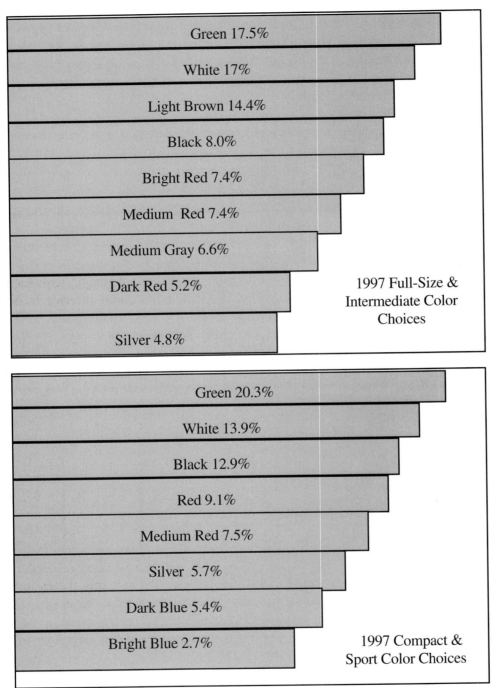

Green 17.5%

White 17%

Light Brown 14.4%

Black 8.0%

Bright Red 7.4%

Medium Red 7.4%

Medium Gray 6.6%

Dark Red 5.2%

Silver 4.8%

1997 Full-Size &
Intermediate Color
Choices

Green 20.3%

White 13.9%

Black 12.9%

Red 9.1%

Medium Red 7.5%

Silver 5.7%

Dark Blue 5.4%

Bright Blue 2.7%

1997 Compact &
Sport Color Choices

The charts on these two pages illustrate the color popularity in various vehicle categories. The big news in color is the astounding change in preference of green. From 1990 to 1997, green went from just about the least popular automotive color to the most popular. White barely held on to its lead in light trucks/vans/SUV's and in the luxury car field (when white metallics-pearls are added). DuPont predicts that the popularity of light browns and other earth tones will increase over the next few years. Courtesy DuPont.

rapidly and can vary from manufacturer to manufacturer.

Industry insiders will tell you that it is common for paint manufacturers to make small changes in the chemical formulation of a particular paint product. The manufacturer's laboratory technicians test whether these changes affect their other products that come into contact with it, but they certainly don't test the effect of the change on another company's paint. In other words, a painter may have good luck using one company's color coat with another company's clear coat for a year; and then without warning, the next paint job can fail because of minor changes in the formulation of one of the paints.

Avoid this by using a well-known paint manufacturer's "system" if at all possible. The savings from buying lower priced components are not worth the risk. If you mix different brands of paint and it doesn't work, you'll have to pay for the materials a second time and start all over. An example of a paint system, DuPont's ChromaSystem, can be seen on pages 90 and 91. The chart literally walks you through the entire paint process, from surface preparation to polishing. Application and safety tips, as well as a list of compatible products, are also given. This instruction sheet is similar to the ones you're likely to get with other manufacturers' paint systems.

Choosing a Color

There are some other tips you can employ to help you decide. Paint chip books are a useful source of ideas. Paint supply stores and many body shops have such books but be careful using them. Take the color you choose outside, and remember that it may look quite different when it is on an

each type of their paint is to be used with another type.

In the past, painters often bought primers, thinners, or reducers from the least expensive source. However,

usually they only had one boundary to worry about: the colored top coat going over the primer. Today, not only are there more layers to worry about but the chemistry of paint is changing

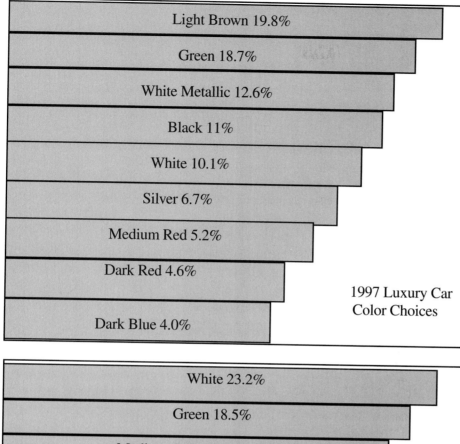

Light Brown 19.8%
Green 18.7%
White Metallic 12.6%
Black 11%
White 10.1%
Silver 6.7%
Medium Red 5.2%
Dark Red 4.6%
Dark Blue 4.0%

1997 Luxury Car
Color Choices

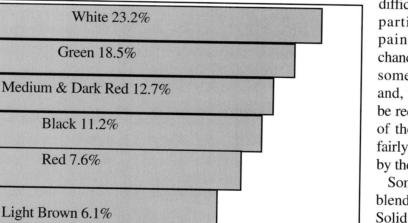

White 23.2%
Green 18.5%
Medium & Dark Red 12.7%
Black 11.2%
Red 7.6%
Light Brown 6.1%
Silver 3.7%
Medium & Dark Blue 2.9%
Teal/Aqua 2.6%

1997 Light Truck
and Vans Color
Choices

original color, check it against an original painted body part after the paint is mixed or against the chip you have selected. Also, remember that the addition of a clear coat will darken the color somewhat.

If the car is a collector car, I strongly advise you to choose the original color. If you just can't stand the original color, try another which was available on that model and year. Even if your car isn't a hot item now, it may be in a few years. There is always a proportion of collector car buyers who want the major items such as paint, motor, and interior to be original.

Selection of a color or paint scheme should also take into account the difficulty of future repairs. This is of particular importance to novice painters because there is a good chance that a mistake will be made at some point during the application; and, therefore, some repainting will be required before the car is taken out of the garage. In fact, touch-ups are fairly likely even with paint jobs done by the most experienced painters.

Some paints are harder to match and blend when spot repairs are needed. Solid colors are certainly the easiest, with black being the easiest of all. However, black also shows defects more and is one of the hardest to keep looking at its best. White is another one of the easiest and, like other light colors, more tolerant of minor defects in bodywork and surface preparation. It is also one of the most popular colors.

Solid, Metallic or Tri-Coat?

Now that you've decided which color, you'll have to decide which type of pigment you want. Solid colors are definitely easier to paint and repair.

entire car than it does on that small chip. Whenever possible, find out what make of car that color came on and go to a dealership so you can see a car painted that color.

Another lesson is that bright or vivid colors often look better on small or sporty cars than on full size cars.

Spread over acres of sheet metal, some intense colors become a little too much for the eye to behold.

Also, don't trust the paint formulation used to mix paints. Today, most colors are mixed either at paint supply stores or at larger body shops. If you want to duplicate the

SAFETY FIRST

I've mentioned safety throughout this book, and I'm going to mention it again. Painting cars can be dangerous! Fumes and particles generated from sanding and paint are highly flammable and toxic. They can destroy your lungs or blow up the garage (and you along with it). If you inhale particles of fiberglass while sanding, they will be permanently lodged in your lungs. They do not "cough" out. Therefore, always wear a particle mask when sanding.

The fumes from the paint and solvents you'll be working with are also highly toxic. Therefore, never spray paint near an open flame such as an appliance with an active pilot light and don't smoke. It sounds like common sense, but many people forget that the water heater located in the garage, or the gas dryer, have pilot lights going all the time. They fill the garage with paint fumes and BOOM!, your garage becomes the world's largest combustion chamber. Furthermore, any electrical equipment you operate must have a "fire safe" motor. If you're thinking of using the cooling fans used in the bedroom--don't. The motors on these fans can produce sparks, which of course is not in your best interest. Get special exhaust fans for ventilating your garage.

Always wear eye protection and particle or ventilated air masks. Do not, under any circumstances, paint without a ventilated paint mask of some sort. When painting, the best system is a fresh air hood. If that's too sophisticated for your budget, then at the very least use a face mask with disposable charcoal filters. Furthermore, make sure that you cover your skin by wearing long-sleeved shirts and long pants--the harmful byproducts of paint can be absorbed through your skin into your bloodstream. The chemicals of today's automotive paints, especially with the two-part enamels, can cause irreparable damage to vital organs, and in many cases, even death. Safety must always be your primary consideration.

Material Safety Data Sheets (MSDS) are specific, detailed listings of the components of products. In the automotive paint field, products that require MSDSs range from the hazardous catalysts used to cure paint to the relatively benign bottles of touch-up paint sold to consumers. Whether you are a professional painter or an office worker, you now have the ability to learn about the nature of products used in the workplace. Ask the manufacturers or suppliers for the MSDS for any product which concerns you. It's important to know what chemicals your lungs and skin are coming in contact with!

However, if you really like a particular metallic color, don't worry too much about choosing it. Many novice painters can do a good job of painting and repairing metallic paints if they have proper equipment and closely follow the manufacturer's instructions. Tri-coat pearls are a different story. They are definitely more difficult to paint and repair. If you want to have your car painted with a tri-coat pearl or Candy™ color or if you need to have some repainting done on your tri-coat paint job, find a painter who has lots of experience with them. It's not a good idea to attempt a tri-coat paint job in the family garage.

Clear Coat or Not?—Paint experts seldom agree, but most will say that a good clear coat will add life to a paint job. One proof is in the manufacturer warranties—the longest ones only cover clear-coated paints.

The reasons not to clear coat are simple: you don't want to spend the extra money; the car didn't originally have it (and you want to keep it as original as possible); you're selling the car; or the car lives a fairly easy, garaged life.

One last tip: buy about 25% more paint than required. Hopefully, you won't need it, but it can be used for practicing your stroke and for touch-ups or future repairs.

PROCEDURE

What follows is an outline covering how professionals repaint cars. It assumes that bodywork, such as dents and rust damage, has already been performed, and that you are going to do the job yourself. An excellent companion to this book, and one that you should read if you're attempting any bodywork and refinishing repairs, is HPBooks' *Paint & Body Handbook*. A step-by-step photo sequence of a complete paint job begins on page 83.

Before getting into the steps involved in a complete paint job, let's cover a few basic rules of preparation.

First, you must have an area to paint in. If this area is going to be your garage, then you'll have to convert it into a basic paint booth. This essentially means a thorough top-to-bottom cleaning; and by cleaning, I mean that the walls and floors should be scrubbed with detergent, not just swept clean. All surfaces must be free

Removal of chrome and trim parts is a hallmark of high quality paint jobs. Some emblems and moldings can be easily (and gently) pried off with a putty knife. If a piece doesn't pry off easily, see if it is bolted or clipped on the other side.

bodywork and sanding, dirt will fall off the chassis, getting into the air in the shop. The more you clean off beforehand, the less chance this dirt will get onto your new paint.

Use high pressure air to blow out dirt stuck under trim pieces and seams. It's best to do this both before and after washing the car.

Dechroming

One of the most easily noticed differences between a high quality paint job and a quickie is the extent of dechroming. Whenever possible, it is better to remove a piece of trim than to mask it off. Removal not only will result in a more professional-appearing paint job but it will also allow you to check underneath the trim for hidden rust. Shops that charge only a few hundred dollars or less for a paint job obviously can't spend much time removing chrome, emblems, and other adornments on the exterior of a car. In some cases, you'll even see cars whose grilles and emblems have been painted along with the rest of the car! They weren't removed or even masked.

The term dechroming goes back to the time when most emblems, bumpers, and trim pieces were chrome-plated. Today, fewer of the trim pieces are chrome, but the term is used to refer to removal of all parts on the body that are not painted the body color.

Actually, some of the parts painted body color, such as flexible bumper covers, also should be removed when doing a high quality complete repaint. In cases where two abutting parts were originally painted separately and then bolted together, there is a crisp seam between the two parts. If those parts were painted while bolted

Corrosion of fasteners is a problem frequently encountered in dechroming older cars. Heating the nuts with a torch is often essential on larger parts like bumper brackets. Several screws had to be sawed off to remove the luggage rack. To prevent this hassle next time, apply anti-seize compound or grease on threads when installing the fasteners.

together, that seam, to some extent, would be filled in with paint. Thus, removal of parts such as lamp housings, bumpers, air dams, and spoilers is desirable even though they'll be painted the same color as the body.

Complete restoration and complete dechroming go hand-in-hand, but these extremes are rarely found in the refinishing of cars used for daily transportation. Dechroming often has a point of diminishing return. In some cases, a lot of work is needed to remove one trim piece, and few people would notice the difference. Therefore, the degree of time and money spent on dechroming is a judgment call that varies with each car and each car owner.

Some parts come off so easily that it is faster to remove them than to mask them. Removal of other parts, such as windshields, may create more problems than it solves.

Removal of body trim pieces not only eliminates the hassle of masking

of dirt and dust, and this includes everything. You should remove or completely cover any item that you don't want coated with overspray. The area will also need to be well ventilated with exhaust fans—fans with fire-safe motors that don't emit sparks. Do not use home-type fans! For more on safety, see the sidebar on page 72. You'll also have to restrict traffic (family members, pets, cars, bicycles, etc.) from entering the garage until you're through.

Washing

A thorough washing is an important first step in any paint job. Dirt, sand, silicones, and oil trapped in crevices can come back later to haunt the final stages. Use plenty of soap and don't forget to wash areas you may normally omit, like hideaway headlights and door jams. Open the hood and trunk and clean out pockets where dirt and leaves may have collected. A trip to a pressure wash is worth the time. Spray under the wheel wells and body pan, too. During

Masking is made faster, easier and safer with new products such as Super Cling Premium Masking Sheeting. It is resistant to paint solvents (no bleed-through) and overspray will not flake off the sheeting. It's available in 12x400 ft. lengths which have no perforations. Courtesy U.S. Chemical & Plastics.

those parts, it also permits preparation and painting behind them. This can increase corrosion protection. Also, if the paint is to be buffed, dechroming allows the easy removal of any orange peel in areas or edges that otherwise would be difficult to reach. Furthermore, removal of trim parts permits you to more easily clean and detail those parts. The condition and appearance of the trim parts will have a lot to do with the overall effect of the new paint job.

Removing Trim—To find out how trim pieces and emblems are attached, look in a service and repair manual. Sometimes special tools will make the job much easier and prevent damage to the parts. Moldings are commonly held on by spring clips or snap clips which can make their removal and installation fairly easy.

If you are unsure of how an emblem comes off, gently slide a putty knife under it and try to pry it off. Many of the emblems on today's cars are simply attached by glue or double-sided tapes. The insertion of a putty knife may be stopped by a pin on the underside of the emblem. Pins are

often used for proper positioning of the emblem. However, if the emblem wasn't attached by glue or tape, the pins may push into a friction clip located on the body panel. Screws or threaded studs with nuts are two other common ways trim parts are attached.

Larger parts, like bumpers and bumper brackets, are fastened with nuts and bolts that are exposed to the elements. If the threads are rusted, it greatly helps to use a lubricant such as WD-40 to help loosen them. Another caution is to be aware of how heavy some bumpers are. When the last bolt is removed, a bumper can come crashing down, causing damage or injury.

Removal of tape or decals is commonly needed on today's cars. A heat gun or a high wattage hair dryer will help soften tapes and facilitate their removal. Use a razor knife to help peel the tape away from the body as it is being heated. Another means is the use of a tape stripe removal wheel powered by a special drill or air chuck. After removal of the tape, wipe the area with a cloth soaked with a chemical glue or adhesive remover and scrape the area with the edge of a plastic spreader.

Rubber weatherstripping needs to be removed or taped when doing a complete paint job. Some weatherstripping just pushes into a channel and is easily removed or installed. This method of attachment is commonly found on trunk lid weatherstripping. Other types of weatherstripping are glued on and require painstaking work with a razor blade or X-acto knife to separate them from the body without tearing the rubber. Take time to bag and label all parts including the weatherstripping. If you don't, when putting the car

back together, you'll waste a lot of time trying to figure out which side a piece went on or which end went where.

Another piece of advice is to put every screw or nut back in place after removing a part. You always think you'll remember which screw went where; in most cases, you won't. Everyone who has dechromed a car has come to the point during reassembly where half the parts are back on the car but the remaining screws won't work—they are either too short or too long. The ones that are needed were used to attach another part. Trust me, minutes spent starting screws or nuts back in place will save hours later during reassembly.

Masking

If a trim piece is not removed, then it must be masked off. The subject of masking could probably be stretched out into a chapter, but a few basic tips are all most people will need to get started. Masking is one of those skills that seems awkward and difficult at first, but proficiency comes quickly with experience, and masking can almost be fun at times. There is much more to masking than simply covering a piece of trim or a part with tape or paper. Proper masking entails covering items with clean, even edges. Some people are blindingly fast (and good) at masking. However, this is certainly a part of repainting where rushing will cost you time. A trim part that takes a minute to thoroughly mask could take an hour or more to remove overspray. In the case of vinyl or convertible tops, a masking mistake that allowed overspray through could cause damage which would be almost impossible to remedy.

MASKING TIPS

1. After laying down a piece of tape, go back and press it tightly to the surface to prevent paint from blowing underneath.

2. If tape won't stick to a surface, wash the surface with wax and silicone remover. If used sparingly, you can also use wax and silicone remover on rubber surfaces.

3. When doing two-tone paint, follow the paint manufacturer's directons so you will know when fresh paint may be masked.

4. Never leave masking tape on a job more than a few days, especially if the car is left outside.

5. Do not remove tape from a wet paint job. Give lacquer or two-part enamels an hour to dry. One-part enamel should dry at leats 6-8 hours.

6. When possible, cut tape when applying it. Tearing tends to lift and stretch the ends.

7. Never pull up on masking tape when removing it. It can lift fresh paint. Peel it back away from the paint and over itself.

8. If masking tape becomes wet, remove it as soon as possible before it hardens and becomes a nightmare to remove.

In haste, one of the simplest things is often overlooked: cleaning the surface being masked. Tape is generally the first barrier to paint

Plastic media blasting is a particularly effective means of stripping the paint off flexible rubber bumpers because they are sometimes damaged by chemical strippers. However, the selection of the plastic media used is critical on plastic and rubber components. Different grades are available, depending on the type of surface to be blasted.

Removing old paint with chemical stripper is serious business, and proper safety precautions must be followed.

overspray, and tape can't stick to a dusty surface. Wipe the surface which is to be taped.

Masking Materials—Masking tape and masking papers come in many widths. The narrower the tape, the easier it will form around curves. Use expensive tape unless you can afford the time to test less expensive brands. 3M is always a safe choice. Good quality masking tape will not allow paint to seep through, it will stick uniformly to the surface, and it will be easy to remove later. The wider the tape, the greater the coverage. Paper comes in several widths. Never use newspaper for masking because it is too porous, and the wet paint can bleed through. Furthermore, the black ink can bleed and contaminate the surface with an oily film.

Masking Procedure—Use 1/4-inch tape for tight curves or hard-to-tape areas. Small items such as door handles and emblems can be masked off with tape only. On large areas to be covered with paper, run a strip of tape around the trim or edges of the area. Add the masking paper, folding the edges of the paper under to match the contour of the item being masked. When the paper is shaped to the item, apply another strip of tape to the paper edges. This makes an effective seal to prevent overspray from blowing underneath. If you need to use more than one piece of paper to cover an area, make sure you tape the seam. A word of advice is to use a double layer of paper at first until you're sure the paint you're using won't seep through one layer.

Mask engine compartments thoroughly. This is important because the overspray goes much farther than you would expect. This is particularly important with paints whose overspray is extremely difficult to remove, such as enamels and urethanes. Lay a drop cloth over the entire compartment and tape paper to the inside of the fenders and cowl. Headlamps, wheels, tires, and bumpers need to be masked off as well.

Be generous with masking until you learn about paint's tendency to penetrate the slightest tape gaps or

PREPARING PLASTIC FOR PAINTING

Twenty years ago, automotive painting of plastic primarily concerned fiberglass bodied Corvettes and Avantiís. Now there are dozens of plastics, and paint doesnít adhere well to some of them unless the proper products and procedures are used. The problem in painting plastics is not so much flexibility today because the trend in automotive use of plastic on exterior parts is away from the very flexible bumper covers which began appearing in the seventies to more rigid materials which hold their shape better, have good surface finishes and cost less. An example of this is TPO which has become one of the most common plastics used for air dams and other parts. TPO is one of the polyolefins (think ìoilyî) the type of plastic which most requires special treatment if the paint is to stick. For details on determining the type of plastic, see the chart on page 20. Then refer to the paint manufacturer's instructions about how to prepare the plastic's surface.

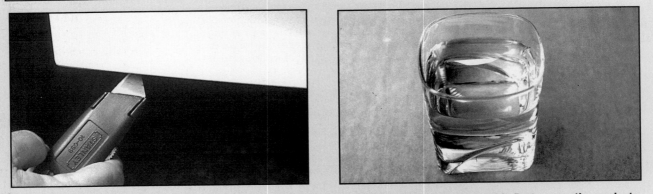

To tell if a plastic is polyolefin, scrape off a chunk and place the sliver in a glass of water. If it floats, use the products specified for polyolefin plastics.

overlapping papered areas. Extra caution is also advised when spraying enamels because overspray can bond very tightly to almost anything it falls on. And, in particular, be concerned about masking parts of the car from which it can be extremely difficult to remove overspray, such as fabric tops.

Surface Preparation

Surface preparation is of critical importance to the durability of the paint job. No matter how good the paint, it won't last if applied over a poor foundation. Although the effects of this stage of work aren't immediately seen in the outcome of the paint job, it accounts for a large portion of the work involved in a quality paint job.

Paint Stripping—For many high quality paint jobs, surface preparation begins with stripping—removal of all old paint. In fact, in some countries, such as Germany, painters are taught to always strip off the old paint on automobiles before any refinishing work is done. Paint stripping is not automatically done in the United States, but it is done more today than in previous years. For tips on when you should strip old paint, see the sidebar on the next page. For more on paint stripping techniques, see the sidebar on page 80.

Although the paint preparation and undercoats don't show (hopefully), they are the foundation for a long-lasting paint job. Some of the changes in paint materials, such as epoxy and self-etching primers, provide greater corrosion protection and durability than ever before. On the other hand, some changes, such as the new composite body materials used on today's cars, require that much more attention be given to which primers and sealers are used. For more information on the preparation of plastic parts, see Chapter 6.

The following is a description of what is typically done in surface preparation. More information on surface preparation and intermediate

YOU MUST STRIP WHEN...

1. The paint shows crazing, cracking, bubbling or peeling
2. You have doubts about the quality of the previous paint work or underlying layers
3. The paint is already too thick
4. The paint warranty requires it
5. You want the paint close to original factory specifications

YOU SHOULD STRIP WHEN...

1. Lacquer primers or top coats are evident
2. It has already been repainted.
3. The car model has a history of OEM paint failure

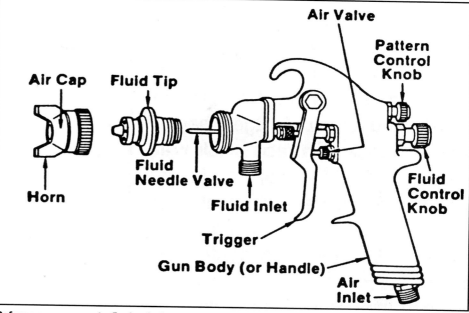

Before you move on to final painting, master the spray gun you are using. Although spray guns may have the paint fed into the air stream by gravity, pressure, or suction, they have many parts and controls in common.

coats are discussed in chapter 2. It is important to get detailed information about the application of each product you use; this is provided by the technical sheets from the paint manufacturer.

Unpainted Body Panels—When dealing with unpainted surfaces, you should begin surface preparation by wiping the entire surface with a wax/grease remover, such as Pre-Kleeno. If the steel body panels were stripped of paint, they should be sanded with 100- to 180-grit sandpaper to remove any remaining materials, smooth out high spots, and give the primer a textured surface to "bite" into. The surface finish left by plastic media blasting or sand-blasting should be excellent for adhesion of primers. Such surfaces should require little or no additional preparation.

Unpainted steel panels should be primered soon after stripping to prevent surface rusting. You'll find

primers covered in detail in Chapter 2, as well as intermediate coats such as primer-surfacers.

Painted Panels—If body panels weren't stripped, the old paint or primer should be sanded with 320- to 400-grit paper. Any nicks, chips, or other defects in the surface should be filled with polyester glazing putty and then block-sanded smooth with 180- to 240-grit paper. The same goes for bare SMC or fiberglass panels.

If the paint has been sanded down to the point where the body panel is exposed, those areas should be spot-primed. Although it is not always necessary, it may be safer to apply primer over all areas which are to be painted, even those that are covered with old paint. This provides a more uniform base for the top coats, and it makes an evenly colored background. It also provides some isolation for the new top coats from the older paints underneath.

Sealers go one step farther to help isolate potential problems caused by

the fresh paint reacting badly to the underlying older finish. Adhesion promoters are another option and are generally employed when repainting over clear coats or other slick surfaces to which the new paint might have difficulty sticking.

If sanding scratches, feather-edges, or other surface defects that have to be covered, primer-surfacers are the next step. They are high-build (thick), sandable primers that are meant to go on heavy and fill any surface defects. They are meant to be easily sanded so that a smooth surface is left for the top coats. Again, for more detailed information on undercoats, see Chapter 2.

Guide Coats—A guide coat of a different color primer can be very lightly sprayed on top of the primer-surfacer to determine which areas need to be sanded. After the areas are dry, sand with 400-grit paper until a smooth surface results. If the guide coat looks untouched, you'll know you missed that area or there's a low

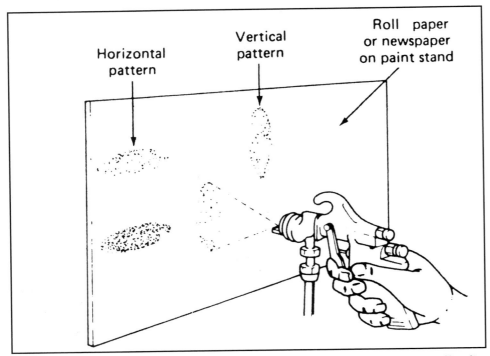

Before beginning painting, the spray pattern should always be checked for its size, uniformity, and the amount of paint material being delivered. Test by spraying on a sheet of paper (masking paper is good for this) or shiny cardboard.

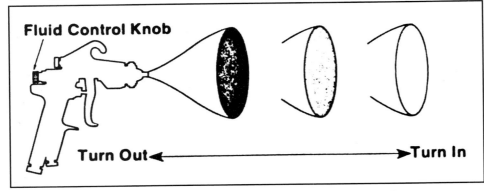

The fluid control knob adjusts the amount, or volume, of paint being delivered.

spot.

Sanding—Use of a sanding block at any stage of paint preparation helps keep the surface flat because the pressure from fingers can create grooves which become noticeable after the top coat is applied. The sanding can be done wet or dry, depending on the preference of the painter. Wet-sanding keeps the dust down and helps keep the paper from loading up. However, it is somewhat messy and the car has to be thoroughly dried afterward.

Final Wipe-Down—Before priming, it is wise to quickly go over the hard-to-reach areas with a scuffing pad, such as a fine Scotch pad. Like sandpaper, it helps to degloss the paint, remove dirt or wax, and make the surface rough to help paint adhesion. In addition, the flexible pad enables the user to get into more difficult-to-reach areas and crevices. Then solvent wipe to remove sanding sludge.

Immediately before any painting, from the initial priming to the final top coats, the car should be wiped with a fresh tack rag. The sticky fibers of the tack rag pick up any remaining loose dirt and dust on the surface. Wad the tack rag up into a ball and gently wipe—or tack—the surface to be painted. Never let the tack rag sit on the car. The varnish in the rag will quickly adhere to the paint. You can find tack rags at paint supply stores.

One other piece of advice: it never hurts to recheck the body for any remaining dents or defects before the top coats are applied. It is well worth the effort to make a diagram of the car and mark every chip or ding before the work begins and then check those areas closely after the prep work is finished. Every painter I know has at one time or another looked at a freshly sprayed car and said, "How did I ever miss that?" Protect yourself so it doesn't happen on your car.

Top Coats

The application of top coats is the part of the paint process where defects and dust come to the surface, literally. Dust control is now a higher priority. During the earlier stages of priming and surface preparation, if a little dust or dirt stuck to the paint, it simply could be sanded off later. In fact, at most body shops, all undercoats and intermediate coats are applied out in the shop or outside, not in the paint booth.

Although you should have cleaned the booth or room prior to beginning, go over it again. One trick often used by experienced painters is to wet the floors and walls after a thorough cleaning, just before they spray paint. Some of the more expensive paint booths actually have running water to help trap contaminants. If it is very humid and the paint is on the verge of

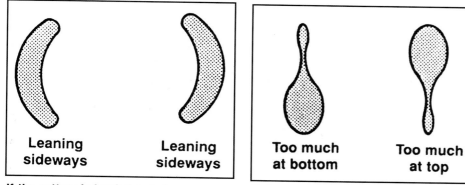

The pattern control knob adjusts the air flow which delivers the paint onto the car.

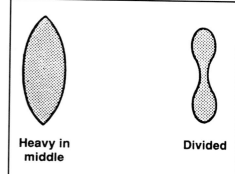

If the pattern is divided or heavy in the middle, check the air pressure at the gun, adjust the pattern, and adjust the material flow.

If the pattern is leaning or is heavy on one side, check the air cap and air horns. Clean if necessary and check the air ports.

If the pattern is heavy on top or bottom, rotate the air cap 180 degrees. If the pattern is reversed, the problem is with the air cap. If the pattern stays the same, the problem is with the fluid tip.

blushing (becoming milky-looking as it dries), wetting the floors is obviously not a good idea.

I cannot emphasize enough the importance of having sufficient lighting when painting. It's very easy to get too little paint coverage, particularly on lower body panels. During spraying, the fumes make it even more difficult to see how the paint is covering. If necessary, after spraying, bring an extra light source into the room or booth to help inspect problem areas.

It's also important to do your best to make certain that dry air is delivered to the spray gun. Change the system's filters and traps, drain the compressor tank, and add a disposable filter just before the gun, if necessary.

Another tip to avoid disaster: don't let anyone spray silicone products anywhere nearby. If your buddy is putting a protectorant on his vinyl interior in the vicinity while you are painting, you'll see more fish eyes than Jacques Cousteau. Paint will not adhere to silicone, wax, or oil of any kind.

Spraying Paint—Take your time at this stage. First, test the pattern of the gun by spraying the paint on a piece of paper. Adjust the spray, material, and the atomizing pressure of your gun to the paint manufacturer's specifications.

If you've never painted before, buy an inexpensive quart of paint and practice spraying it, preferably on a spare body panel, although a piece of shiny cardboard will do. Spray guns

operate best when held 8 to 12 inches away from the surface. If held closer, air pressure will ripple the paint; if held farther away, the paint will go on too dry (too much solvent will evaporate before the paint hits the surface) and cause orange peel, or dry film, and can alter the color.

Begin the first stroke outside of the boundary of the surface to be painted. Pull the trigger and start the airflow, then squeeze it all the way to release the material just before the gun crosses over the surface to be painted. You need to develop this sense of timing. Pass across the surface in one full, long stroke. Keep the gun equal distant from the panel all the way across. Do not fan the gun by waving your wrist—keep it square to the surface. Lock your wrist and arm, using your body and shoulders to pull the gun across the surface. This forces you to maintain the distance and angle from the beginning of the stroke to the end.

Move your stroke at a rate of speed that will put down a full, medium-wet coat. If you go too slow, the paint will run. If you work too fast, the paint will be too thin and dry.

The next pass should begin by overlapping 50% of the previous pass, by directing the center of the spray pattern at the lower or nearest edge of the previous stroke. Repeat this procedure, alternating from left to right, right to left, until the entire panel is coated.

Painting the Car

After mastering the stroke, it's time to paint the car. Follow the paint manufacturer's directions so you'll know how many coats to apply and how long you should wait between coats. Flash time is the time required for thinner and solvents to evaporate so that the next coat doesn't create a run. Most paint manufacturers will list the flash time.

If you're painting the entire car, start inside with the door jambs, trunk, hood, fender flanges, and engine compartment (if it's being painted) and work to the outside panels. For step-by-step details, see the sidebar on page 83.

Buffing

If the top coat you applied was lacquer, you'll need to buff the paint. In the case of spot repairs, shops sometimes buff the paint the same day it is sprayed so that the customer can pick up the car as soon as possible. However, over the following weeks,

PAINT STRIPPING METHODS

Paint stripping has become more necessary in recent years due to problems with paint delamination and because it is often required by the new paint warranties. Because of this increase, there have been improvements in paint stripping methods. Chemical strippers, sand blasting and hand sanding are the traditional means of stripping, and they will continue to be popular. However, new variations on these old themes promise savings in time, money, effort and clean up.

Chemical Baths Steel bodies and steel panels which have been stripped by dipping in a chemical bath, such as Redi Strip, are beautiful to behold. Their surface finish and cleanliness is remarkable, and this method has been the choice of many restorers. One major advantage is that immersion in a chemical bath enables stripping of rust and paint from hidden areas, such as the insides of frames or body panels. No other process does this. But it can also be a disadvantage in some situations. For example, it may be extremely time consuming and difficult to apply new rust proofing or sound deadening materials in hidden areas. Care must be taken to remove all stripper from these hidden areas so it doesn't attack the paint later. Also this method of stripping is expensive compared to other processes. The chemical dipping of a body shell can cost well over a thousand dollars. Additional labor costs are incurred because it is necessary to disassemble the body and remove dissimilar metals. The limited number of chemical dipping businesses also requires the expense of trucking the body and parts to and from their facilities. Chemical baths are also limited to the auto parts which can be stripped. Fiberglass and plastic parts, of course, aren't candidates for this type of stripping but care must also be taken with steel parts. Check with operator of the stripping center, to see if dissimilar metals such as aluminum or copper must be removed before dipping.

Chemical Strippers: These have advantages in that they are convenient to use, and they require a minimum of equipment. However be careful where you use them. The chemicals are often too strong for certain plastic body parts. When stripping fiberglass or plastic panels, the stripper may eat into the panel itself. Read the product literature and ask someone who has experience in stripping and refinishing that type of part. Some of the plastics and rubbers used on flexible bumpers and fascia components are even more susceptible to chemical damage. In some cases, the car manufacturer provides technical bulletins which recommend the preferred method of stripping. One major disadvantage of chemical strippers has been the clean up and disposal of used stripper and paint. A new generation of chemical strippers aims to help with that problem. The "dry"' chemical strippers go on wet like conventional strippers, but they dry and then can be flaked off. Clean up involves sweeping the used stripper and paint off the floor. Clean up is not only easier, it is less likely to create problems with governmental agencies, which are becoming increasingly concerned about what is flushed down the drain. Another caution about chemical strippers: so eye and skin protection is essential, as well as a mask to avoid inhaling the fumes.

Sand-Blasting: There are few methods as effective as sand-blasting for the spot cleaning of rust pockets on car bodies. One of the major drawbacks, however, has always been the dust and mess which sand blasting creates. New spot sand-blasters attack this problem by surrounding the sand-blasting nozzle with a large vacuum hose to suck up the

lacquer continues to dry as its solvents evaporate. As it dries, the paint sinks to some extent and dulls up a little. When an entire repaint is done in lacquer, some shops recommend that it not be sanded and buffed for at least six weeks. Having the car outside, and in particular in the sun, speeds the drying. Lacquer actually continues to dry and dull even after 10 weeks; but,

at that point, the change is so small that routine polishing or an occasional light buff should keep up the shine.

The majority of two-part and catalyzed enamels dry shiny and don't have to be buffed. However, if they are to be buffed, it should be done within about 24 hours. After that, it is much more difficult to do. One more caution about buffing: be very careful

of edges on the body because it is extremely easy to buff through the paint there. The subject of buffing is covered in detail in Chapter 5.

Reassembly

An experienced and careful painter or body man will have done a lot of preparation for the reassembly work before applying the top coats.

sand, paint and debris. In use, the vacuum is turned on, the blasting nozzle assembly is held against the car and then the trigger can be pulled to start the sand-blasting. A boot or brush seals against the contours of the body to keep the sand from blowing out and around the shop. Most units require 110 volt power for the vacuum and about 20 CFM for the air supply. The units are compact and easy to use, but the process is slower, and is not the fastest choice for stripping large panels or complete bodies. Sand-blasting an entire car is very a time consuming process unless it is done by a business which has high volume equipment. Unfortunately, such businesses usually do more of their blasting on heavy equipment and buildings. Also, they get paid by the job. The faster they strip something, the more profitable the job is. Be aware that the high pressure and volume of industrial sand blasters can heat and warp body panels if the operator is not careful. This can be an expensive lesson.

Plastic Media Blasting: A relatively recent development in the art of stripping paint off cars is the use of tiny plastic beads instead of sand for the blasting material. Called plastic media blasting (PMB), the plastic is harder than the paint but softer than the underlying metal, therefore it can safely remove the paint with minimal abrasion to the base. The first major use of PMB was the stripping of paint off jets. For one thing, the aluminum skins of airplanes are relatively fragile. Another important consideration was the increasing cost and difficulty of disposal of the thousands of gallons of used chemical stripper and water which resulted from the previous methods.

Plastic media was relatively safe, clean, dry and recyclable. Meanwhile, in the automotive industry, thinner sheet metal and increased use of SMC, TPO and other plastic for body panels gave additional reasons to utilize media blasting. Today the types of plastic media used in stripping have become more specific as experience has been gained using this technology in automotive applications. A media blaster may have separate types of media for steel bodies, for fiberglass panels and for urethane parts. Refinements in blasting equipment also are taking place. One example is the multiple venturi nozzle which allows air to be drawn into the high pressure blast. The effect of the extra air is to disperse the media more uniformly in the pattern. This reduces the "hot" spot at the center of the pattern and directs more abrasive to the outer edges so that a larger area is being stripped.Some of the major auto manufacturers are recommending the use of media blasting to strip the OEM top coat when paint delamination has occurred. An experienced operator can remove just the top coats and leave the primer relatively untouched. The cost of blasting an entire car will vary with its size and the number of coats of paint, but an average car costs about $500.

Future Methods: Other methods of paint stripping are being experimented with and may become a greater part of automotive refinishing in the future. In place of plastic media, walnut shells have been used and they offer the advantage of being biodegradable. In a similar vein, starch blast media makes use of starch extracted from wheat. Still more basic is aqua stripping which uses water propelled at very high pressures from 35,000 to 50,000 psi. Water, in another form, is used in crystalline ice blasting for paint removal. Another type of ice, dry ice, (frozen carbon dioxide) creates a stripping process where the medium disappears. The dry ice turns to gas. More exotic technologies employ the use of lasers, and experimentation has even been done with sponge blasting where small pieces of sponge carry media or chemicals to surface, and the sponge is recycled and reused.

PAINTING FRAME OFF RESTORATIONS

On Sal Carbone's '72 LT-1 Corvette roadster, all of the body painting was completed before it was lifted off the chassis. The chassis was then restored and repainted, and the finished body reassembled. This method eliminates the overspray on the restored, painted chassis. Courtesy Sal Carbone's Restoration Parts Outlet, Bolton, CT.

Although car aficionados universally agree that a collector car should be painted the original color, the type of paint is open to a little more debate. Some purists call for repainting with nitrocellulose lacquers on those cars which originally were painted with nitrocellulose lacquers. However, as mentioned previously, the types of paint applied at the factory are different than the types of paint available to body shops and restorers so exact originality isn't possible in any case. From a practical stand point, on a high quality paint job, it's not easy to tell the chemical composition of an automotive paint just by looking at it. I've never seen a judge, no matter how experienced, be certain whether a paint is nitrocellulose or acrylic lacquer, or even if it is urethane. In some cases it is questionable whether an observer can tell for certain if a car is clear coated.

Considerations such as matching the orange peel and the defects of factory paint jobs are relatively new to the field of automotive restoration. Perfection in restoration used to mean perfection in paint and detail. Even today, many of the big money cars such as Duesenbergs and Cadillac V-16's are what some people would call "over restored." The paint on the insides of hoods and fenders is often flawless in finish and gloss.

Up into the eighties, the common philosophy of restoration was that the cars should be restored or rebuilt to the degree of paint finish the factory would have wanted them to have. Frames and engine compartments were treated to dazzling perfect paint. At some point, a group of car enthusiasts took a new look at this and decided that restoring means restoring the cars to the way they actually were, flaws and all. Corvette restorers, in particular the Bloomington Gold Certification and the National Corvette Restorers Society (NCRS), were among the first to put this new philosophy of restoration into systematic use.

Restorations which adhere to this philosophy are much more expensive to complete. People can spend months researching exactly what the composition and supplier was of the paint which was originally used on the frame. Only you can decide the type of restoration you want for your car, and to what degree you'll go for authenticity.

The description frame-off restoration is popular in car collector circles and it refers to a restoration in which the car's body was lifted off the frame to permit thoroughly cleaning, painting and restoring of the underside of the body and the frame. It's also used to describe restorations of cars which don't have frames, such as Mustangs. Frame off, at the least, should mean that all suspension, brake, drivetrain and all other parts which are bolted to the body are removed and restored to their original condition.

This level of restoration presents a problem because it is nearly impossible to keep overspray and dirt off a restored chassis, drivetrain and engine compartment through the whole process of restoring and repainting the body. One of the techniques that has evolved is restoration and repainting of the body before the chassis restoration is completed.

In this procedure the body is raised to permit installation of new body mounts where appropriate. If a different frame is going to be used, the body will be installed onto it at this stage. After the body is tightened down and secured to the fame, the bodywork begins. The alignment of doors, hoods and trunk lids is made perfect by adjustment or by trimming or building of the adjacent body panels. Then all the remaining body work and repainting is done. Only after painting and buffing is completed, is the body removed.

Then the chassis and drivetrain get their full restoration and repainting. When the body is once again united with the frame, hopefully the only extra work the paint on the car will need is a quick polish or buff in any areas chafed or marked by the straps which were used to hoist the body.

Specifically, he will have made sure that every body part that was painted off the car lines up and fits properly on the body. The same goes for moldings, bumpers, and even emblems.

Although this dry run of fitting the parts to the car takes a little extra time, it avoids the very real possibility that you'll discover at the last minute that one or more parts won't go on the car properly.

The new fender you replaced might not fit the old molding, or it might have its emblem holes in a slightly different position. When the new taillight housing is bolted to the fender, it might show that the curvature of the fender and the curvature of the housing do not match. Even such simple tasks like drilling or enlarging holes are much better done before the final paint is applied.

Another tip is to use duct tape to cover the edges of bumpers or other parts which might scrape the paint as they are moved into position.

Use taps and dies to clean threads when they are rusted or binding up. Using an anti-seize compound, grease, or thread locker also will help prevent corrosion of the fasteners, and it will greatly aid any future removal of these parts.

And one last lesson from experience: Don't over-tighten parts which touch the paint. As the saying goes, "Tight is tight and too tight is cracked."

THE COMPLETE PAINT JOB

1. After dechroming, the car was driven to West Coast Technologies in Tampa, Florida, to have the old paint stripped by plastic media blasting. Steve Wilson first tested a few places on the body to determine what adjustments were needed for the air flow and plastic media. Equipment like his, which permits adjustments to be made during blasting, is highly desirable when stripping plastic or fiberglass body parts.

2. Seldom will a car be stripped of paint without an unpleasant discovery or two for the owner. Extensive previous collision damage was revealed on the lower half of the left door. The steel door frame had rusted underneath. End result: a good replacement door had to be found before we could proceed with painting.

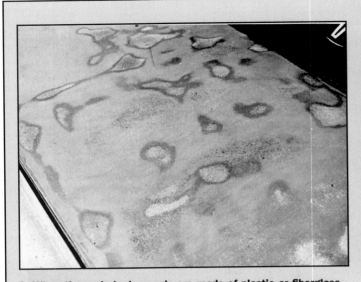

3. When the car's body panels are made of plastic or fiberglass, it is wise to stop before every bit of paint is blasted off. The few remaining areas of paint were easily removed with a sander. Plastic media blasting is not fool-proof, particularly on non-steel panels. Severe damage easily can be done by over zealous blasting, an inexperienced operator, or selection of the wrong media. Whenever any type of paint removal by blasting is undertaken, you or your body man should be around at the start to inspect how it affects the panels.

4. After all stripping, fill in any areas with spot putty and sand off any remaining paint spots.

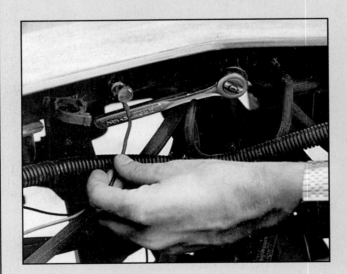

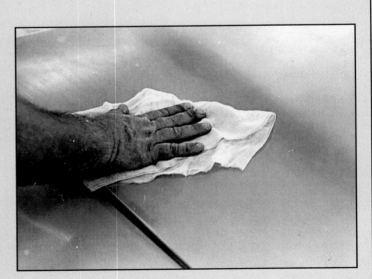

5. After any body work or spot repairs have been made, blow the car off and retape it. Don't forget to mask off the engine compartment, wiring harnesses, and lamp sockets. For example, it would be impossible to remove any overspray from the grooves of this wiring harness cover. A few minutes of extra masking can save hours of trying to remove overspray.

6. Prior to applying the first coat of primer, wipe the car down with a tack rag. If there's a possibility of oil or silicone contaminants, you should wipe the car down with a pre-cleaner.

7. Glassofix epoxy primer was used as the first primer because epoxy primers have excellent adhesion. Therefore, they are often chosen as the initial coating on unpainted body panels.

8. If the body was bare steel, such as this early Thunderbird, an etching primer would have been chosen for the first coat because of its ability to "bite" into the steel and provide the best corrosion protection.

9. The flexible front bumper was not bolted tightly to the body so that it could be sprayed separately. It required a special plastic primer, 934-0; but, prior to priming, Glasurit's solvent prewash was used to clean and soften the material for better adhesion. It is important to identify any plastic parts to determine what they require for primers and cleaners. In particular, polyolefin parts need special attention. To help identify plastic parts, see the chart on page 20.

10. Paint thickness gauges don't work on plastic or fiberglass, therefore, an uncoated steel test panel was taped alongside the body (arrow) to help judge how thick each paint layer was being applied. Of course, on a steel-bodied car, the readings can be taken directly on the panel after the paint dries.

11. Two coats of the epoxy primer were sprayed to achieve a thickness of about 1-1/2 mils. After the primer cured, Russ Rasmussen of Precision Collision in Clearwater, FL, dry-sanded it with 320-grit to flatten the surface, remove dirt, and prepare for primer-surfacer.

12. Three medium-wet coats of a two-part primer-surfacer, Glassodur Primer Filler MS 285, were applied. Because two-part paints cure by chemical reactions instead of by evaporation, there is little shrinkage later and less chance of underlying sand scratches or the borders of filled areas becoming visible. The primer-surfacer was tinted the color of the top coat to help provide more uniform coverage.

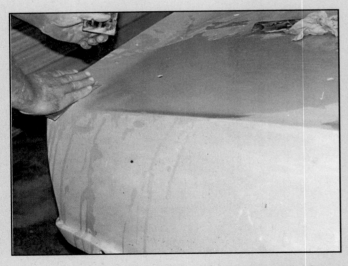

13. Two-part primers "dry" quickly like lacquer-based primer-surfacers, but they offer a more stable foundation for the top coats. 400-grit paper was used to wet-sand the primer-surfacer smooth and level.

14. After wet-sanding, it's time to clean up and retape/mask the car. Gina Bertsche used high pressure air to thoroughly blow off every inch and crevice on the car.

15. The car was remasked and taped with new paper to minimize the chance of dirt or dust blowing onto the top coats. The underneath of the hood and the engine compartment were thoroughly masked so that the hood could be opened to permit painting the edges and rain gutters.

16. The deck lid was removed so that its edges and the rain gutter area on the body could be painted. Those areas would have been difficult to paint with the lid on—the surface would have been dry and grainy. In small areas like these, the paint can be applied wet enough so wet-sanding is not needed.

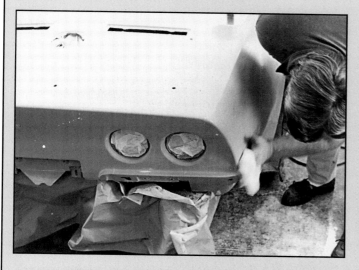

17. Just before you spray the color coat, wipe down the surface with a tack rag once again.

18. A clear coat/base coat system was used. Glasurit's top system 54 uses a polyester base coat which needs no activator. It dries quickly so that if any dirt blows onto the paint, it can be lightly sanded after about 15 minutes and then resprayed. Also, once the base coat is dry, the clear coat can be applied as heavy or wet as desired without affecting the base coat.

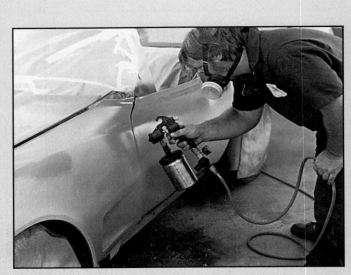

19. The top coats were applied by Norb Kwiatek, a BASF systems specialist with 22 years experience. Norb used an Accuspray HVLP gun. Note how clear the air is—a tribute to the HVLP's ability to reduce overspray.

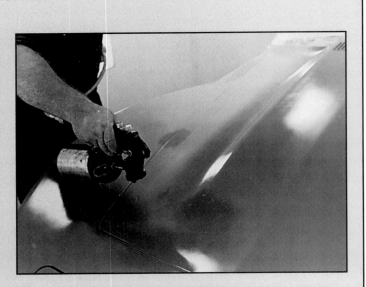

20. Coverage was very good with the first color coat, even though that required only the contents of the spray gun cup, about a quart of mixed paint. It helped that the primer was tinted the same color, and the HVLP gun helped by getting nearly all the paint in the gun onto the car. The first color coat was applied light to medium to reduce the chance of fish eyes and other problems that can occur when the first coat is applied relatively wet.

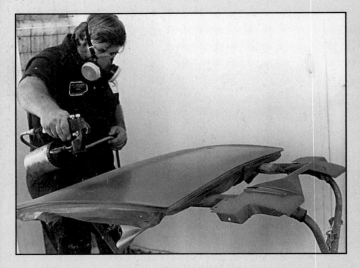

21. The deck lid and other body panels, grilles, and trim pieces were set up on stands in the paint booth. This provided better visibility and access, particularly to the lower body parts.

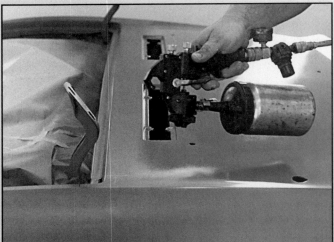

22. A second coat of color was applied to insure complete coverage and to bring the thickness of the base coat to the recommended 1/2 mil. The second coat can be applied as soon as the first coat flashes off (dulls down), which is less than the time it takes to go around the car when spraying. The second coat was applied medium to wet.

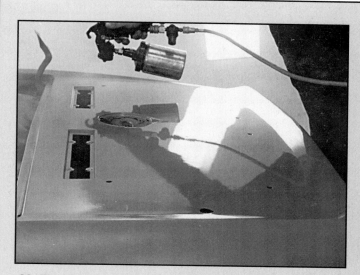

23. The clear coat was applied shortly after the second base coat flashed off. The Glassodur 54 system paint is a two-part clear based on acrylic and polyurethane resins, and it has sun blockers to prevent destruction of the base coat by ultraviolet light. As you can see, application of the clear coat imparts a high gloss from the very first coat.

24. As Norb moved forward around the car, you can see the difference between the clear-coated areas and the relatively dull-looking base coat (at the front). Paint designed specifically for base coat applications must be clear coated.

25. A second wet coat of clear was applied after the first coat flashed off. The recommended paint thickness is 2 to 2-1/2 mils after buffing. Therefore, if a lot of sanding and buffing is needed, a third coat of clear should be applied.

26. The last coat of clear was applied wet so that it could flow out and minimize orange peel. With clear coats, it is not much of a problem if the paint is applied so wet that it gets a run or a sag in some places. They can be easily sanded out later. The car was left in the booth for several hours to minimize the chance of dirt or pollutants affecting the paint before it cured. The level of gloss did not decrease as the paint cured; and the orange peel was so minimal that in many cases (especially when trying to duplicate a factory finish), sanding and buffing would not be needed. Also, it's likely that the paint will stay looking good—BASF provides a lifetime warranty for the Glasurit 54 system when applied by a certified shop.

THE CHROMASYSTEM™

Surface Preparation

Cleaning
1. Wash entire area with soap and water.
2. Use Prep-Sol® 3919S or Kwik-Clean™ 3949S to remove silicone, tar, wax, polish and grease.

Spot Repairs & Light Dents/Dings
1. Clean, sand and featheredge with 220-320 grit paper or finer.
2. Use Final-Fil™ 2290S Polyester Glazing Putty to fill very small dings, key scratches and other minor imperfections. (Apply directly over clean sanded metal or sanded cured finishes. Finish sand with 220-320 grit paper.)
3. Prime.
   — For bare metal, apply VariPrime® 615S for improved corrosion resistance.
   — For fill, apply Fill 'N Sand™ 131S or 181S or Waterborne Primer-Surfacer 210S.
   — For maximum fill and performance, use URO® Primer-Filler 1120S or 1140S.
4. Wet or dry sand the repair area with 400-600 grit paper. Use 1200 grit or finer for the clear blend area.
5. Final wipe with Lacquer and Enamel Cleaner 3939S or Kwik-Clean 3949S.
6. For base/clear repairs, apply Mid-Coat Adhesion Promoter 222S over the entire OEM panel and beyond any blend area. (Allow 15 min. dry time before top-coating with CHROMABASE.)

New Replacement Panels & Parts
1. Clean, then sand with 320 grit paper.
2. Final wipe with Lacquer and Enamel Cleaner 3939S or Kwik-Clean 3949S.
3. Apply 1-2 coats of Prime 'N Seal™
— Activate Transparent 2600S or Gray 2610S by mixing 1:1 with Spot & Panel Activator 2603S or Overall Activator 2605S.

Panel & Overall Refinishing
1. Clean, sand and featheredge with 180 grit paper or finer.
2. Use Final-Fil 2290S Polyester Glazing Putty to fill very small dings, key scratches and other minor imperfections. Final-Fil may be applied directly over thoroughly dried Prime 'N Seal 2600S or 2610S for improved corrosion resistance. Finish sand with 180 grit.
— Apply Final-Fil directly over clean metal or cured finishes that have been sanded with 180 grit paper.
— Or apply directly over thoroughly dried Prime 'N Seal 2600S or 2610S for improved corrosion resistance. Finish sand with 180 grit paper.
3. Prime.
   — For bare metal, apply VariPrime 615S for improved corrosion resistance.
   — For fill, apply Fill 'N Sand 131S or 181S or Waterborne Primer-Surfacer 210S.
   — For maximum fill and performance, use URO Primer-Filler 1120S or 1140S.
4. Final sand (wet or dry) with 320-400 grit paper.
5. Final wipe with Lacquer and Enamel Cleaner 3939S or Kwik-Clean 3949S.
6. For optimum appearance, seal with your choice of:
   — Prime 'N Seal Transparent 2600S or Gray 2610S
   — Sealer 9140S
   — VelvaSeal®

Rubber & Plastic Replacement Parts
Refer to the DuPont Plastic Refinishing Guide (H-17650).

CHROMABASE Basecoat Application

Mixing
1. Shake or stir CHROMABASE base color thoroughly.
2. Select and shake the Basemaker® that's right for your spray conditions.
3. Mix color thoroughly 1:1 with Basemaker.

Basemakers	Super Fast	Medium	Slow
	7160S	7175S	7185S
	(60°–70°F)	(70°–80°F)	(80°–90°F)

Spot & Panel Repairs	Overall Refinishing
30-40 psi (siphon gun)	45 psi (siphon gun)
25-35 psi (gravity-feed)	35-45 psi (gravity-feed)
6-8 psi (HVLP)	7-9 psi (HVLP)

1. Spray medium coats. (For spot & panel repairs, extend each coat a little further than the previous one.)
2. Apply 2-3 coats with 5-10 minute flash time between coats.
3. Allow 15-30 minutes dry time before applying clear.

Two-Toning
1. Flash first base color 30 minutes, then tape.
2. Apply second base color, remove tape, and flash 30 minutes before applying clear.

CHROMACLEAR Clear Coat Application

Mixing
1. Select the Activator-Reducer that's right for your needs.
2. Mix CHROMACLEAR 4:1 with Activator-Reducer. Spray viscosity is 17-19 seconds in a DuPont M-222 (#2 Zahn) cup.

		Multi-Use	Super Productive	High Glamour
Clears		7500S	7600S	7800S
Activator-Reducers	(fastest)	7565S	7655S	—
		7575S	7675S	7875S
		7585S	—	—
	(slowest)	7595S	7695S	7895S

3. Use the CHROMACLEAR mixing stick to measure accurately. Stir CHROMACLEAR immediately after activating.

Spot & Panel Repairs	Overall Refinishing
25-45 psi (siphon gun)	45-55 psi (siphon gun)
30-40 psi (gravity-feed)	40-50 psi (gravity feed)
6-8 psi (HVLP)	8-10 psi (HVLP)

1. Spray 2 medium coats with appropriate flash time between coats.

	Multi-Use 7500S	Super Productive 7600S	High Glamour 7800S
Flash Time:	5-10 min.	1-3 min.	5-10 min.

If blending is required, use CHROMACLEAR Blender 7601S.
2. Remove tape when touch-dry.
3. Dry time:

	Multi-Use 7500S	Super Productive 7600S	High Glamour 7800S
Dust Free	15 min.	2 min.	15-25 min.
Air Dry to Deliver/Polish	Overnight	4-6 hrs.	Overnight
Force Dry to Deliver/Polish (30 min. @140°F)	4-6 hrs.	2 hrs.	4-6 hrs.

4. If polishing is required to remove dirt, lightly wet-sand with 1500 grit paper; polish with DuPont 1500S. Follow with DuPont 3000S if needed. (Do not use heavy-duty compounds or coarse paper.)

CHROMABASE®, CHROMACLEAR® & CHROMAONE™

Courtesy

CHROMAONE Single-Stage Color Application

Mixing

1. Mix 3:1:1 with 7005S Activator and the Reducer that's right for your needs. Spray viscosity is 18-20 seconds in a DuPont M-222 (#2 Zahn) cup.

Activator	7005S		
	Spot/Panel	*Mid-Temp*	*High-Temp*
Reducers	7075S	7085S	7095S

2. Use the CHROMAONE mixing stick to measure accurately. Stir CHROMAONE immediately after activating and reducing.
3. Pot life is 2-3 hours.

Spot Repairs	**Panels & Overall Refinishing**
25-35 psi (siphon gun)	45-55 psi (siphon gun)
25-35 psi (gravity-feed)	40-50 psi (gravity-feed)
6-8 psi (HVLP)	8-10 psi (HVLP)

1. Apply 2-3 coats to achieve desired hiding & match.
2. Spray each coat to achieve flow. Flash 5-10 minutes between coats.

Blending

After the Last Coat of Color (Single-Gun Method):
1. Apply two coats of color, extending the second beyond the first.
2. Immediately over-reduce the remaining color 200-300% with CHROMACLEAR Blender 7601S.
3. Apply light coats of the mixture at the color edge, using 15 psi at the gun.

Between Coats of Color (Two-Gun Method):
1. Load color in one cup and color-Blender mixture (over-reduced as shown above) in a second cup.
2. Apply first coat of color. Apply mixture at the color edge, using 15 psi at the gun.
3. Repeat for second coat of color.
4. Repeat for third coat if desired.

Dry Time:

Dust Free — 30 min.

Tape Free — 6 hrs.

Air Dry to Assemble — 6-8 hrs.

Air Dry to Polish/Deliver — 12-24 hrs.

Force Dry to Polish/Deliver — 1 hr. (30 min. @ 140°F)

Polishing

If polishing is required to remove dirt, or to better match the OEM texture:
1. Wet-sand with 1200 grit paper or finer.
2. Polish with DuPont 1500S. Follow with DuPont 3000S if needed. (Do not use heavy-duty compounds or coarse paper.)

Air-dry: Allow 12-24 hours before polishing.
Force-dry: Allow one hour cool-down, and polish within 24 hours.

SAFETY

Before using any DuPont Refinish product, be sure to read all safety directions and warnings. WEAR A PROPERLY FITTED VAPOR/PARTICULATE RESPIRATOR approved by NIOSH/MSHA for use with paints (TC-23C), eye protection, gloves and protective clothing during application and until all vapor and mist are ex-hausted. In confined spaces, or in situations where continuous spray operations are typical, or if respirator fit is not possible, wear a positive-pressure, supplied-air respirator (NIOSH/MSHA TC-19C). In all cases, follow respirator manufacturer's directions for respirator use. Do not permit anyone without protection in the painting area.

VOC Compliance

These directions refer to the use of products which may be restricted or require special mixing instructions in VOC regulated areas. Follow recommendations in the VOC Systems Chart for specific mixing instructions.

Compatible Products

UNDERCOATS

■ **VariPrime® Self-Etching Primer**

Regular	*Converter*	*Fast Converter*
615S	616S	620S

■ **Prime 'N Seal™ Non-Sanding Primer-Sealer**

Transparent	*Gray*	*Panel Activator*	*Overall Activator*
2600S	2610S	2603S	2605S

■ **URO® Urethane Primer-Filler**

Beige	*Gray*	*Activator*	*Converter*	*Fast Converter*
1120S	1140S	1125S	1130S	1135S

■ **Fill 'N Sand™ Acrylic Primer-Surfacer**

Gray	*Red Oxide*
131S	181S

■ **VelvaSeal® Acrylic Sealer**

Neutral Cream	*Neutral Red Oxide*	*Gray*	*Translucent*	*High-Hiding Red*
1984S	1985S	1986S	1989S	1990S

MISCELLANEOUS

■ Final-Fil™ Polyester Putty 2290S
■ Sealer 9140S
■ Mid-Coat Adhesion Promoter 222S
■ Flex Additive 9250S

VINYL

■ DuPont Vinyl Color

8

CUSTOM PAINT

The direction of custom paint is seen on Brian Dotterer's seriously aggressive Chevrolet S-10: lean, mean and clean. Brian chose Sikkens Autobase toners to produce the brightest red around on the body and then used DuPont Chroma Premier to paint the graphics in shocking Corvette Grandsport Blue. The clear coat's so wet looking, you'd better have a lifejacket on if you go near. Photo by Chris Richardson.

Custom painting can change the image of a car more than any other cosmetic modification. Put a dazzling custom paint job on a common sedan and you'll find a crowd gathered around it wherever it is parked. The same car sans the special effects would be overlooked by passersby.

And the attraction of custom paint goes beyond the cult of car enthusiasts. At car shows, the true "gearheads" will be salivating over superchargers and chrome independent rear suspensions; but everyone, even those dragged along against their will, will stop to admire the best of custom paints.

A custom paint job can be produced either by using uncommon paints, such as metal flakes or candy systems, or by using common automotive paints to produce artwork such as murals or graphics. And in this field where out-doing the other painters is a passion, the tricks of custom painting

are combined in every way imaginable. To bring a little order to this naturally wild field, we'll look at the most popular custom paint systems first.

CUSTOM PAINT SYSTEMS

Competition among car manufacturers to produce exciting and appealing cars is intense, and they know that one of the best ways to attract customers is to put spectacular paint on their cars. Because of this drive to produce more exotic colors and paint schemes, the paint systems previously labeled as "custom" are more commonplace on new cars. This has already happened to paint systems such as clear coating. In the recent past, clear paint was used to finish only the best custom paint jobs; but now it comes from the factory on nearly all new cars and light trucks. The same popularization of pearl paint jobs has also occurred, to a lesser degree.

Experienced customizers are tending toward what I call refined radical. That is, major reworking but the changes are functional and they blend in. Visible examples are the 1997 Z-28 hood scoop formed into the stock hood, the custom molded grill, the Trans Am scoops mounted backwards and blended in to cool the rear brakes, PIAA Projector Beams and coordinated paint scheme on the 17-inch wheels. The modifications which aren't visible here are equally exciting: a sealed 1988 Corvette Challenge motor applying power through a 1988 Corvette independent suspension with 2.59 gears. Photo by Chris Richardson.

Wild custom paint jobs are available from the factory today. BASF's Extreme Colors contain pigments which actually change color when viewed from different angles. And this is no subtle shift in shade: one person can be seeing red while a person a few feet away sees blue! First available on the 1996 Mystic Mustangs, these are now available to refinishers in five colors in both the Diamont and Glasurit. 3 quarts will provide a sufficient basecoat for most cars and no special application techniques are required. Courtesy BASF.

Candy Colors

Candy colors are really more of a system of painting than a separate color. The starting point of a candy paint job is a reflective base coat such as gold or silver. It is opaque and applied in multiple coats until you can't see the primer underneath. The next coat is the candy coat and it is a tinted transparent paint, like a colored cellophane. For an example, I'll use gold as the base coat and red for the candy coat.

Actually, the candy coat is painted on in a number of coats. Each coat darkens the paint job a little more because it cuts down on the amount of light reflected by the gold base coat. Each successive coat makes the paint look less gold and more red. Candy paint jobs are finished off with a clear coat of paint, making them a tri-coat system. The clear is particularly necessary with candy paints because if there weren't any clear, polishing or buffing of the paint would wear down the candy tinted layer and make the paint lighter in those spots.

The problem in application is that it is very difficult to make the candy coat perfectly uniform in its thickness. For one thing, during the spraying of paint, you must overlap the areas being sprayed; and any differences in the thickness of the candy layer where the pattern overlaps can be easily seen in the lightness or darkness of the color. It takes a very skillful painter to apply candy coats without ending up with a blotchy paint job. If the tinting of the candy coat was very weak, such that 10 or more coats needed to be applied, it would be easier to get uniform coverage because the overlapping spray areas and other variances could be averaged out. However, that could lead to a very thick paint job prone to cracking and crazing, especially on a car that is parked daily in the sun.

The second major problem with candy colors is that it is difficult (some would say impossible), to repair any problems. Spot repainting and blending of a candy coat is extremely difficult because you are seeing through the candy coat, and the line where the old paint meets the new can never be perfectly uniform in thickness. Even if a problem that needs repainting lies on a separate panel, such as a hood or door, it is still

A dazzling iridescent-like custom paint called Prizmatique is offered by PPG in 24 dazzling colors. PPG says it contains holographic particles like on some credit cards, and each flake has the ability to create five different colors which results in a meandering array of color shifts. The colors are impressive in any light, but they are amazing in the sun. If you're into custom paint, you will want to look at color samples of these. Courtesy PPG.

Four-Coat Systems

If you think candy colors test a painter's patience and skill, imagine what four-coat systems will do. As the competition for exotic automotive paint escalates, the next tier is the application of two transparent tinted layers over a reflective base coat. The four coats then are the base coat (such as gold or silver), the first transparent layer (this can even be a black transparent, if you can imagine such a thing), the second transparent layer, and finally a clear coat. The same considerations in applying and repairing candy colors apply to the four-coat systems.

Pearls

The excitement of pearls is that they can produce paint jobs that change color as they are viewed from different angles. As mentioned in previous chapters, pearl paint has traditionally been accomplished by

very difficult to exactly match the depth of paint previously sprayed.

To make the situation worse, candy paint jobs are often on customized cars that had bodywork where panels were blended together. This eliminates seams, thus, a problem on the rear fender might require a total repainting of the car. This is not just a worry for the car owner, it is also a problem for the painter because it is quite common for at least one or two problems or errors to occur during the various stages of applying a custom paint job. Some very experienced painters will not do a candy paint job because there is just too much of a chance of a problem developing.

Because of the application and repair problems of candy paint jobs, they are not likely to become common with car manufacturers in the near future. Even at car shows, true candy paint jobs are not in the majority; so

when you gaze upon one, appreciate not only its beauty but the skill of the painter as well.

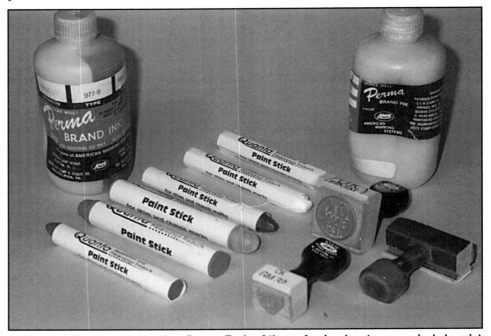

Custom painting means more than flames. Tools of the professional restorer now include paint sticks, inks and custom-made stamp pads. These are used to reproduce the assembly and inspection marks originally applied by the factory on suspension components, radiators, firewalls, etc. Courtesy Final Finish, Branford, CT.

This lime green pearl Calloway Camaro shows that a custom paint job doesn't need wild patterns to be dramatic. Having an absolutely flawless finish with a specially formulated color will captivate all who see it. Photo by Final Finish, Branford, CT.

I like to see a custom paint scheme carried over into the interior, and it is particularly appropriate for fun vehicles like this custom minitruck.

adding the mica particles that produce the pearl effects in a clear paint which is then applied over the base color coat. A typical clear coat finishes off the job, making it a tri-coat system. This is the principle method traditionally employed by custom painters to apply pearls, and it is still the most common type of custom pearl paint found today.

However, mica particles that produce pearl effects can also be blended into the color coat to produce a degree of color change without having a separate pearl layer. Car manufacturers call these blends pearl which means that you can't always tell if the paint job has a separate pearl layer (and therefore is a tri-coat system) or not. We'll describe the tri-coat system as "true" pearl paint and use it to describe the effects available with pearls.

In the automotive paint industry, pearls are described as nacreous pigments. The mica platelets can be easily oriented in parallel layers when the paint is applied. If they weren't oriented in the same direction, light would be reflected and refracted at all angles; therefore, the paint wouldn't look different when viewed at varying angles. However, when the mica platelets are arranged in overlapping layers, only part of the light is reflected as it contacts each platelet; and the rest of the light goes through the platelet and is partially reflected off the underlying layers. The reflection of light from these many layers produces the shimmering luster called pearlescence.

Color Effects—The exciting effects of pearl paints also come from their ability to produce color changes. A pearl layer that has no color or pigment in itself can produce colors just as a soap bubble or an oil film on water can. This comes from the interference effect of light reflected from different surfaces of thin films. In the case of pearl paint, the thin films are mica platelets dispersed in a clear or transparent paint. The relative amount of mica is very small, often two to five percent of that paint layer. Some pearls work best when they comprise only one to one-and-a-half percent of the transparent paint layer.

Two colors are seen with most pearl pigments: the strongest color is the one reflected from the film and the other is its complimentary color which is seen after transmission through the film. The relative proportion of the color striking your eye changes according to the viewing angle. One color will be more prominent when the paint is viewed straight-on (called face or specular viewing angle) and the other will be more prominently seen when the paint is viewed at a side angle (called the diffuse or flop angle).

The difference in color at different viewing angles is described as the paint's travel or flop. A similar change is seen with metallic paints. Proportionately more light is reflected by the metallic flakes when viewed straight on than when viewed at an angle. This is why metallic paints look lighter when viewed from the

NEW FRONTIERS IN CUSTOM PAINTING
By Jon Kosmoski, Founder, House of Kolor

There is a lot of excitement in the field of custom painting because of the brilliant new pigments that the researchers are discovering. One example we are experimenting with is a pigment which is a deep blue when viewed head on, yet a strong red takes over when it's viewed on an angle.

There's a breakthrough in metallics, too. Until now the metallic components have been primarily silver, but a new process of coating them with iron oxide makes them look like little chunks of pure gold.

The pearlescents are also making dramatic improvements; they are getting brighter and more vibrant each year. They colors are becoming much cleaner, and less "gray", and they are making the pearls of just a few years ago look pale by comparison.

On the OEM or factory side there are radical changes too. Chevrolet offered the first factory "candy" type paint as an option on their 1994 S-10. It was a raspberry color and was termed a "tinted clear".

In fact there has been so much progression to glamour paint jobs from the manufacturers that it almost seems that they are taking over the territory previously traveled only by custom painters. They have really begun to appreciate how important the paint is to the sale of their cars.

It is rumored that other major manufactures will also be coming out with candy-type paint on their vehicles. One impact of this for the future is that all painters will have to master the techniques of applying and blending tinted clears and candy paint jobs because they'll have to be doing that to repair the new cars.

Even though the factory cars have made so many advances in their glamour paint jobs, the field of custom painting will continue to have a lot more excitement to offer. For one thing, factories can only use a small number of exotic pearls or candies because the dealerships and jobbers won't want to have to stock many special ingredients. The custom paint supplier however can make use of hundreds of new pigment, pearls, and metallics. You are going to see wild new paints, and our "Kosmic Glow" pigment which glows in the dark is just one of them.

face and darker from the side. However, metallic particles only reflect light—they can't change it into different colors like pearls can. Therefore, the travel or flop of pearl pigments can be much greater than metallics. Color samples of pearls show this dramatically. Rotate the chip away from you and it becomes an entirely different color.

The colors produced by mica can be altered by increasing the thickness of the TiO_2 (Titanium Dioxide) or Fe_2O_3 layers deposited on the surface of the mica platelets. As the thickness of the layer is increased, the interference color will change from white to gold and then red, blue, and green. The color effects can be further changed by adding color absorbing pigments. For example, if certain green pigments are added to a gold pearl, the color will look gold head-on and green when viewed at an angle. In the same way, a red pigment could be added to a blue pearl to produce a paint which looks blue head-on and red at an angle.

Base Color—Another choice in a true pearl paint scheme is the base color. The lighter the base color, the more subtle the pearl effects. The amount of light reflected from a white base coat is so great that it overpowers much of the pearl color effects. The same pearls applied over a darker color, particularly black, can produce a more noticeable color effect. Why then are so many of the factory tri-coat pearl paint jobs white? One reason is that white is car buyers' favorite color, and there is little the manufacturer can do to jazz up white except to add a pearl coat. The message hasn't always gotten through to the customer, however. I've occasionally heard new car owners complain that their paint job looked a little yellow, not realizing it was the gold highlights of a pearl tri-coat.

Experimentation with pigment combinations and the development of new mica coatings has produced an explosion of exciting new pearl paints,

If people were asked to draw a car or truck with a custom paint job, they probably would draw flames. Few themes have been so popular and enduring. Flames require skillful layout with masking tape.

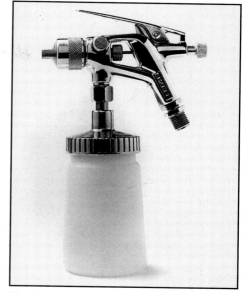

The air brush is the tool of mural makers and other custom painters. It is not much different than the ones used to air brush T-shirts. Photo courtesy Sharpe

and the future for these types of paints is very bright. As dazzling as the pearl paints are by themselves, they are often used by the custom painter in combinations to make patterns or overlays of many colors. Because these patterns and colors spring forth from the paint when the car is viewed from different angles, pearls can be both subtle and dynamic in a way no other type of paint can be. In spite of their growing popularity with car manufacturers, their appeal to custom painters has not diminished.

Metal-Flake Paints—Metal-flake paints, as mentioned in Chapter 1, are like metallic paints on steroids. The metallic particles are so large they can be seen individually, and different color flakes can be mixed to produce a kaleidoscope effect. As spectacular as they are, metal-flake paints aren't as common a choice for the custom painter as they were in the early sixties. Perhaps their widespread use in other manufactured items such as boats, helmets, and toys took away some of the glamour.

Many colors and varieties of metal-flake paints are still available from specialty paint suppliers such as House of Kolor. You'll always find metal flake paint jobs on some of the most exciting cars and trucks at custom car shows.

PATTERNS

The nineties have produced a trend of custom paint schemes that rely more on the special effects of the paint itself than on patterns such as flames, murals, and geometrics. Perhaps this is just evolution; automotive custom painting became the rage in the fifties and sixties. Today's custom paint jobs seem to be striving more for a classy, rather than cluttered, look.

However, bold patterns will continue to be a part of the custom paint scene. One reason is that they help make a car more identifiable at a distance. This is particularly important on race cars. A sponsor who pays several hundred thousand dollars a year wants his car to be recognizable, even when it is going over 150 mph.

Another important virtue of custom paint patterns is that many of them do not require a complete repaint as pearls, metal flakes, and candies do. A car owner can simply add patterns to a good existing paint job.

A dramatic multi-color paint scheme such as on some NASCAR vehicles fits this bill. A black cherry pearl, although beautiful close up, wouldn't quite have the same effect.

Flames

Flames are still popular; some people say it's a general nostalgia trend; I think it's just that they are classic. The pattern is bold, racy, and well-suited to automobiles.

Layout—Flames are relatively easy to lay out. Experienced custom painters tape out the borders free hand. First-timers are advised to use an erasable marker to set down the pattern. Once the lines look right, they can be followed with narrow masking tape. Next time you are at a car show, examine the flames more closely. The

Mural themes are as varied as the owners, and they remain a popular category of custom painting. The classic landscapes and "Dungeons and Dragons" style themes are still common.

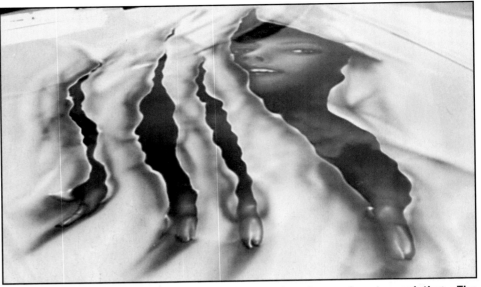

Murals display perhaps the most artistry of the various forms of custom painting. The technical ability and imagination of some murals is striking.

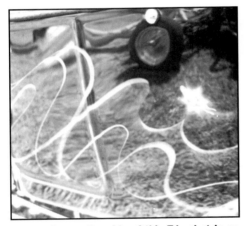

The design on the side of this T-bucket is an example of the kind of fine detail work an air brush can do.

Here's a variation on the flame theme. The flames are outlined, but not filled in.

use of color and shading by some master painters really brings the art to life.

Gradations

Gradually blending automotive paint from one color to another is one of the skills mastered by only a few of the best custom painters. Even some of the best professionals in the business find it difficult to blend without blotchiness or curtains that show where the transition from one color to another occurred.

An artfully done blend is beautiful to behold; and the more you know about them, the more you'll appreciate the skill it took to produce a perfect gradation. The other side of this, however, is that if you haven't done this before, practice off the car. Color gradation isn't one of the loudest looking custom paint effects, but it is one that requires a lot of patience and skill to achieve.

Murals

All custom painting can be considered art, but murals are the closest to the common notion of that word. The popularity of murals may have waned a number of years ago, peaking with the custom van craze of the late sixties and seventies, but they are still part of custom painting and will be around as long as people put paint on cars.

Although some of the scenes portrayed in murals have become trite, nearly everyone will stop and look at a good mural. Also, no other form of custom painting offers as great a

Lace is one of the forms of custom painting that went the way of hula hoops. Although it's relatively easy to paint, it just doesn't seem to fit automotive applications like flames do.

freedom of expression.

Another advantage of murals is how radically you can change the effect of a car, truck, or van by simply adding a mural. In that respect, it can be one of the fastest, cheapest, and easiest methods of custom painting.

To get ideas for murals, visit car shows and page through car magazines. Art books and magazines can also provide great source material. If drawing isn't your strong suit, show the scene or concept you envision to an artist. From my experience, people who do pin striping frequently have an art background, plus they have paints that will stand up in automotive applications. That is a critical consideration. Dyes and pigments or paints that are used for other types of artwork may not stand up to the sun, or they may not stick well to your car's finish. After being painted, the mural should be clear-coated to increase its durability; but make sure the paints are compatible. The mural will be destroyed if the solvents in the clear coat dissolve the mural paints.

Geometrics

With the application of a single extra color, a geometric pattern or stripe can make a bold difference in the appearance of a car. Not only that, this type of custom painting can be seen and recognized from a distance.

Because it is the shape of the pattern which is the essence of this form of custom painting, the other factors

matter less. It doesn't require an exotic paint like candy or metal flake, nor the skills of an experienced painter, nor the drawing ability of an artist. If you can lay out a pattern on the car with tape, you're halfway there. In this respect, it is not only fast and inexpensive compared to other types of custom painting, it is also easier to do yourself.

Look at custom-painted cars at car shows to gain a good source of ideas. Once you have a few designs in mind, try drawing on a sketch of the car. You'll be able to work out a lot of details that way, and you may come up with a better way to enhance the effect.

Fads—One form of geometric pattern that has continued in popularity over the years is a series of stripes or panels which decrease in length or width as they go down the side of a car. It gives a modern or high-tech look to the car and imparts a sense of motion. On the other hand, one form of geometric pattern which has not continued in popularity is

Waves, splashes, and drops have been a popular theme and the talents of some painters at producing 3-D effects make some of theme spring off the car.

Even though it has no flames or graphics, this Calloway Speedster features perhaps the most exquisite of custom paint: a four color system. After a color base coat, a different color is applied, followed by a transparent mist coat of a third color, topped off with the clearcoat. Paint aficionados know how difficult it is to apply the multiple colors so that the shades are perfectly even to the eye. Photo by Final Finish, Branford, CT.

A nice combination is seen in this neon light band which seems to run behind the wider color stripes.

lace. A lace pattern was easy to create—all the painter needed to do was lay a piece of lace or patterned cloth on the car's surface and spray over it. The lace acted like a masking template and, after spraying, it was removed, leaving the old color where the lace lay. You won't see much of it at car shows today. Lace has gone the way of hula-hoops.

Modern Themes

The three-dimensional effects custom painters are now achieving are simply incredible. Through talented use of shading and shadows, some of the new paint schemes seem to spring right off the body. The 3-D techniques coupled with the popular patterns of drips or droplets give a great appearance of depth to custom-painted panels. Another popular custom paint theme is the "heart beat," a horizontal line interrupted by up and down peaks imitating a line on an EKG monitor. Perhaps punk rock also has influenced today's paint schemes in the form of dramatic "rips" and "tears" air brushed on the sides of cars and trucks. Only time will tell if the custom paint themes of the nineties will have the staying power of their popular predecessors, like flames.

Since the fifties and the birth of the hot rod movement, custom painters and car enthusiasts have been creating techniques and themes that are still popular today. And, although some custom paint schemes, such as flames, may have appeared over 40 years ago, their popularity and appeal is timeless. Today's custom colors are more brilliant than they've ever been before, and the paint chemists say the best is yet to come.

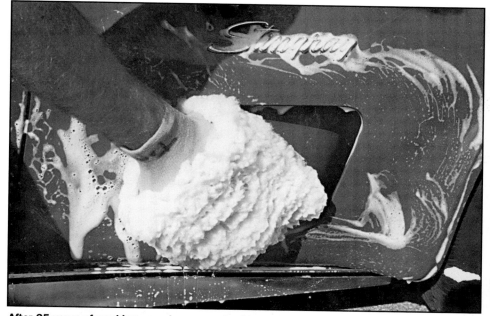

After 25 years of washing cars, I was surprised to see how this new mitt made the job easier. It holds so much soapy water, you can wash the entire car with only a few dips in the bucket. Plus, you can quickly flip it over on your hand to use on the other side. TIP: Mark the wristband on one side to identify that side for use exclusively on the dirtier lower panels of the car. Use the other side for top panels.

Cleaning not only makes automotive paint look better, it helps it to last longer. Acids, salts, and other corrosive chemicals are an inevitable part of the environment in which automobiles must live. Common enemies of auto paint include acid rain caused by pollution from factory smoke stacks, road salt spread by highway departments to melt snow and ice, and natural pitfalls such as bird droppings and splattered bugs. The damage begins as soon as these chemicals contact the surface of the paint, and the corrosive effect is accelerated when water is added. Every time the nightly dew falls on a car, a chemical stew is created. If the paint is not occasionally washed, each spot of chemical contamination eats a little further down into the paint.

Accumulations of dirt and road film also create damage because they soak up moisture, and thereby keep body surfaces moist. Areas inside the wheel wells that can trap leaves and dirt are the most prone to rust. Such pockets fill with dirt and can hold moisture for days. Water is a powerful catalyst for the chemical process of rusting and greatly accelerates it. For example, a piece of bare sheet metal can go weeks in a dry environment without a trace of surface rust being visible. Wipe a little water on the same piece of steel and, in a matter of hours, rust will appear.

Although it sounds contradictory, one of the reasons for washing a car is to keep it drier. By removing the accumulations of dirt that absorb and hold moisture, the rain and dew will dry faster from the car's body.

Soaps

What is the best type of soap to use? Automobile manufacturers, paint manufactures, and major auto wax manufacturers all recommend that you use as mild a soap as possible. For one thing, much of the bright work and trim parts commonly used on cars today are made of aluminum. These parts are particularly susceptible to the chemicals in strong

Using a hose without a spray nozzle has always been wasteful of water. Now it's illegal in certain parts of the country. This handle cost just over a dollar, and the pressure stream it produces helps speed up spraying and rinsing.

After washing the top panels, move on to the lower panels. Note the wash pail/storage unit here, designed to keep all materials for cleaning your car in a neat, self-contained bucket.

When washing, rinse the mitt or cloth frequently to avoid grit or sand buildup which may scratch the paint.

soaps and can be permanently stained or etched by them.

The safest choice is to select a car wash soap made by one of the major wax manufacturers. In fact, if you're using a particular wax, it would be wise to use the car soap of the same brand. Hopefully, a manufacturer's soap will be formulated so as not to dissolve and remove their wax from the car. Soaps specially formulated for cleaning cars have another advantage: the inclusion of non-spotting additives. Westley's Car Wash is a popular choice. It is mild enough so it won't harm most waxes.

For those who don't wax their cars, liquid dish detergent is a common choice for soap. Although it's readily available, it is stronger than most car wash soaps. Automatic dishwasher soap is even stronger, and it is definitely not recommended.

Regardless of what type of soap you choose, don't go overboard on how much you use. The more you use, the harder it is to rinse off. Plus, the more soap that goes down the drain, the

worse it is for the environment.

The soap should not be so strong that it dissolves every dirt or tar spot on the car. It's much better to use a separate cleaning rag with a dab of a stronger cleaner, such as bug and tar remover, to remove the tough spots. To minimize damage to the finish or the wax, use a relatively weak soap solution to wash the entire car and use a stronger cleaner for spot cleaning any remaining dirt.

Washing Tips

There are many different routines used in washing a car. However, sticking to one particular routine makes the job go faster and helps prevent missing spots on the car. Here are some suggestions from painters and detailers who have it down to a science.

1. Find a shady spot. The longer it

It's a good idea to use a separate rag for cleaning the wheels and tires. Why? Some brake pads produce a dark, corrosive dust that accumulates on the wheels. The dust can be so corrosive that it will etch and dull the trim rings or aluminum wheels within a week. Also, the chemicals in whitewall tire cleaners are often quite strong. Use a separate rag to prevent getting such harsh chemicals on the body paint. Rub and rinse the sidewalls immediately after using any tire cleansers to prevent discoloration of the rubber.

takes for the soapy water or the rinse water to dry, the easier and better it is for you. Also try to find a spot out of the wind. If sand or dirt blows up from the ground and gets on the car during washing or drying, the resultant scratches can mar the finish.

2. Rinse the car, preferably with high pressure water, before washing it. This is to wet the dirt so it can begin dissolving and softening, to rinse off dirt and sand before a washcloth is dragged over the paint, and to cool down the car. (It's always better if the soap doesn't dry and bake on a hot hood or roof). It's also a good idea to go around the car twice on the initial rinse. First, to soak the surface and next to spray off any loose dirt or sand.

3. Start from the top. Although it's

WASHING AND DRYING CLOTHS

SPONGES: Natural sponges are among the best items for washing cars. Although they cost more than synthetic sponges, they last much longer—often for many years. The bigger the sponge, the better, because it will hold more soap and water and thereby allow you to cover more area before returning to the wash bucket. Whatever you do, don't use the type of kitchen sponge that has a rough pad on one side. It is too easy to make a mistake during washing and accidentally use the wrong side. This surface can really scratch. It can even permanently scuff the chrome finish on bumpers or trim parts.

T-SHIRTS: Old clothing or T-shirts are also acceptable as wash cloths, but be sure to cut off any buttons, snaps, rivets, or zippers. The best wash cloths are soft, and the larger the weave the better because dirt particles picked up during washing will work their way into the weave and minimize scratching.

CHAMOIS: A natural chamois is a piece of suede-like leather, oiled and tanned to make it soft and pliant. Once it has been wetted down and wrung out, it will soak up water like a sponge but will leave the surface dry and streak-free. Plus, unlike a towel or cloth, it won't leave behind lint clinging to the paint. A less expensive alternative is the synthetic chamois. Some of the synthetic chamois work remarkably well and often hold up better than the natural variety—also, they cost about a third as much. The Absorber picks up more water than a natural chamois and it stores away wet, which you'll find is another advantage.

DRY CLEANING CLOTHS: Dry clean your car? Well, almost. A type of cloth called a dry cleaning cloth has been available for years. This is a soft cloth treated with a cleaner to help remove light films and dirt from cars. It is used by some car dealers who find it easier to wipe down the dust that accumulates on the cars overnight instead of doing a complete wash to every car on the lot. Although dry wash cloths shouldn't be use on heavily soiled cars, they certainly are much faster and easier for a quick, light cleaning. If there is any grit on the car, it may scratch the finish. If you have a dark-colored car or if you're very picky about its finish, be cautious when wiping down the car with a dry cleaning cloth.

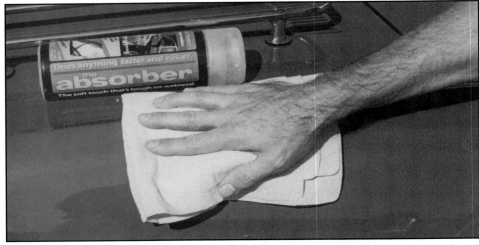

Chamois are perhaps the best way to dry off a car and prevent water spotting or streaking. A good sized, natural chamois, however, costs about $15 and does wear out. The Absorber is a synthetic chamois which soaks up 50% more water, costs less, and lasts longer. My Absorber has lasted seven years so far, plus it has the convenience of being able to be put away damp.

Fine steel wool, 0000 for example, works well for cleaning chrome and stainless steel parts. WARNING: Use the steel wool before washing the car. Little steel particles fall off and land on the paint while you are scrubbing. If they sit for very long, dew or moisture in the air can cause them to rust and leave brown stains in the paint.

better to do most things from the ground up, this doesn't apply to washing cars. For one thing, the dirt and sand is usually accumulated on the lower areas; and the dirtiest area should be washed last to minimize the chance of sand getting caught in the washcloth and scratching the upper surfaces. In fact, some aficionados (particularly those who own black or dark colored cars) use at least two separate sets of washcloths and two chamois; one set is used on the lower areas, and the other is used only on the upper surfaces. The other obvious reason for starting at the top is that everything rinses downward. It makes little sense to wash or rinse the bottom areas and then wash or rinse the areas above them.

4. Wash the roof and windows first. If the soapy water is drying very quickly, stop and rinse it off. Then start at the driver's side door and work toward the rear. Why? So the hood, which is usually the hottest part of the car, gets washed last and gets rinsed off immediately afterwards.

5. Use plenty of water, and keep turning and checking the washcloth or sponge to keep sand or grit from accumulating on it. Dunk and squeeze it out after washing part of the car, especially after use on the dirtiest areas.

6. Keep bug and tar remover nearby. Whenever you come upon a spot that won't wash off with soap, try cleaning it with a rag and a little bug and tar remover. This type of cleaner is petroleum-based and leaves an oily film. Therefore, after the spot is removed, wash the area with soap and water to remove the film's residue.

7. Lightly rinse the car. If you didn't go overboard on the soap, it won't take much water to rinse off the soap. Also, depending on the condition of the water in your area, the water spotting might be less of a problem if the soap isn't 100% rinsed off.

8. Do the tires and whitewalls last. The tires and wheels are usually the dirtiest part of the car. In many cases they are laden with dark, corrosive brake dust

from disc brakes. Spray on a little whitewall cleaner and then use a soft brush, such as a nail brush, on the whitewalls or raised white letters. You may be surprised at how little cleaner and scrubbing is necessary. Immediately after this, wash the sidewalls or the cleaner may later turn the rubber a dingy brown color. If any cleaner gets on surrounding paint or trim, wash or rinse it off immediately. Many tire cleaners, such as Westley's Bleche-White, spray on and wipe off without any scrubbing, or with very little scrubbing, depending on the condition of the whitewalls. Although whitewall tire cleaners are easy to use, you must be careful if you have aluminum wheels because some cleaners can cause permanent damage if they are allowed to remain on the wheels. Some of these cleaners are strong enough to harm nearby freshly painted or lacquer painted surfaces, too, so be careful spraying whitewall cleaners when it is windy. Special wheel covers, or a piece of cardboard, can be used to protect your hubcaps and rims when applying whitewall cleaners. Also, try to keep the rag on just the whitewall when wiping off the

Meguiar's Quik Detailer is a spray cleaner that can be used when a full washing isn't necessary or possible. This helps save water and extend the time between washes. The manufacturer says it also enhances the shine and leaves a protective finish.

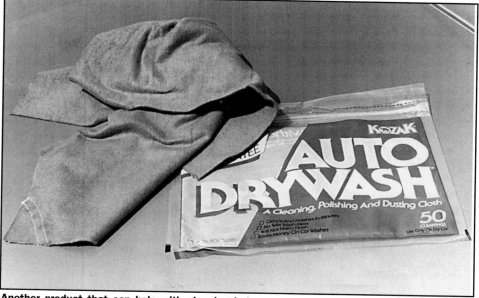

Another product that can help with cleaning between car washes is a "dry" cleaning cloth. Kozak's Auto Drywash has long been used by car dealers to quickly dust or clean the cars on their lots. With any cleaning system, however, be careful not to rub grit into the paint's surface, particularly on dark-colored cars.

Turtle Wax's Bug & Tar Remover is one of the most useful spot-cleaning products for your paint. Kerosene can also remove oil and tar spots, but it is not advisable to use strong cleaners on fresh paint jobs, particularly lacquer ones.

cleaner. When you're through, rinse the wheels thoroughly to help avoid streaking.

Once your tires have been cleaned, you may want to use a tire dressing to enhance their appearance. One brand of tire dressing, No Touch, comes in a 15-oz. can which will do about 16 to 20 tires. After you spray it on, it foams up and then slowly dissipates. The tires are left with a very "wet" look. However, it is not a cleaner, so you'll have to use the conventional whitewall cleaner mentioned above for cleaning deep dirt from the whitewalls or letters.

9. After cleaning the tires and wheels, it's time to chamois the rinse water off the car body. Whether natural or synthetic, a chamois is the best way to dry the paint. In some regions of the country, the water supply has so many chemicals in it that letting the car air dry leaves ugly water spots. Try taking the car for a quick lap around the block to blow off a portion of the water or use an air compressor. Another technique you might want to try is to go over the car twice with the chamois. It may be necessary to use a window cleaner and paper towels to make the windows and mirrors streak-free. The paper towels can then be used for a quick wipe of the door jam area.

Special Cleaners

Bug and tar remover is a petroleum-based product that makes removal of the inevitable road tar spots and streaks much easier. Turtle Wax is a popular brand, but there are others, and all work about the same. Many other petroleum-based solvents found around the house will also work. However, be careful and test them on the inside of the trunk lid or another out-of-the-way area to make sure they don't harm the paint. Also, be cautious of volatile petroleum distillates, such as gasoline, because they can harm delicate finishes like lacquer and fresh paint.

If a spot is stubborn in coming off, take your time and let the solvent work. The safest thing to do is use a little elbow grease and continue rubbing. Try scraping off the spot only as a last resort. Even relatively soft tools made of plastic or wood can

"Brushless" car washes are thought by many people in the industry to be the kind least likely to scratch a car's paint. At this car wash, soft cloth is used in place of brushes for cleaning the upper surfaces of the car. Much of the rest of the washing is accomplished by high pressure sprays. Even if the operation is described as "brushless," brushes may be still be employed for manual scrubbing or for mechanized cleaning of the lower body panels.

gouge the paint.

Removal of adhesive left behind by oil change stickers, bumper stickers, and the like is made easy by 3M's General Purpose Adhesive Cleanser, part number 308984. In fact, this is such a useful and multi-purpose product that you'll find uses for it everywhere. It cleans off tape marks and many other types of residue, including tar and silicone.

Another multi-purpose product that works well for cleaning certain adhesive residue is WD-40. Before washing the car, some mechanics recommend spraying WD-40 into the insides of the door locks (where the key enters) to help repel moisture and lubricate the mechanisms.

Car Washes

Automatic car washes have two potential dangers. The first danger is that the brushes may scratch your paint. You never know if the vehicle that went through the car wash shortly before you had just come back covered with mud and sand from a hard day four-wheeling!

A second possible drawback to automatic car washes is damage to exterior parts such as mirrors, antenna, wipers, and trim pieces. In fact, many car washes have a signs posted warning of this danger and disclaiming any liability for it. Check your car for loose or fragile moldings before trying a car wash. At the very least, make certain the antenna is retracted before entering an automatic car wash. It may be necessary to shut off the radio to retract your power antenna. If you have a non-retracting antenna, you may find that it's easy to unscrew and remove the mast.

To put this in perspective, many cars are washed only by automatic car washes year after year, and their finishes still look OK. However, if you have an exceptional finish and want to keep it looking its best, it should be hand washed to be on the safe side.

WAXES

Are you bewildered about what type of wax to buy? Don't feel alone. When you walk into an auto parts store, you are confronted by an entire wall full of products to care for your car's paint. The automotive wax industry is intensely competitive, with hundreds of different brands and products vying for your dollar.

Car owners generally want the answers to three basic questions:

1. Does wax do any good?
2. What type of wax or polish should I buy?
3. How often should I wax my car?

While the questions are simple, the answers are not simply found. One reason why there is so much contradictory information is that many millions of dollars are spent on advertising to mold your opinions. Fierce competition among manufacturers has led to a lot of conflicting information that often ends up confusing even the most informed consumer. A byproduct is the formation of myths about wax and its use, a few of which I'll try to dispel.

COMMON MYTHS

The most common myth is that when water beads up on a car's finish, that's proof of a protective coating of wax. The truth is that water can bead up on an entirely unwaxed finish.

Although water beading is not a sure sign that a painted surface has wax, it is a sign that the surface is in a relatively healthy state. When water no longer beads on a clean, painted surface, it is because the surface has become relatively rough. The individual imperfections in the surface are too small to see; but these tiny cracks, pits, and holes allow the water to stick. The water adheres, penetrates, and spreads out like a paper towel soaks up water.

There are many myths about wax and other car care products. One of the most common myths is that water beading on paint proves that it has a good coat of wax and is protected. After four years without a single application of wax or polish, water still beaded on this polyurethane paint.

Carnauba wax has long been a favorite of automobile enthusiasts, and it is now available in an aerosol can to make application a little easier. Courtesy Eagle One .

Does Wax Protect?

People have widely differing opinions about most subjects in the field of automotive paint, and waxing is no exception. On one hand, the only people who are absolutely certain that automotive paint needs to be waxed regularly are the people who manufacture and sell, or apply, wax products. On the other hand, it has been generally assumed that waxing protects painted surfaces, and millions of dollars are spent on waxing and wax products by people who care about cars.

Extending Paint Life—The best urethane and other two-part paints are incredibly durable without any application of wax. Solvents as strong as lacquer thinner can be poured on some factory urethane paint jobs with no effect. So be wary of demonstrators who show how durable paint is after waxing if they don't show that the paint is fragile before the product is applied.

On the other hand, the argument can be made that the paint lasts longer on cars that are waxed and pampered. But just because cars frequently waxed often have paint that appears to hold up very well, this doesn't mean the wax extended the paint's life.

One example of an alternative reason for longer paint life is that a frequently waxed car is more likely to lead a sheltered life—literally. For example, it's a safe bet that a higher percentage of Ferraris are waxed and garaged than are Ford pickup trucks.

Another alternative reason for longer paint life on pampered and waxed cars could be extra washing. People who wax their cars more often than others also are likely to wash them more. Cleaning dirt, salt, and other chemicals off a car's paint does a lot to protect the finish.

Painters and other professionals in the field of automotive refinishing generally agree that frequent waxing won't hurt the paint, and, at the very least, it will keep the paint clean.

Selecting a Wax

There are many brands of wax available on the market today. Most of them have labels spouting impressive words like polymer technology, pure carnauba, silicones, natural waxes, resins, and glazing. All manufacturers have tests that claim their brand is better than the other. But the best advice is to try several products yourself, then select the one that is easiest to apply, looks the best, and lasts the longest. Other suggestions are to ask a trusted fellow car enthusiast or your local body shop which brand they recommend, and then try the product yourself.

If a product takes too much effort to apply, you probably won't use it very often. Some of the non-wax polymers and glazes contain silicones and go on very easily. This ease of application makes them very popular. Another

Liquid Glass has gained a loyal following over the years. It's a non-wax liquid polish that is easy to apply. Courtesy Liquid Glass.

Cleaner/waxes are designed to bring life back to slightly weathered or dull finishes and leave a coat of wax for protection in one step. Courtesy The Wax Shop

Some waxes are tinted to match the popular basic colors. One advantage is that they help to make less visible the wax build up that is inevitably left behind in crevices. Courtesy Colour Wax.

product many experts in the industry highly recommend is one of the oldest—carnauba wax. This wax is made from the carnauba palm tree in South America, and you'll find a pure carnauba wax product offered by many of the top names in the car care business. Carnauba wax in its purest form is thought by many to be the most durable and most protective type of wax.

One-Step Cleaner/Waxes—One-step cleaner/waxes typically contain a mild abrasive. Such products are a compromise between a cleaner and a wax, and they are intended to save the time it takes to do each operation separately. Because it is a compromise, a cleaner/wax may not do as intense a cleaning job as when cleaning is done as a separate operation; and the level of wax protection may not be as great.

However, few people will take the time to completely clean their car with a hand polish and then do a separate waxing operation. Therefore, these products fills a useful niche. A one-step cleaner/wax is the best choice for people who have a slightly dull or worn finish and want to get a little more gloss and protection without making a big project out of it.

Waxing Applicators

Don't beat yourself up trying to find a particular type of cloth recommended on wax manufacturer's label. I drove to over a half-dozen automotive and auto paint stores trying to find a 100% cotton terry cloth. So if you can't find one either, don't despair—there are suitable alternatives.

T-Shirts—Elsewhere in this chapter, I recommended T-shirts as a good choice for washing your car. They are also good for applying and buffing wax. Advantages are that T-shirts are inexpensive, are easily found, and are easily cleaned and reused. Closely examine any articles of clothing; and then cut off buttons, zippers, rivets, and anything else that might cause scratches. Use only soft, preferably 100% cotton cloth. Large weave and

fluffiness is also a plus because any grit picked up by the cloth will work its way into the weave and thereby not drag along the painted surface.

Diapers—Some car care purists won't use anything but a well-washed soft cotton diaper (available from a diaper service) for polishing. However, be careful of the stitching. I recently bought a package of new "cotton" diapers and found that the stitching was nylon thread. The nylon left minute scratches in the paint I was polishing. If you want to test the thread or stitching in any piece of cloth, clip out a short piece of thread. Hold it with tweezers or pliers and bring a match or lighter under the end of the thread so that the flame is about an inch away. Nylon thread will shrink up and its end will melt into a ball. Cotton thread will turn brown.

Shop Rags—Avoid using mechanic's shop rags on paint. Not only are they rough and sometimes contain harsh chemicals, they may have metal particles stuck in the weave. Check with your local auto body supply store to see if it has boxes of rags made specifically for waxing and polishing. A ten-pound box costs about $15, and it certainly saves time searching for clean rags.

Specialty Polishing Cloths—Cheesecloth is just a very loosely

If you're lucky, even nasty looking layers of grime sometimes can be removed to reveal sound paint underneath. This grime was removed with a cleaner first.

woven soft cloth. Terry cloth is a fabric made with short loops of thread on the surface.

Specialty polishing cloths can be excellent. They all have the advantages of the softest cloths, along with the disposability of paper. The only disadvantage is the cost, which may not be worth the difference they make on your finish. If you are happy with what you are using, there is little advantage in changing.

Waxing Cautions

If wax has some value for sealing out chemicals, it also has the possibility of sealing in or trapping chemicals. Freshly painted areas continue to undergo chemical changes and solvent evaporation for many weeks. In particular, it is important that the excess solvents are allowed to go through the outer layers of paint and evaporate. If they don't escape, they will form bubbles at the boundary between layers of paint. This could push the paint layers apart, causing delamination in those specific pockets.

To help avoid this, some car manufacturers and painters recommend that you do not wax new or freshly painted cars for about two months. If you have just bought a new car, check your owner's manual for recommendations about waxing. If your car has just been repainted, ask the painter what the paint manufacturer recommends.

Silicone—The tiniest amounts of silicone cause problems when repainting. If your car is scheduled for a spot repair or a complete repainting in the near future, you may want to choose a wax that doesn't have silicone as an ingredient. Some refinishers maintain that there is nothing to worry about if the painted surfaces are properly cleaned. Other painters say it is nearly impossible to eliminate all the silicone. Even if it is removed from the car's body, a particle of dust with silicone can create a blemish during painting.

Frequency—How about too much waxing? TV ads warn of wax build-up on kitchen floors, but that's not a problem discussed regarding cars! Although wax build-up on cars is not a problem, the wearing down of paint could be. If you frequently use a power buffer, or if you often use a polish or a cleaner/wax, be aware that you are removing paint. Most polishes and one-step cleaner/waxes contain abrasives that remove paint. If they are used too often, you could wear through the color and into the primer.

Too much buffing or polishing with abrasives creates problems with clear coated cars, too. Even though you are not removing color by buffing or polishing, the protective clear coat layer is being worn down. That allows more UV light to penetrate and damage the sensitive underlying color coat.

Be particularly aware that wearing through the paint is much more of a problem on peaks and fender creases.

Many car care products combine two functions in one. Visual Perfection takes another tack and supplies two products in one package. The polish is said to contain resins which help fill swirl marks and small imperfections. After its application, a Gloss Enhancer is sprayed on and wiped off. Courtesy Eagle One.

It is best to use only a minimal amount of pressure (or none at all) when polishing or power buffing near edges and high spots on the body of the car. It is so easy to go through the paint in these areas that many professionals tape edges and seams to prevent the power buffer from even touching these areas.

Abrasives—Don't trust the label when it comes to describing the abrasive content. One manufacturer may choose to call a particular ingredient "abrasive" while another manufacturer may not. Every fluid or paste is abrasive to some extent, even pure water. If you have any doubts about that, look at weathered rock formations.

If your finish is glossy and slick without the use of a one-step cleaner/wax or polish, then there is no need to use one. Look for a wax that says it is non-abrasive or that it is formulated for use on clear coats. Then test it on the car. It should wipe

Dulled Black trim or black bumper moldings that have been scratched or faded can be brought back to new with sprays such as Mar-Hyde's Black Satin. Clean the parts thoroughly, and then mask adjoining surfaces carefully to prevent black overspray where it's not wanted.

on smooth without any gritty or abrasive feel. If the car is not clear coated, little color should come off on the rag. If the car is clear coated, try rubbing the wax on a clean, painted surface under the hood or in the interior (areas that have probably not been clear coated) to make sure that a lot of color doesn't come off on the rag. If the wax passes this test, it shouldn't remove any of your clear coat.

WAXING TIPS

Wash the car before waxing. If you don't, you risk scratching the paint by rubbing the surface dirt around while applying the wax. After washing the car, dry it thoroughly with a chamois. Natural chamois are great but the synthetic ones last longer, absorb more water, cost less, and can be put away damp.

Frequently look at the surface of the cloth to see if it has picked up any

dirt. You don't want to get any dirt into the bottle of liquid wax. With paste wax, if the surface begins to feel gritty, scoop off the upper layer and throw that part away. Use a separate rag for lower panels and more heavily soiled areas. Make sure that you wax one small area at a time. In other words, apply the wax to one panel, for example, a front fender, then buff it off completely before moving on to the next panel.

Watch out for the sun. Waxing a car in the sun can become a major disaster to the final appearance of your car. Direct sunlight dries the wax faster than you can remove it, and the result is streaking. This is especially true with one-step waxes and quick liquid waxes which seem to dry and streak upon contact in the hot sun, leaving your car looking like a bleached blonde with a bad frosting job. If wax bakes on during application, it can take hours of hand rubbing with a second application of paste wax or cleaner/wax to get rid of the streaks.

A shady spot under a tree is great for waxing your car, but be careful that the tree doesn't drip. This can be another permanent paint mauler if the sap is left on. By the time you get to the back of your car, the newly waxed front may be decorated with pine syrup!

Overhead wires are great resting areas for birds with full digestive tracts. Bird droppings can quickly eat into the finish of your paint. Remove such deposits immediately, when possible. For spot-cleaning, soak a paper towel in water or use a glass cleaner, if necessary. It's better to have a few shallow surface scratches from the spot cleaning than the deep etching in the paint that bird

droppings can create.

POLISHING OR RUBBING COMPOUNDS

Polishes and polishing or rubbing compounds are all designed to remove the deteriorated top layer of paint and create a smoother, slicker surface. By themselves, they add no degree of protection, other than the benefits of a very thorough cleaning. In general, rubbing compounds are the most abrasive, and polishing compounds are less abrasive. Products labeled "polish" generally have the smallest abrasives.

However, there is plenty of overlap among manufacturers on the labeling of products. One company's polishing compound might be as abrasive as another company's rubbing compound. Unfortunately, there is no grading system commonly used for polishes and compounds like there is for sandpaper.

The comparison of different products is further complicated because the abrasive in some products breaks down into a finer abrasive as it is used. It starts off relatively gritty but, as it is rubbed into the finish, the grittiness disappears and a smooth finish results. If you stop rubbing before the compound breaks down, the surface will still have scratches from the abrasive.

The effect of a polish is also different depending on whether it is applied by hand or with a buffer. Reading the labels can help in some instances, but usually you have to test the products to find one that is suitable. The advice of painters, counter men, and even the manufacturers is often of limited help in choosing which brand or which

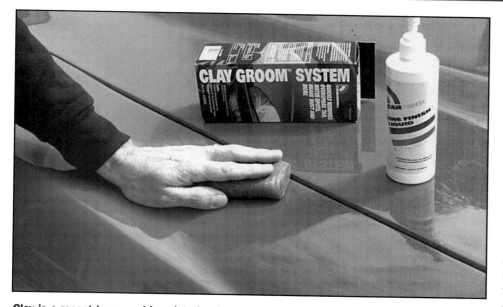

Clay is a recent buzz word in paint cleaning, especially for removing light overspray. A blob of the special fine grained clay is held in your hand and rubbed over the finish.

product you should buy because their experience has been primarily with professional usage by power buffers on newly refinished cars.

You may have to choose a few products to find the best one for your car's finish. It may help to start with a manufacturer who has a line of products that are graded or described in terms of their relative abrasiveness. At least then, you have a means of comparison which will give you a better chance of getting a slightly less abrasive product on your next purchase.

Chapter 5, *Finessing,* recommends specific products that have worked for me when restoring damaged finishes. Even if you follow someone's recommendations and the product or system isn't polishing like it should, it might not be your fault. Like paint manufacturers, wax manufacturers change their formulations from time to time. For example, Turtlewax changed its popular "ColorBack" polish to a much less abrasive formulation.

Restoring Dull Finishes

If your car's paint is dull and you polish it to a good shine, will that shine last? Finishes that have been slightly dull ever since the paint was applied have a good chance of staying glossy once they have been polished or buffed. Lack of gloss is due to surface imperfections and roughness which absorb light or reflect light randomly.

In cases where the paint has always been dull, the surface roughness is due to problems in the paint's application, not the paint's deterioration. Either too much orange peel occurred on the final coat, or the paint sunk unevenly into the undercoats, or the final coat was applied too dry. Another possibility is that the paint was lacquer, and it was buffed too soon or not buffed at all. In any of these situations, a good polishing or buffing (with wet sanding beforehand, if needed) will usually produce a shine that lasts.

However, when a paint that once was shiny has deteriorated to a dull or rough finish, it means that chemicals

and/or sunlight have etched away the top surface and have probably penetrated into the deeper layers. This will be difficult to restore. But with the cost of repainting the car so much higher than cleaning and waxing the existing paint, polishing is certainly worth a try.

Cleaning using a polish or polishing compound, whether by means of a buffer or by hand, will remove the deteriorated upper surface of the paint. Removal of this weathered surface paint decreases the depth of the remaining scratches and pits. After waxing, these surface imperfections are partially filled with the wax, and this provides a degree of protection at the paint's most vulnerable, thinnest points.

The one rule to follow is to use as little abrasive as possible when cleaning a damaged finish. If a polish will do the trick, don't use a rubbing compound. Not only will the more abrasive products remove more paint, they'll leave deeper scratches which then need to be removed. Again, if your paint doesn't require use of a polish or a cleaner/wax, don't use one. If there's dirt build-up that won't come off with normal washing, try rubbing the area with a good bug and tar remover before polishing. If sufficient cleaning of the finish can be done this way, it will take off less paint and the job will be easier to do.

If the car remains outdoors and exposed to the same environmental conditions that caused the paint to deteriorate, it is certain to continue to break down. When the paint dulls down in the same areas within only a few weeks after polishing and waxing, no amount of effort, or type of product, is likely to stop the breakdown.

The finish on this BOSS 429 is superb. Notice how "wet" and "deep" the gloss looks. This should be the type of finish you're trying to achieve. Photo by Michael Lutfy.

However, if a car leads a relatively pampered life, for example, always garaged and seldom driven, then older decaying paint can sometimes be brought back to a glossy finish and maintained in good appearance for years. This is particularly valuable for collector cars, where authenticity and originality is prized, not only for historical purposes but also for enhanced resale value.

In such cases, extraordinary efforts to preserve original paint are often justified. One key factor is to use as little abrasive and buffing as possible because this removes paint. In most cases you'll never know how much color is left until you buff or rub through into the primer. Slightly dull paint is almost always preferable than paint that is buffed through or blotchy.

A second key factor is to keep the car out of the sun and the elements. Original factory paint jobs will last almost indefinitely if the car is kept clean and garaged.

GLAZES AND SEALANTS

Car dealers, detailers, and some auto body shops sell a service called paint glazing or paint sealing. The process usually involves washing the car and using a buffer to apply a product on the paint. The cost of this can run into the hundreds of dollars. At this price, you should examine its cost versus benefit.

If a warranty is given, see what it actually covers and what reimbursement you receive if the paint has problems. If the warranty is limited to a pro-rated reimbursement of the money you spent, it's not much warranty or much protection.

Unless you see proof otherwise, be wary of such high-priced services. As yet, I have seen no paint manufacturer nor any car manufacturer who recommends such treatments. If glazes or sealants were of great value, it seems likely that manufacturers would make them part of their paint warranty programs.

What does an auto paint professional say about sealants? I asked a friend who not only owns a rust-proofing shop that sells paint sealant, he's also a painter and car collector with many years of experience. Because his services carry a warranty, his customers bring back their cars yearly for inspection. His observations are that sealants usually won't last a full year on a car which sits out in the elements. However, the type of sealant he sells is applied with a power buffer and appears to last longer than wax. What this means to a car owner is if the glazing or sealant is reasonably priced and if it's likely you won't wax your car, the convenience can be worth the price. For another perspective on the claims and composition of paint care products, see the sidebar by Bud Abraham on the next page.

COMPOSITION OF PAINT CARE PRODUCTS
by Bud Abraham, President, Detail Plus Systems

Polishes—By a polish, I mean a product that is used as a second step after the compound to remove swirls and polish the paint. It would also be used as a first step on a good paint finish to create a high shine. A "good" polish would contain light abrasives to remove swirls, oils, solvents, and silicones for ease of use. To remove swirls, a polish must be used with a high speed buffer and finishing pad. If you use an orbital to remove swirls, at best you will only fill them; and after three or four car washes, they will show as the filler washes away. On a particularly good finish, especially a clear coat, you could use the polish with an orbital as a first step to clean and polish the surface before wax or sealant application. For tips on using buffers, see page 41.

Glazes—What is a glaze? Someone tell me! There are a good number of detail chemical companies out there that sell glazes, and I would like to hear their definition of a glaze as it differs from a polish, wax, or sealant. This is a challenge to set the record straight. As I understand, a glaze is a product formulated to be easy to apply and remove while providing a high shine. The durability is limited to a few short weeks. In terms of composition, it is made up of some oils, solvents, silicones, and very little, if any, wax. It is a product designed for use on dealer cars to provide a "quick and dirty" shine. Therefore, in my opinion, a glaze has no place in a detail shop where the customer is paying top dollar for protection as well as shine. If I am wrong, please, chemical manufacturers, set me straight.

One Step Products—While these products, as I understand them, could technically fall into the glaze category, they differ in that they do contain cleaners as well as glazes. Their purpose is to provide a quick, one-step cleaning and shining of the painted surface. They can be used with a high speed buffer and finishing pad or applied with an orbital. If a cleaner glaze/one-step product is used, nothing more should be done to the vehicle. If the finish is unsatisfactory after its use, then you have used the wrong product or applied it with the wrong tool and pad. Again, the cleaner glaze products were primarily designed for use on dealer cars where all that is needed is a quick, high shine. (Given the finish is in good enough condition to justify only a one-step product.) They can also be used for detailing cars where you sell a simple wash and wax, express detail, "hand wax," or other such low cost services. Remember, if you use a cleaner glaze, by definition, it is not necessary to wash or seal the finish afterwards.

Waxes—Waxes are available in pastes, creams, or liquids; they can contain natural or synthetic waxes; by name: carnauba, paraffin, or synthetic carnauba. They will also contain oils, solvents, and silicones. Their purpose is to provide protection and enhance the shine left by the polish. There is really no major difference between pastes, creams, or liquids other than the amount of water or solvent in the formulation. The more water, the softer the product; the less water and more solvent, the harder the product. Which is better, I will leave to the manufacturers to answer.

Sealants—Teflon, Amino Functional Silicones, Liquid Glass, Polymer Resins, Siloxane, and a host of other high-tech sounding names are used to describe paint sealant. What is true and what is false is beyond me. How they work is even more confusing. For example, "sealants bond to the paint finish by an ionic bonding. The paint finish is positive, and the sealant negative, causing this bond . . . ." Or, "The molecules of the amino functional silicones are shaped like corkscrews and when applied to a clean paint finish these molecules bore into the open paint pores . . . ." Others claim to have no waxes, resins, silicones, or polymers, but a revolutionary Siloxane which, once cured, turns to a liquid glass protecting the paint finish "like nothing else can . . . ." If any area is more confusing and downright misleading, it is the area of paint sealants. Do paint sealants really contain Teflon, the invention of the DuPont Company? As one official from DuPont told me, about one-tenth of 1% of total volume. Does it do anything to enhance the durability of the sealant product? No!!

Silicone—Silicone is found in many car care products for the interior, and it is also an ingredient in some waxes, polishes, and sealants. Silicone makes the finish feel slippery, and it helps the product go on easier. However, silicone products are banned in most body shops. The chemical property that makes them slippery also prevents paint from sticking to them. If there is a minute amount of silicone on a car when it is being painted or if a dust particle with silicone falls on the surface, the paint will pull away, leaving a crater, or fish eye. If you don't plan on any repainting, perhaps that won't be a problem.

Compounds—Rubbing compounds, as they have traditionally been called, come in soft pastes or liquids and include a variety of different types of hard to soft abrasives that might include silica, diatomaceous earth, or even talc, depending on what the formulator is attempting to achieve with the product. In general, compounds fall into three categories: heavy, medium, or light. In addition to the abrasive, they include solvents and oils, in varying degrees, and a number of secondary elements. Their purpose, used in conjunction with a high speed buffer and cutting pad, is to correct a paint surface irregularity. Obviously, the heavy duty compound is used for severe oxidation, scratches, etching, or orange peel. You should never use a heavy duty compound on a clear coat finish.

The light duty compound differs from the other mentioned compounds in terms of the type of abrasive used in the product. It has abrasive, however light, but it is in the product. However you try to shake it out, a light duty compound can offer "chemical" cleaning of a good surface that is stained; elimination of light surface scratches and water spots; and finally, a product you can use on scratched or spotted clear coat finishes. If you have a product that can do all this, why would you need one especially for clear coats? Think about it! The formulation we use has an extra amount of mineral oil to keep the product "wet." That is, it does not dry quickly when used with a high speed buffer and this helps prevent burning. It also reduces the amount of product needed to buff the surface.

The effect of the sun is seen in the deterioration of the paint on this Jeep's hood. The dark top coat has oxidized and worn off to the extent that the gray primer is now exposed.

If you were to ask car owners what conditions damage paint the most, the answers would frequently be "heat" and "harsh climates." Although neither of these conditions benefit automobile paint, they are not the villains that prematurely ruin your car's finish.

The proof of this is obvious upon closer examination. Take heat, for example. Under-hood temperatures are usually so hot that you can't touch parts without getting burned. The firewall, inner fenders, and engine parts experience this heat daily. Also, they are steeped in some of the nastiest vapors, including gasoline and oil fumes, antifreeze (ethylene glycol) and acid vapors from the battery.

Nevertheless, the paint on the firewall stands up very well. Clean the dirt and oil off a 10-year-old firewall and you'll often see beautiful paint. If you see any flaking of paint, it is because there is often little or no surface preparation on inner fenders and engine parts. In fact, many times they were dipped or sprayed without first being painted with a primer.

PAINT ASSASSINS

Harsh climates that have more than their share of rain, sleet, and snow are also perceived as being harder on paint than they really are. But, in reality, automobile paint jobs are less likely to crack and fade after a few years in damp, rainy Washington State than in sunny Florida. Cold weather is a fooler, too. When you are experiencing the bitter cold of temperatures far below freezing and the wind chill factor makes it feel even more frigid, then everything you touch in your car, from the seats to the rubber weatherstripping, seems brittle. Most people think the same would be true of the paint. However, auto paint is less likely to become cracked because of the icy cold of a Minnesota winter than it is because of the extreme conditions of an Arizona summer.

What then are the chief villains of automotive paint? In every parking lot, you'll see cars with paint that is cracked and crazed, or faded and dull, or bubbling and peeling. The worst enemies of your car's finish can be

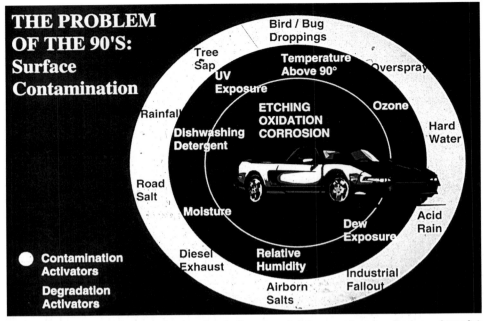

THE PROBLEM OF THE 90'S: Surface Contamination

- Contamination Activators
- Degradation Activators

Bird / Bug Droppings
Tree Sap
UV Exposure
Temperature Above 90°
Overspray
Rainfall
Ozone
Dishwashing Detergent
Hard Water
Road Salt
ETCHING OXIDATION CORROSION
Moisture
Dew Exposure
Acid Rain
Diesel Exhaust
Relative Humidity
Industrial Fallout
Airborn Salts

The chart lists many of the environmental challenges paint faces and makes it clear why paint has a better chance of lasting if it is cleaned regularly. Courtesy Meguiar's

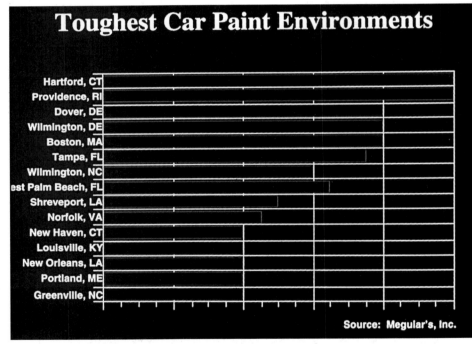

Toughest Car Paint Environments

Hartford, CT
Providence, RI
Dover, DE
Wilmington, DE
Boston, MA
Tampa, FL
Wilmington, NC
West Palm Beach, FL
Shreveport, LA
Norfolk, VA
New Haven, CT
Louisville, KY
New Orleans, LA
Portland, ME
Greenville, NC

Source: Megular's, Inc.

Some regions of the country are tougher on your paint than others. Remember, that these are only averages; local conditions such as a nearby airport, smoke stack, insecticide, railroad etc. can significantly impact your paint. Courtesy Meguiar's.

summarized in four categories: sun, acid rain, rust corrosion, and thick paint. Thick paint is covered in detail in Chapter 12.

Sunlight

Sunlight, or more specifically the sun's ultraviolet (UV) radiation, is the chief cause of paint failure in many parts of the country. Sunlight is composed of many different wave lengths of electromagnetic radiation. The shorter the wavelength (the higher the frequency), the higher the energy the radiation will deliver to the molecules it strikes. Ultraviolet radiation is powerful. Fortunately, most of it is filtered out by the earth's upper atmosphere. However, the UV radiation that does get through is the portion of sunlight that causes the most harm to your paint.

The level of UV radiation can be rather low on some bright, sunny days and can be very high on some hazy days. The intensity of UV radiation is dependent on latitude, time of year, and time of day because all three determine the angle of the sun to the ground. The smaller the angle, the more atmosphere the sunlight has to travel through, and the less UV makes it to the ground. In short, when you can see medium or long shadows, there is not enough UV radiation getting through to worry about.

This basically means that sunlight isn't a problem in the early morning or late afternoon. Sunrise and sunset will have little effect on your skin or on your paint. Northern latitudes have much less of a problem with UV light, particularly in fall, winter, and early spring. However, southern midday sun is a destroyer of paint jobs.

Acid Rain

While in some regions of the country the sun is the major villain to auto paint, in other areas it is acid rain. Acid rain is a catch-all term usually applied to airborne contaminants from sources such as factory smokestacks. They are brought back down to the ground dissolved in water droplets during rainfall or in the form of overnight

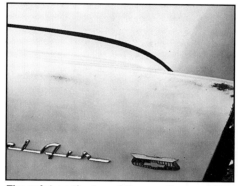

The paint on the top of the rear fender of this 1956 Chevrolet has worn down to the primer. Again, the primary paint assassins were the sun and the elements. Also, the nitrocellulose lacquer applied by the factory wasn't as durable as the acrylic lacquers which came into use just the next year.

Sun was a contributor to the dulling of the paint on the flexible rear bumper of this car, but it wouldn't have happened so fast if not for the flex agent added to the paint. Note that the paint is still in good condition on the adjoining panels.

Here's what tree sap can do when left on the paint. As you can see, it has etched its way into the factory paint on the front of the hood. To help save your paint, clean sap, bugs, bird droppings and other natural hazards off as soon as possible. Don't wait for a complete wash job; use a paper towel or rag and cleaner, if necessary. It's better to risk a few shallow scratches from cleaning than permanently embedded spot damage.

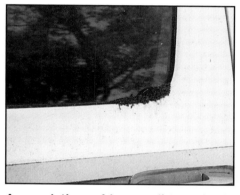

Accumulations of leaves, dirt, or debris rapidly accelerate destruction of your paint. The chemicals in leaves can quickly stain or etch paint, and built-up dirt holds moisture on the paint which will catalyze rust.

It's a little late to repair this paint chip. Rust has already eaten completely through the body panel. If that isn't bad enough, rust streaks also have stained the paint on the side of the car.

condensation (morning dew).

Hopefully, the nineties will continue to see progress towards decreasing the levels of industrial pollution; but keep in mind that there are other sources of chemical damage to paint besides acid rain. This category also includes industrial chemicals which can be wind blown, such as fertilizers and insecticides.

Natural Hazards

Even non-industrial chemical sources can be hazardous to your paint. For example, splattered bugs, bird droppings, and dead autumn leaves have the ingredients for a destructive chemical stew. For example, when wet leaves sit on a car's finish for a few days, chemicals can etch down into the paint. In some parts of the country, this is a common problem for new cars sitting on a lot. If the leaves aren't cleaned off frequently, the damage can be so severe that repainting of hoods, roofs or trunks is necessary.

Bird droppings can also be surprisingly destructive to automotive finishes. One problem is that they usually land on the flat top panels where they puddle up and bake into the surface. A similar problem is caused by harsh water that lands on a car's finish and then bakes in the sun. In some areas, the water used for lawn irrigation is very harsh, and you never know when those automatic sprinkler systems might start spraying. Surface defects from acid rain, bugs, and bird droppings often can be finessed out. To learn how, see Chapter 5.

Rust

As long as there is water or salt on the roads and in the air, and as long as cars are manufactured of steel, there

Rust is probably the number one cause of premature paint failure in the rust-belt states. Here's a good example of how paint will continue to blister and peel when a small break in the paint is not properly touched up.

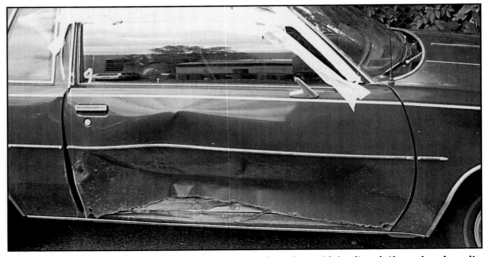

Rust doesn't just destroy the appearance and paint of a vehicle, it quietly undermines its structural integrity. The bottom edge of this door easily tore away during a minor collision. It would have provided more protection if not for the rust. The rust, by the way, was hardly noticeable before the accident.

will always be the threat of rust. Although there have been major advances in undercoatings and corrosion-resistant materials, rusting is still a cause for concern, especially for car owners in the rust-belt states which extend from New England through the Midwest and northwest regions of the United States. The problem is equally severe in the eastern regions of Canada. The extensive use of salt and sand on the roads to make icy winter driving safe has a powerful effect on steel car bodies. The salts are such a catalyst to rust that actual rust-through of body panels can happen in as little as a few years.

Water is also a catalyst for rust, and in areas of the country that are arid, steel car bodies can last virtually forever. Car collectors desire California and Arizona cars for good reason. Depending on what part of the state of California cars come from, they can be almost untouched by corrosion no matter how old they are. For car enthusiasts living in the rust-belt, the extent of the difference in corrosion on car bodies has to be seen to be believed. You can see absolutely rust-free 40-year-old cars sitting outside in junkyards in Arizona and New Mexico. Their interiors and rubber parts will be cooked, but their steel bodies are in great condition.

PAINT PROTECTION SERVICES

Car owners are more concerned about their paint than ever before. Two good reasons for this are the rapidly increasing cost of paint work and the harsher environmental conditions paint is subjected to. At the same time, a number of new services and products have been developed. Let's look at the latest means of paint protection along with standard services and products.

Rust-Proofing

The subject of rust-proofing is a basic and literally underlying concern to automotive paint protection. Although the use of plastics and aluminum is increasing in automotive body panels, virtually all car bodies and frames are still made of steel. And if the steel rusts, the paint goes. In some parts of the country, as explained in detail in Chapter 12, rust is the first problem car owners are likely to see with their paint. Underlying rust is also the most expensive problem to see in your paint, and if the rust damage is severe, it will cut short the life of your car.

New Car Warranties

The change by car makers to lighter, unibody construction has intensified the significance of automotive rusting because the only things holding these cars together are thin sheet metal panels. This is one reason why today's new cars come with extensive rust-through warranties. The majority of car bodies are now dipped in tanks containing special corrosion-fighting primers, and therefore the bodies have paint electrodeposited in areas where a spray gun could never reach. Today, there is also much more extensive use of galvanizing on one or both sides of exterior body panels. Advances such as these are so effective at combating the rust problem that car manufacturers have provided rust-through warranties for as long as nine years.

Although it looks like this van was sprayed with rust-proofing on the outside by mistake, it's actually been protected from the rust-proofing overspray by a water-soluble coating that will later be washed off. Similar spray-mask coatings can also be used by painters to protect against paint overspray.

Exclusions—If you own a car or truck with a rust-through warranty, find out if inspections are necessary to keep the warranty valid. Also, be sure to touch up chips or scratches so they don't begin rusting and possibly void your warranty. If you are buying a new car, check the small print to see what the conditions of the warranty are. Some of the exclusions are so loosely worded that the warranty would be very limited if it was strictly interpreted. The warranty may contain wording that excludes common environmental conditions like "humidity" or "exposure to salt." An exclusion that is a personal favorite of mine is "normal deterioration of sheet metal," whatever that means.

In spite of the exclusions, new car warranties may provide more than sufficient coverage for the length of time you are planning to keep the car. Chrysler has provided rust-through warranties that cover their vehicles for seven years. However, if there are important exclusions or limitations in the warranty, or if you're planning to keep the car well beyond the warranty

period, additional rust-proofing is a service you will want to consider.

Aftermarket Rust-Proofing

Aftermarket rust-proofing varies to a large extent, depending on who is doing the work. Rust-proofing primarily involves the spraying of anti-corrosion coatings on the underneath of the car and inside its interior body panels. When sprayed, the coatings are liquid and they are formulated with a viscosity that enables them to seep into crevices and between overlapping pieces of metal. Because of this, the cars must sit for a few hours after being sprayed so that the excessive undercoating can drip off. Then, the remainder will set up and the overspray can be cleaned off.

Although the coatings thicken up after a few hours, a good rust-proofing coating will never harden to the extent paint does. It must remain somewhat sticky so that it will adhere to the body panel's surface and not peel off or crack for many years. Because it is so important for the coatings to completely adhere to the body, the car

should undergo a thorough, high-pressure spray cleaning of the undercarriage before the rust-proofing is applied. When you buy a new car, rust-proofing should be done as soon as possible because surface rust or build-up of road film will also interfere with the adhesion of the coatings. In fact, the warranty may not be available if the rust-proofing is not done within the first few months.

Interior body panel areas are also sprayed with the rust-proofing coatings. Such areas include the inside of the doors (where the window mechanisms are located) and the entirely closed-off areas such as the door pillars and rocker panels. It is necessary to drill holes into some enclosed areas to enable the spraying of the coatings into those areas. After the spraying is completed, small plastic plugs are pushed into the drilled holes to close them off. These round plastic plugs are a tell-tale sign of aftermarket rust-proofing and can usually be seen in the door jam areas when the door is opened.

The coatings are sprayed under high pressure and a variety of nozzles or tubes are employed to reach into hard-to-get-at areas. The areas which are coated vary on different types of cars, and a good rust-proofing service will have diagrams of all new cars to show the locations where holes must be drilled.

After applying the rust-proofing coatings, any parts removed for better access to the body, such as carpets or door panels, should be reinstalled and all unwanted overspray should be cleaned off. The odor of the coating may be noticeable for a few days, just as an occasional drip of coating may appear. Before and after your car or truck is rust-proofed, inspect the

These plastic plugs were installed to seal off holes that were drilled to enable aftermarket rust-proofing material to be sprayed into enclosed sections of the body. The corrosion resistance of today's galvanized and e-coated steel panels are responsible for the long rust-through warranties that many vehicle manufacturers provide, which have reduced sales of aftermarket rustproofing. Now if you see plugs on late-model cars, it's as likely to be from paintless dent repair.

interior trim panels for their fit and to spot any missing or loose fasteners.

Maintenance—To maintain a rust-proofing warranty, you may have to take the car back for an annual cleaning and inspection. Therefore, choose a location that will be convenient for you. In rust-belt areas, the inspection is best scheduled for the spring because the rust-proofer should perform a high pressure water spray and then blow off the underneath of the car before the inspection. Cleaning should also include opening up of drain holes and removal of leaves and debris from lower fender areas and pockets. A thorough cleaning of the underneath of the car alone will add years to the life of your vehicle and is worth a nominal charge. The vehicle will then be put up on a lift and any critical areas or areas of undercoating that have worn thin will be resprayed or touched up.

Check the warranty to see what actually is covered if rust-through does occur years later. For example, reimbursement for the full cost of the rust repair is certainly preferable to a partial reimbursement of the original rust-proofing charges. Also be aware that some states require that repairs of rusted areas be accomplished by welding in new steel, not by just covering up the hole with plastic body fillers. In any case, you should make sure that any rust repairs eliminate the problem and not just cover it up temporarily.

Dealership Paint Protection & Rust-Proofing—Salespeople at new car dealers are sometimes motivated to sell buyers additional paint protection or rust-proofing services. Some will even employ "scare" tactics to get buyers to pay for this additional protection. The reason is that these services are almost pure profit. The cost of materials and labor can be less than 25% of the price charged to the car buyer.

Therefore, don't be surprised if a salesperson tries to sell you these additional services even if the car has an extensive factory rust-through and paint warranty. Read the factory warranty very carefully to see if there really is any need for the extra rust-proofing or paint protection. If you decline the dealership's optional services, but when you go to pick up the car you are told it was "mistakenly" or already done, do what a friend of mine did. If they try to charge you for it, tell them to take the rust-proofing off or paint protection off. Tell them you didn't order it, you don't want it, and you won't pay for it. If they don't agree, then the deal is off. The dealership, of course, cannot remove the rust-proofing or glaze, and they will absorb the cost rather than lose the sale of the vehicle.

Collector Cars—There is another thing to consider about additional rust-proofing on collector cars in the future. A large percentage of, if not most, collectors don't want aftermarket rust-proofing or undercoating on collectible cars. Aftermarket or dealership rust-proofing could lower the value of the car. For the majority of cars, however, additional rust-proofing will, if anything, increase resale value.

Sound Deadening—The factory rust-through warranties appear so extensive on cars today that some people will wonder why aftermarket rust-proofing services still exist. For one thing, additional rust-proofing provides something in addition to increased rust protection, and that is sound deadening. The extra coatings sprayed on the underneath and interior body panels of the car will absorb more road and tire noise and deaden outside noise.

This can justify the cost of additional rust-proofing for owners of all types of cars, luxury to compact. In some cases, the thinner steel on today's unibody cars can make road noise unpleasantly loud. Rust-proofing can help reduce the level of road noise somewhat. If you feel you don't need any additional rust-proofing but would like the level of road noise reduced, some businesses such as Ziebart will apply just sound deadening at a reduced cost.

Whenever you're paying for a service you can't actually see, it's wise to deal only with someone who has a good reputation—and that advice certainly applies to rust-proofing. However, with rust-proofing, it is also wise to think about whether the person doing the rust-proofing will be in business years from now, because that's the only time a rust-proofing warranty will be of value to you. With many new car dealerships going out of business, that could be an important consideration.

DIY Rust-Proofing

A number of undercoating and rust-proofing products are available to the do-it-yourselfer (DIY). They range from convenient aerosol products to thick liquids that must be sprayed with high pressure air guns. The two general categories of such products are undercoatings and rust converters.

Undercoatings—These are thick liquids that produce a rubbery coating when sprayed onto body panels. They aren't good looking, most are a dull black, and they all produce a surface that has the look of deep orange peel or is even bumpy. Some are actually foamy, and the thick coating they produce helps to absorb sound and protect inner fenders from sand and gravel kicked up by the wheels.

It is very important that the undercoating you choose stays soft and flexible. If it dries out and becomes hard or brittle, it can crack or

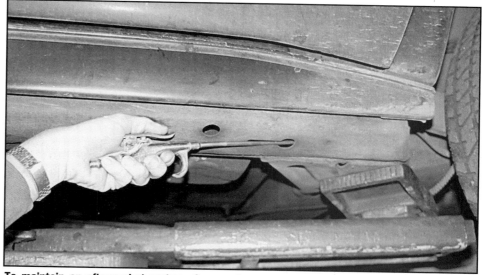

To maintain an aftermarket rust-proof warranty, you may have to bring the car back for an annual cleaning and inspection, which should include opening up drain holes and cleaning them with high pressure water spray or air to remove all leaves and dirt prior to inspection. This is equally valuable if you don't have a rust-proof warranty.

shrink and pull away from the body panel. If this happens, water seeps in under the under-coating and will actually accelerate rusting. Apply the wrong undercoat, and you can make your car rust much faster. The same condition occurs if the surface is not adequately cleaned. If there is any oily film or loose dirt, it must be thoroughly cleaned off before the undercoating is applied. If it is not, the undercoating can't adhere to the surface and the undercoating may actually seal water into the body. Again, this would be worse than no undercoating at all.

Oil—If you can't thoroughly clean an area, don't undercoat it. This particularly applies to the insides of body cavities or frames. The spraying of paint or rust-proofing compounds inside a frame will accelerate any rust damage. However, there is an alternative for these trouble spots— oil. Did you ever notice that any area of the car that was covered with a light film of oil doesn't rust? Oil is remarkably effective at penetrating and adhering to even the dirtiest

surfaces. It will seep in between overlapping pieces of sheet metal on the car's body and will penetrate any open areas in the welds of frames.

A simple but very effective method of protecting hard-to-clean areas of the car's body starts with removing as much accumulated dirt or debris as possible. High pressure air and a blow gun with 1/4 inch tubing as an extension works well in tough-to-reach locations. After whatever degree of cleaning you can muster, use a pump-type oil can to squirt oil into the area. Any engine oil will work. Use as heavy an oil as convenient, but beware that some gear oils have a nasty stench. Don't be stingy in applying the oil, it is far cheaper than any degree of body or frame repair. The excess oil will simply drip off.

Use of oil works well on boxed frame sections, the lower portions of doors, and even rocker panel or wheel well areas. Like professional rust-proofing, it may be worthwhile to drill holes to permit the application of oil in otherwise inaccessible parts of the body.

Slide in bedliners are an effective way to protect the paint on truck beds. If you live in a wet climate, make sure water doesn't stay trapped under the liner and hasten rusting.

However, car manufacturers and paint manufacturers agree that cleaning helps prolong paint life, and waxing helps clean paint and also helps keep it clean. A good cleaning and waxing once or twice a year undoubtedly will help your paint last longer, particularly if the car is not garaged most of the day. If you don't like to do that chore yourself, it is worth the money to pay a reasonable price to have your car thoroughly cleaned and waxed at least once a year.

The only drawback to using oil as a rust preventative on body parts is if repair or repainting has to be done later. In that event, it may take some additional effort to clean the body parts so that primers or fillers can adhere. Caution should also be used to avoid soaking any rubber parts with oil. Some types of rubber deteriorate faster when they are in constant contact with oil.

Rust Converters—Rust converters are liquids that can be sprayed on bare metal even if it has already rusted. The rust converter chemically alters the steel and rust so that further rusting is stopped, or at least slowed down. Rust converters do not have the sound-deadening properties of undercoatings. However, many rust converters can be painted over, which is a big advantage over undercoating.

Before spraying rust converters, it is important to mask or cover up any areas that may be damaged by the overspray. The same applies to undercoatings but many of them are petroleum-based and therefore can be easily wiped off paint, glass, or rubber if the overspray is removed shortly after the undercoating is sprayed. Oil doesn't pose much of a problem if it

gets on nearby parts; but you certainly want to avoid getting oil, undercoating, or rust converters on any fabrics such as convertible tops, vinyl, seats, or rugs.

Sealers and Glaze Coats

Paint protection services such as waxing, sealing, and glazing are offered by all detail shops, most car washes, and many dealerships and body shops. However, there is no objective way to tell how effective these services are or how much value they give for the money. It would be great if there were some way to separate the "hype" from the "help" on these services, similar to the ratings used on some car care products.

Unfortunately, the car owner will hear a lot of claims and see little objective data. Some question whether paint protection services such as waxing and sealants do any good.

Car manufacturers and paint manufacturers both risk thousands of dollars of loss on each paint job they warranty, but neither requires regular waxing to maintain the warranty, as regular maintenance is required for the drive train warranty.

PAINT PROTECTION PRODUCTS

The increased concern and awareness of today's car-care conscious consumer has spawned an industry of products designed to protect a car's finish from damage of any kind. Many of the following products can be purchased at automotive retail outlets, through mail order, and in some cases they are offered as options by new car dealerships. You'll have to weigh the relative pros and cons of each before deciding if they are right for you and your car.

Bed Liners

Paint protection on pick-up truck beds has always been a problem. The chipping and scratching of paint on the inside surfaces of a pick-up truck bed can be solved by using a plastic bed liner. The liners are formed to fit a specific model and size of bed and can be removed for cleaning underneath. Liners keep harsh chemicals away from the sheet metal of the bed. That can be a serious problem if fertilizers, salts, mortar mix, or other chemicals are occasionally carried in the truck.

Another option for protecting truck beds is the new spray-on bed liner coatings which are remarkably durable and chip resistant. This is what the spray-on bedliner looks like when it's dry. Bob Belling chose a black coating for his red 1953 Studebaker truck. Courtesy Yankee Auto/Truck, East Hartford, CT.

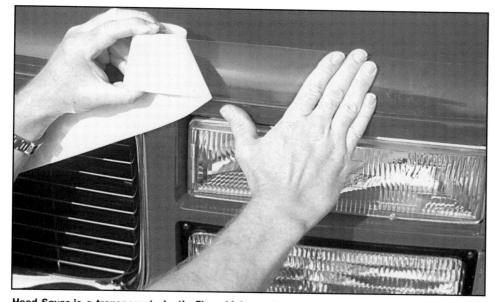

Hood Saver is a transparent plastic film which can be applied to protect paint in the trouble prone areas such as the front of hoods. It is available in 2.5 inch wide rolls which make installation easy. Just clean the surface, apply the tape and trim off the excess. Courtesy ALLSaver Tape Products

A serious disadvantage is that water can become trapped under the bed liner and that can make the bed rust out faster than if there were no liner at all. In some parts of the country, it rains so seldom that this is not a problem. However, if you live in a wet region of the country, you may want to periodically remove the liner, especially after heavy rains, to dry the bed underneath.

Spray-On—One exciting new solution is spray-on bed lining coatings. Some of these coatings are incredibly durable. Their resistance to chipping and scraping is far superior to factory-applied paint. Proof of their durability is that many counties and municipalities are having these coatings applied not only to their pick-up trucks but also to heavier equipment, including dump trucks.

There are only a few choices in the color of the coating, depending on the manufacturer. Gray and black are two colors commonly available. One of the advantages of the spray-on coating, as opposed to a bed liner, is that the coating is bonded to the paint so that it cannot trap moisture. Non-skid coatings can also be applied to help prevent falls on any areas where footing could become slippery.

Bras

Automotive paint on the front of cars suffers terribly in certain regions of the country. There are so many chips on the front bumper and forward edges of the hood that these cars look like they were blasted with shotgun pellets. This can occur in dry areas of the west where sand and gravel frequently blow on the road. A similar problem exists in hot, humid areas where the number of insects is so great that you can't count them as they splatter on the car. As mentioned before, bug "splat" can cause chemical damage to your paint.

A front end cover, often called a bra, is an effective means of preventing paint damage caused by gravel and bugs. This protection comes at a cost over and above the initial purchase price of the vehicle. The material of the bra must contact the paint or the air turbulence will cause it to abrade the paint to some extent. Choose a bra that is snug fitting and well tailored to your car. Examine the paint occasionally to make sure paint abrasion isn't a problem. The bra material shouldn't stretch and loosen up so that it flaps around when the car is moving, or dirt and sand can become trapped between the bra and

The star, or spider-web, pattern of cracks is typical of paint damage caused by a stone striking a panel from underneath, thrown up from below by the tire. That's one of the reasons why most cars have inner fenders. On cars that don't have inner fenders, such as many Corvettes, a thick layer of undercoating can be applied to the underside of the fender to help prevent this type of paint damage on the top side.

The design and integration of stone shields and bug deflectors now make them an attractive as well as functional, addition to your vehicle. Before you buy, check the installation method. It's best to avoid drilling holes on outer body panels, and make sure the parts won't flex and rub on painted surfaces when buffeted by high wind at cruising speeds. Courtesy MacNeil Automotive Products, LTD.

the paint.

Minor abrasion of the bra rubbing the paint underneath will only cause the paint's gloss to diminish. If that occurs, use a paint cleaner or polishing compound to bring back the shine. Refer to Chapter 5, Finessing, for more information on products and procedures for finish restoration.

Be careful about using a bra on a freshly painted car. Not only is the paint softer and more easily damaged by wear, water trapped under the bra could cause problems if it bakes in the sun.

Screens and Shields

Screens are another means of limiting paint damage caused by bugs and gravel. Screens are generally less expensive than fitted bras, and they do less to change the appearance of the car. In addition, some people do not like the masked look of bras. Screens also help keep bugs out of the radiator. In some regions of the country, the number of flying insects is so great that they can eventually clog up the cooling fins of the radiator and air conditioning condenser.

The same cautions apply to screens as to bras. Occasionally check the areas where the material contacts the paint to be sure abrasion isn't becoming a serious problem.

Hood shields and deflectors offer another option for paint protection. The design of some cars is such that the only painted body parts exposed to gravel and bug damage on the frontal surface of the car is the area above the grille and headlights. This can be the front portion of the hood or the front fascia. A number of aftermarket manufacturers have custom-tailored plastic shields or deflectors to protect these parts. Some of the deflectors extend up above the hood to change the airflow and thereby also help prevent bugs from splattering on the windshield.

Owners of some popular car and truck models have a wide assortment of designs and colors to choose from.

In choosing a shield, consider the mounting hardware. If possible, it is best to avoid drilling holes in painted steel body parts because that can create a foothold for rust. For the same reason avoid hardware that clamps onto painted steel parts because it might crack or chip the paint.

Gravel Shields—The paint can be protected on certain parts of the car by installing custom-tailored guards or shields over the body paint. For a number of years, adhesive overlays have been attached directly to the paint on vulnerable portions of some European cars such as Porsches. Another type of shield is made of formed clear plastic and can be removed. Aftermarket manufacturers have produced these for the trouble-prone areas of certain cars such as the "dog leg" area behind the door on 1968 to 1982 Corvettes. Again, these provide protection while the car is driven but require no permanent

Mud flaps not only help prevent paint chips, they keep vehicles looking cleaner longer by shielding the lower panels from road spray and the effect of puddles. These flaps came from an auto parts store and only took an hour to install. I used a paper template to help make holes in the flap at the same location as the factory wheel well screws so that no holes had to be drilled in the metal panels—which can void rust-through warranties.

attachment.

Mud Flaps

Mud flaps aren't noted for their beauty, and many people think they look tacky. However, they can prevent paint chipping and abrasion on lower body panels. Not only can they save the paint, they can help prevent build-up of mud and dirt underneath the car; and they help prevent stones from being thrown by your rear wheels into the windshield of the driver following you. That's why they are required by law on larger trucks and trailers.

The use of wider tires and the curving body lines of some cars have resulted in areas of the body where the paint is blasted off by gravel and road spray. The ground-effects styling of some newer cars has helped reduce this problem, but on many cars the paint doesn't have much of a chance on the lower body panels.

Although some people make their

The wider performance tires used on many new cars stick out and hurl stones or sand at body panels. Clear plastic removable mud flaps are one solution. Another solution is a contoured clear plastic shield to overlay the trouble-prone areas such as the "dog-leg" on this early Corvette.

car's mud flaps a fashion accessory by embellishing them with lights, reflectors, and insignias, mud flaps can be less ostentatious. Flat-black rubber flaps can be cut and tailored so that they blend in fairly unobtrusively with the tires and underbody of the car. Some flaps are easily removed so that they can be used during everyday driving and then taken off for car shows or photo opportunities. Mud flaps or stone guards can also be made

of clear plastic. If they are kept clean, they can be almost invisible.

Running Boards

Big tires and high ground clearance expose the lower portion of truck bodies to paint damage. The problem is more severe on 4-wheel-drive and off-road vehicles. Running boards can protect the paint from low-lying brush or rocks and gravel thrown up by the tires. More varieties of running boards are available now than ever before. Brushed aluminum and chrome are common, and running boards can be inset with rubber strips or even running lights.

Nerf Bars

Heavy brush and small trees can inflict serious damage to the lower portions of doors and cabs on vehicles which are used off-road. Nerf Bars are a popular means of protection for these areas. Made of large diameter steel tubing, these bars extend out below the door and cab. Although they don't provide as much protection from rocks and gravel as running

Body Saver transparent tape is an excellent means for protecting the finish on today's painted bumpers from stone chips. It can help prevent scrapes and scuffing of the paint if your car encounters "touch" parking. The tape can be removed with aid of a hair dryer to heat and soften the adhesive. Courtesy ALLSaver Tape Products.

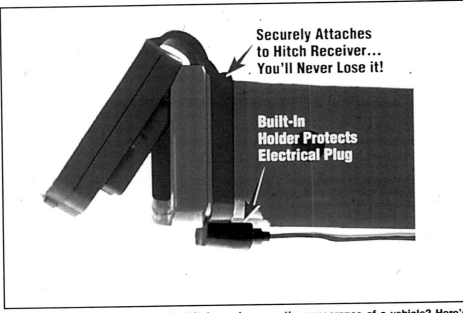

Securely Attaches to Hitch Receiver... You'll Never Lose it!

Built-In Holder Protects Electrical Plug

How often does a rusty dirty trailer hitch receiver mar the appearance of a vehicle? Here's a new fix that takes only a few seconds to install. HitchHider is the first receiver cover which permanently attaches to a hitch receiver. It completely covers the unsightly receiver but stays attached when the hitch is being used—no more storing a dirty greasy receiver cover inside your vehicle. It also holds the standard 4 wire connectors, keeping them clean and corrosion free, plus preventing the wires from dragging on the road or getting torn off.

boards, if properly mounted they can be as strong as a roll bar and prevent dents from trees, banks, and boulders.

Close encounters of the off-road kind also can be damaging to the front of a truck or sport utility vehicle. Grille guards can help not only the grille but the paint on the front of the hood. Typically, they are made of strong tubing and bolt to the bumper.

Door Edge Guards

It is surprising how fragile paint is on the edge of a door. The slightest tap against another car, a wall, or an object in the garage will inevitably chop a substantial chunk of paint from the door edge. Edge guards not only provide excellent protection for your door, they also protect the paint on the car next to you by absorbing the blow.

New car dealerships often have custom-molded door edge guards made to fit the contours of specific models. Auto parts stores and mass merchandisers carry flexible door edge moldings which can be bent, as necessary, to fit the shape of your doors. In either case, make sure the molding fits snugly, is securely attached, and that there is enough clearance between the molding and the adjacent edge of the car body when the door is closed. The clearance should be at least the width of a credit card, preferably two. Remember that as the car goes over bumps, the body flexes and the door gaps can close. If a door edge molding comes loose or if there is insufficient clearance, the molding can wear or chip the paint on the body and create the problem it was meant to prevent!

Body Side Moldings

The sides of a car's body are susceptible to damage from handling, specifically, the handling of doors on cars parked next to you. This type of paint damage is particularly upsetting because it is completely needless. And unfortunately, it's nearly unavoidable if you have to park next to other people. On one hand, a ding in one's door is not of cosmic importance, but it really steams a person who appreciates their car's finish and takes care of it. Body side moldings can do a lot to help prevent, or at least minimize, such damage.

In the fifties and sixties, the careless opening of a door usually resulted in

The wide, thick rubber trim pieces (called cladding or body side moldings) which run down the side of many cars today are the best protection from door paint chips caused by careless people who park next to you. Unfortunately, even these sometimes are not sufficient protection for your car from the abuse of others, as this door demonstrates.

Two more paint protectors are seen in this photo. The lip of the tailgate is protected by a metal shield because that is an area prone to damage. The tie-downs also help the paint—they prevent heavy cargo from sliding around.

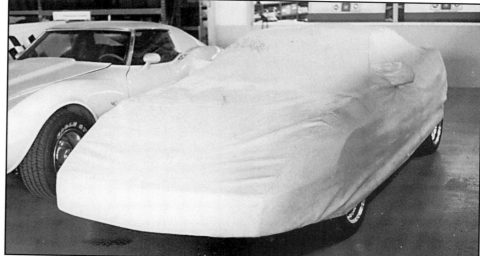

It is possible to get tailored car covers at a reasonable price for more popular cars. Note the pouches for the mirrors.

only paint damage. Today, however, the use of thinner sheet metal for the outer body panels makes shallow dents and creases a common outcome of these parking lot clashes. The best protection is to use the widest, thickest body side molding you can stand the sight of and attach it to the farthest protrusion of the door. Even that isn't sufficient in some cases. Take a walk through any parking lot and you will see cars with door dents underneath protective side moldings.

If you apply door moldings yourself, use tape or soft crayon to mark a straight line down the sides of the body to aid in positioning. After attaching the molding, slowly open the door to see if there is a clearance problem between the front of the door and the fender. The molding may have to be cut at an angle or trimmed. Although moldings that attach by adhesive occasionally come loose, they still have the advantage of not having to have holes drilled in the car body. Again, such holes provide a

foothold for rust. Another problem is that the space between the molding and the body can trap dirt and water. Tightening the molding's fasteners also can crack the paint and create further opportunities for rust or blistering.

Roof Racks

Racks are usually added for the sole purpose of transporting objects on top of the car, and they can actually create paint problems. Again, holes drilled into the body, or fasteners can accelerate rust at those locations. However if you frequently carry things strapped to the outside of your car, racks are an effective way to minimize paint damage finish which is usually instantaneous and irreversible. When carrying objects, make sure nothing solid contacts the finish; use soft clean blankets (the thicker furniture moving pads are even better) or even cardboard if necessary to keep any part of the object you're transporting from contacting the paint directly. Some temporary racks come with rubber-covered mounting clamps which don't

do as much damage to the paint as ones that are bolted on. This type also has the benefit of being easily removed in the future.

Tailgate Guards

Pick-up trucks are especially vulnerable to paint damage on the upper lip of the tailgate and the top surface of the sides of the bed. Metal or plastic protectors which are formed to the contours of the tail gate can be an attractive and very functional addition. Protective strips or rails do a similar job of protecting the paint along the top side of the bed, and rails can also be used to help tie down the cargo. Just keeping the cargo from falling over or sliding around does a lot to save the paint inside a pick-up truck bed. If side rails aren't used, tie downs and eyelet's can help prevent shifting of cargo and thereby prevent paint damage as well.

Car Covers

There are almost as many kinds of car covers as there are kinds of cars. A little research and planning can make the difference in whether the cover

Custom made-to-fit car covers can be obtained for a price for just about any shape car. This thick, felt-lined cover from **Beverly Hills Motoring Accessories** was made to fit the body contours of a 1959 Cadillac, and it cost under $200.

helps or hurts you.

The first question to ask yourself is the intended use for the cover. Car covers are desirable even for collector cars that are garaged most of the time. A cover will keep the dust off the paint and chrome so that the car looks its best any time you wish to show it. Also, the car has to be cleaned less often, which is not only a major savings in time and effort, it is often to the car's benefit. Show chrome and flawless black or dark colored paint jobs can get scratched incredibly easy. In many cases, the less they have to be cleaned the better.

A third benefit of covering stored cars is the protection against bumps and scrapes. Whether the potential damage is from children and other traffic in your garage or from work going on in a commercial building, having a layer of soft material on the side of your car can prevent disfiguring scrapes, scratches, or gouges. Therefore, if inside storage is the main use of the cover, having a thick material (such as a heavy fabric

with a soft liner) may be your best choice. However, such a heavy cover may be too bulky for use on a car which is driven often. It is more difficult to put a thick cover on, and it takes up a lot of space in the trunk!

If the cover will be frequently used outside, it is important that it fits snugly. Elastics or draw strings are needed so that the cover can be tied

down to prevent it from flapping excessively in the wind. Too much movement can allow the paint to be abraded or allow the cover to tear.

Outdoor use also requires a cover material that will breathe. It is inevitable that the cover will get rained on at some time and, if the moisture can't escape, the cover can do more harm than good.

A car cover can also be an enhancement to an expensive car. In that case, having the cover custom-made and fitted to the body style is an important consideration. Some car marques are popular enough so that a fitted cover is available off-the-shelf. Corvettes, Porsches, Mercedes, Camaros, and Mustangs are prime examples. Other marques are sufficiently in demand that manufacturers who specialize in making car covers already have a pattern for them. If you order a cover, they will cut it out and sew it up for you at a reasonable price.

Before ordering the cover, decide if any special features are needed. Examples of special features are

This cover looks securely fastened, and it is. The problem is that wind caused tugging on the cords which were used to tie down the cover. Two weeks later, the cords had already abraded the paint. It's ironic that the method used to protect the paint can cause damage instead.

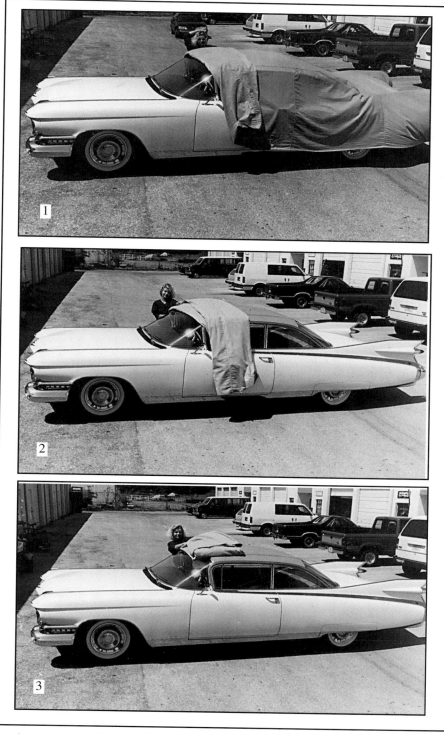

CAR COVER PROCEDURE

Car covers should be removed and installed correctly. This not only makes putting it on easier, but it also helps prevent scratching the surface of the car. Begin by folding the front half over itself until you reach the middle of the roof (1). Repeat the procedure from the rear (2) and when the rear reaches the roof, fold the rear half over the front half. Finally, fold the passenger side up onto the roof, then fold the driver's side over it (3). The cover is now folded small enough to store easily, and by using the same system every time, you'll know which end is which when you place it back on the car and unfold it.

pockets sewn in for the mirrors, a hole or boot for the antenna, a zippered flap on the side for easy entrance to the driver's side door (particularly useful when the car is transported in certain types of enclosed trailers), or grommets for tie-downs or a security lock.

Very inexpensive covers are likely to be quite thin. Some covers are so thin and have such a large weave that dirt and dust will filter right through them. Cheap covers probably won't fit snugly either; they usually come in only a few sizes. And in the case of plastic covers, they probably won't last very long in the sun. In fact, some plastic covers will become brittle and disintegrate after only a few months in the sun. They also tear easier.

However, inexpensive covers are

You're looking at the best paint protection from sun, acid rain, and birds. No, it's not the fresh coat of wax Rick Tousley just put on his 1965 GT-350R. It's the garage. A garage obviously can't protect your vehicle's finish from paint assassins while it's on the road, but it's the most fool-proof protection for your car the remaining 95% of its life. Photo courtesy Rick Tousley.

sometimes the best choice, again, depending on the intended use. For example, if your car has to spend a few weeks in a body shop or garage, a cheap cover might provide the most economical protection for overspray, dirt, and grease.

Types of Fabrics—Cotton flannel fabrics breathe, allowing air to circulate through them. They are soft and easy on the car's paint and wax. They have no fluid resistance so they should only be used in the dry environment of a garage.

Cotton/polyester fabrics have poor fluid resistance and they trap heat and moisture. Their stiffness can harm your paint and remove wax, and they can also fade. When they are treated with a chemical repellent, they lose their ability to breathe. Nylon fabrics have the same deficiencies as cotton/polyester.

Plastic films should be avoided because they don't breathe, they trap heat and moisture, their stiffness can damage your paint, they shrink in the cold and stretch in the heat, and they provide only minimal hail and nick protection. Vinyl films should also be

avoided when used outside for the same reasons.

Composite covers made from several layers of material combine the best qualities of each type. For example, covers made from Kimberly/Clark's Evolution 3 fabric is made in four layers which allow the cover to breathe, repel fluids, and provide protection against hail and nicks. Another benefit is that some covers will not rot or mildew if folded and stored while wet.

There is a new DuPont material, called Tyvek that is offered by Budge, that provides superb temperature protection. Independent tests have shown that on the hottest days, a vehicle covered with a Tyvek cover won't heat up more than 10 degrees above the outside air temperature. By comparison, with other car covers, it can reach 160 degrees inside, and with no cover, as much as 190 degrees.

If you only plan to use a cover in the garage, then a cotton cover may be sufficient. If the car is kept outside or if it will be trailered, then a multi-layer fabric may provide the best means to keep the car's finish clean, dry, and scratch-free.

A variety of paint and body enhancements transform the pedestrian Monte Carlo into a sleek pace car for the 1998 Brickyard 400.

PAINT & BODY ENHANCEMENTS

There are many methods available today to enhance the appearance of a car's paint, as well as change the appearance of the entire car. The subjects in this chapter range from ways to transform a daily driver to a street racer (at least make it look like one) to subtle changes designed to personalize your car and highlight that glorious paint job.

PAINT ENHANCEMENTS

The difference between the appearance of today's glamour paint jobs that come from the factory and the best high quality repainting is often little more than the degree of orange peel on the surface of the paint. A high quality paint job done by a body shop or restorer typically includes wet-sanding of at least the final layer of paint. The sanding is used to remove all orange peel and produce a finish that is free from any surface irregularities. After sanding the top coat of paint, the car is, of course, buffed to bring back the gloss.

Buffing will definitely enhance a car's paint, and it is covered in detail in Chapter 5, Finessing. In short, the finish is block-sanded with a very fine paper, such as 1200 grit, until the orange peel is removed. Then the car is buffed or polished with a very fine compound, followed with an even finer polish to remove any scratches and swirl marks. The last step is the one that removes the least paint, and that step alone can do wonders in bringing life back to a somewhat weathered finish. The methods described in this chapter will focus on specific products that are added to your car's paint or body to enhance its appearance.

Pin Striping

Pin striping has been used to enhance automotive paint since the days of the first motor-powered carriages. In fact, pin stripes appeared on carriages before they were motor-powered, when they truly ran on "horse" power alone. Pin striping is an easy and relatively inexpensive way to personalize any car, but it also can do a lot more. Pin striping is used frequently to hide flaws in paint jobs and thereby cover up problems

Detailed pin striping such as this design is an art form, especially when done freehand. But there are other methods for those less artistically inclined.

without the cost and trouble of repainting. It is also used to cover up the border line where two different colors adjoin.

Stripes have an aesthetic value, too. They can add life to a boring paint job and provide a pleasing visual break on large single-colored body panels. On some body styles, stripes are an effective way to dramatize the body lines of that particular make. If you are considering adding pin stripes to your car, look around at car shows to see what others have done with similar cars. Sometimes stripes bring out a car's character and uniqueness while a different placement of stripes may only clutter up the car's appearance.

Hand Painted Striping—Pin stripes painted with a brush are never perfect, and that is, oddly enough, part of their appeal to many enthusiasts. Stripes painted with a brush are not always perfectly straight and their width may vary, too; but this can be viewed as a greater degree of artistry and craftsmanship than the machine-cut

stripes made of tape. For some people, it's like the preference for paintings instead of photographs on their walls.

Aesthetic considerations aside, painted stripes have another advantage over tape stripes: they have less of an edge to trap wax and therefore are usually smoother and

cleaner looking. Plus, being paint, they can be as glossy as you want them to be. One of the biggest advantages of hand-painted stripes is the flexibility in designs and colors. The painter can mix whatever shade you want, create the tightest corners, make any design, and vary the width of the stripe.

The cost, however, is more than a roll of tape. Depending on the extent of pin striping desired and the reputation (or current workload) of the striper, the price can range from $50 to well over $200.

Machine-Painted Striping—"Fast, Accurate, Easy" is how Beugler describes their pin-striping tool, and that sums up the main advantages of using a tool as opposed to a brush. The tool permits all the advantages of painted stripes, including mixing whatever color you want. It also provides a more uniform stripe width than brushes, but to vary the width you have to change the wheels that apply the paint. With the tool, you can

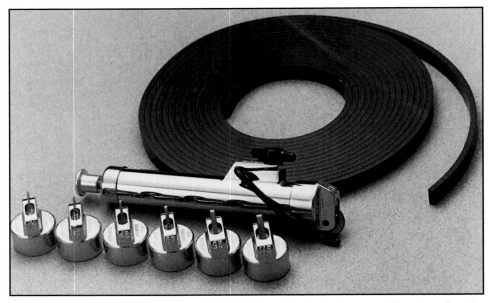

For those people who have neither a steady hand nor the desire to use masking tape, Beugler makes a pin striping tool that rolls the paint onto the car's finish. Interchangeable heads have different width wheels to produce different width stripes. Courtesy S.B.Beugler Co.

The optional sixteen-foot magnetic guide strip helps produce a straight line on steel body panels. After changing to a narrow roller, a thin stripe can be added next to the first one. Courtesy S.B.Beugler Co.

PAINTING STRIPES WITH BRUSH & STENCIL TAPE
Courtesy Finesse Pinstriping

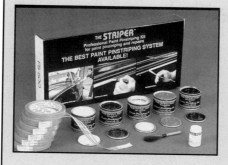

1. The STRIPER pin striping kit includes paint, brush, brush oil, and rolls of precut stencil tape. This allows you to choose different combinations of width and spacing for dual stripes.

2. Thoroughly clean the surface to be striped, preferably using a cleaner labeled "paintable." Choose where the stripes are to be, and then position the tape on the body. Stand back and examine the positioning before pressing the tape firmly onto the body.

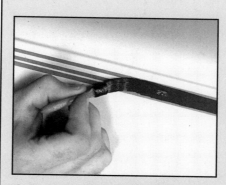

3. Peel away the clear layer of tape on which the stencil tape was held. Apply the pin striping color of your choice with the brush. Take your time and check for complete coverage by the paint.

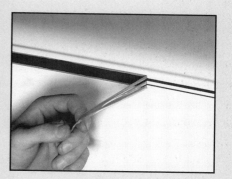

4. Carefully peel the stencil tape off the car body. The pin striping paint should be dry enough to drive the car within a few hours, but it shouldn't be washed for a day or two.

not produce patterns as intricate as you can with a brush.

Masking Kits—Another way to obtain the advantages of painted stripes while avoiding the cost of tools or the fee of experienced pin stripers is to mask the areas before applying the paint. After cleaning the surface, the tape is applied to the body. One advantage is that you can move it around until the placement looks good. Next, the paint is brushed on, and finally the tape is removed. The edges are sharp and straight, and these stencil-like tapes can be used to make double lines with different widths.

Clear Coating—There is always the possibility that pin stripes will be worn down or removed by washing, waxing, or polishing. Weathering is also a concern because of the type of paint sometimes selected for pin striping. And even if the stripes hold up, they always produce a noticeable ridge on top of the paint. All of these problems can be cured by coating the stripes with clear. In the course of repainting or custom painting, the stripes can be applied over the color coat before the clear coat is applied. After the car is sanded and buffed, you won't feel the edges of the stripes, and they will benefit from the protection provided by the clear coat.

This, of course, is a little more inconvenient than waiting until the car is completely painted, and therefore it can cost more if you're paying someone to do the work for you. Plus, it is not possible to change the striping. When the pin stripes are applied on the surface of the paint,

If you're uncomfortable about applying painted pin stripes, you may consider vinyl tape. Tape packages are relatively easy to apply and offer a wide variety of designs. Courtesy Ziebart Tidy Car.

surface should be thoroughly cleaned so that the stripes will adhere adequately . Use a paint cleaner or polish that contains no silicone, wax, or sealant. In fact, you should use a wax and silicone remover. If the product's label makes any reference to its providing paint protection, select another product. If the label says that it is "paintable" or that you can paint over the surface after using it, that's the type of product you want.

Decals

The use of decals has increased greatly in recent years. However, they are by no means new—decals were popular with owners of muscle cars of the sixties and seventies. The large Firebird decal on Pontiac's Trans-Am in the seventies is a popular example.

You can radically change the look of a car or truck in an hour's time by applying decals to the paint. In addition, they are relatively inexpensive and usually can be removed later with no permanent damage or alteration to the paint.

Today there is an incredible variety

you can always buff them off later if you get tired of them, or if a buyer doesn't want them on the car.

Vinyl Tape—Decorative tapes are a fast, easy, and inexpensive method of striping a car or truck. There is a wide variety of tape available for pin striping. Different widths, colors, and combinations are found at any auto body supply store and most traditional automotive parts stores. They are so popular that large, non-automotive retail chains often have them in their automotive departments. Some tape packages have an assortment of different designs you can use for the beginning or end of the stripes, and precut initials for the doors are also available.

The ease of application is a particular advantage of tape stripes. If you don't like the alignment when you are putting on a tape stripe, you can lift and reposition it. If you decide it's not the right place for the striping, you can simply pull it off and try another location.

Removing Old Tape Stripes—If tape stripes have been on the car for

quite a while, a new tape removal wheel and tool helps make the job much easier. After the stripe is removed, the area should be thoroughly wiped with an adhesive remover. Painted stripes can be wet sanded and buffed out, but care should be taken to remove as little of the car's paint as possible.

Surface Prep—Before application of stripes, whether painted or tape, the

This street machine uses subtle enhancements to accentuate the lines of the Camaro, and draw attention to the blower poking through the hood. Photo by Michael Lutfy.

The factory ground effects on these Pontiac Trans-Ams have more than cosmetic value; they can help reduce paint chips on the lower body panels caused by rock or gravel kicked up by tires. Top photo by Nina Pfanstiehl.

of decals available, from factory packages at car dealerships to any number of custom patterns from aftermarket vendors. The latter can be found in specialty automotive parts catalogs, and many are advertised in car magazines. Write to the decal manufacturers or car parts catalogs to see the full line they offer.

Factory Decals—The decals that come on cars from the factory are primarily available only through the parts departments at new car dealerships, and they often can be pricey. However, some of the most popular ones, such as the aforementioned Firebird Trans-Am hood decal, can be obtained at a lower, aftermarket price through other sources.

One concern with factory decals is that they aren't kept in stock forever. If your car suffers some damage to a body panel that has a decal, a replacement decal might not be found. Then the options would be to strip off all the remaining decals or have someone airbrush a reproduction on the car. The latter won't be cheap, and a close match is not likely. A matching problem can also exist even if a new decal is found. The remaining original decals may have faded considerably. TIP: If either of these potential problems worries you, one solution is to buy a complete set of replacement decals to have on hand in case any of them are discontinued.

BODY ENHANCEMENTS

Body enhancements such as rear spoilers, air dams, rocker panels, and louvers first began appearing in the sixties, as manufacturers tried to make their muscle cars more appealing than their competitors' by installing "aerodynamic" body kits developed by factory racing teams. Perhaps the most telling example of how far they were willing to go can be seen in the Dodge Daytonas and Plymouth Superbirds of 1969 and 1970, with their huge rear wing and flared rear quarter panels, which were originally developed to create downforce for the high speeds generated at Daytona and Talledega Raceways. These body items did the job on the raceway, but on the street they were merely cosmetic appendages. Similar (though less radical) body kits and spoilers developed for NASCAR and Trans-Am racing eventually trickled down to the street car.

But today's body kits are much more understated, with more thought given to how they flow with the stock body design. Such enhancements, although marginally functional at the speed limit, nevertheless provide a racy, sporty look giving the illusion of speed and performance. Car manufacturers now offer optional sporty versions of models that generally consist of at least a rear spoiler. Of course, many kits are available from the aftermarket industry to fit most any car, and these kits generally must be painted before they are installed on your car. If you have to paint any kits, go back to Chapter 6, *Paint Repairs*.

Cosmetic changes can also be made by replacing the factory panels with custom aftermarket pieces. If you are lucky, the replacement panels can be painted to closely match the original color on the adjoining body panels and save them from having to be painted.

Spoilers

Rear air spoilers have been one of the most popular add-ons for years. Although it's not likely they'll make any difference in the car's handling at normal road speeds, the performance look appeals to many car owners. A wide variety of spoilers exists, ranging from the rather delicate looking ones often found on BMWs to the mutant-looking rear appendage nick-named the "whale tail" often found on Porsche 911s.

Installation—If the spoiler needs painting, follow the steps on spot repainting in Chapter 6, *Paint Repairs*. But before you buy the spoiler, find out what is necessary for its attachment. Many models require the drilling of holes in the existing body panels. Also, hold the spoiler up to the car body and test its fit before painting it, even before buying it, if that is possible.

If holes are drilled in body parts, there are a number of cautions to observe. If the body panel is steel or aluminum, you should paint or undercoat the edges of the holes to prevent corrosion. If you don't, after several months or a year, you may find that the paint is blistering and peeling off near the attachment points. Also be careful when attaching the spoiler, because over tightening the fasteners may crack the paint.

You may not want to prick-punch the body panels before drilling because that alone may crack the paint. However, be sure to use some means of preventing damage to the surrounding paint. No matter how carefully or tightly you hold the drill, it can "run away" and tear up the paint before the hole is started. Holding a thick rubber washer on the paint and inserting the drill bit in its center can help keep the drill from getting away.

Ground Effects

Ground effects were first used on high-speed race cars when it was learned that reducing the amount of air that goes under the car reduces its drag. Ground effects were first used on street-driven cars when their owners customized them to reproduce that racy look. Now, like factory-installed rear spoilers, ground effects packages are a common sight on upmarket models.

Unlike rear spoilers, ground effects may actually do some good at highway speeds. The reduction in drag can somewhat improve the car's fuel economy. Before you get out your checkbook, however, remember that any gas savings won't be as great as the cost of purchase and installation of an aftermarket package. Though partially functional, ground effects on street cars are primarily installed for appearance. Also be forewarned that air dams are easily damaged by curbs, speed bumps, parking lot tire stops, and driveways or entrances angled sharply to the road surface. Also, because of their close proximity to the ground, ground effects kits are more prone to chipping.

The same caution applies to ground effects as to spoilers: find out how they attach. If you must drill holes and use screws or bolts, the same cautions apply here that were mentioned for attaching rear spoilers. If they are applied with an adhesive, remember that the installation will be basically permanent and the panels cannot be removed without damaging the paint surface. Therefore, it is even more critical that you find out how well they actually fit your car. The best way is to ask someone who recently installed the same ground effects made by the same manufacturer. Don't rely solely on the advice of the people selling the parts—their idea of a good fit may be much different than yours. At the very least, hold the parts up to your car, or better yet, attach them. Do this as soon as you get them

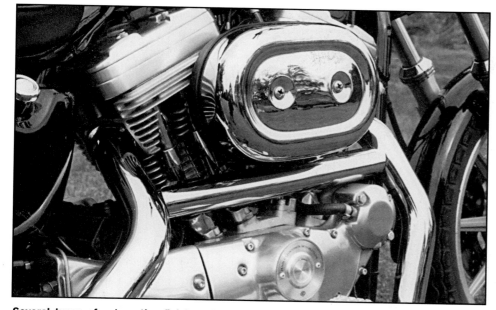

Several types of automotive finishes that come on aftermarket parts can be seen on this Harley Davidson: paint, chrome-plating, cadmium plating, polished aluminum, and anodized aluminum.

and certainly before you paint. Don't forget to try opening the doors to make certain there is enough clearance.

Some aftermarket custom body parts fit very poorly and would require extensive work even to be usable. If you order them by mail, deal with a reputable company that offers to refund your money if they don't fit.

Painting Body Enhancements

The saying "Less is More" can apply to automotive body colors, too. For years, painting grilles, bumpers, and other trim parts the same color as the car's body has been a trend. The idea was to reduce the visual clutter and produce a look popularized by some European car customizers. Taken too far, this can produce a car that resembles a lump of colored clay. As cars become smaller, their height increases relative to their length. Their appearance goes from long and lean to stubby and blob-like. Designers

have added a number of styling features, such as bigger rocker trim and larger beltline moldings, to help break up the height of the car's side panels. In the wrong places, painting such trim pieces the same color as the car can make it look chubbier.

Black-Out—Black-out, on the other hand, refers to painting trim parts or sections of a car body with black paint that can lend the car a sleeker appearance. So another trend has been to black-out grilles, bumper parts, and trim pieces. In some applications, this can make the car look leaner and longer. On 1984-1996 Corvette coupes, for example, if the windows are darkly tinted and the small section of body-colored roof panel is painted black, the only parts of the car that remain body-colored are less than three feet from the ground. The car then looks longer and lower.

Blacking-out can do more than just change the appearance of the car. It is also an easy way to repair paint damage. If you want to avoid the problems of matching paint on some

of the lower body panels, painting them black is an easy solution. Whenever they get stone damage or are scuffed, they can be retouched more convincingly because black is relatively easy to match.

Anodizing and Chrome-Plating

No discussion of exterior body enhancements would be complete without the subject of chroming and other platings. If exterior metal parts aren't painted, they are typically chrome-plated or anodized.

Anodizing—Anodizing is a surface treatment that can only be done on aluminum alloy (lightweight) parts. The anodizing is done in a tank by an electrochemical process; it is not sprayed on like paint. The surface of the aluminum is chemically changed, typically to a depth of only a few 10 thousandths-of-an-inch. However, this can provide a considerable amount of corrosion protection. This outer layer can also be dyed or tinted, and the colors can range from black to gold to brilliant blues.

To test to see if a part is not anodized, touch the leads of an ohm meter or continuity tester on the surface. The anodized layer does not conduct electricity, therefore if current passes, it is not anodized. If current does not pass, the part could be anodized or painted. Other clues are that either anodized or painted surfaces can get small cracks and subsequent corrosion, but typically only paint will peel or chip. Orange peel is another clue to the existence of a clear coat of paint.

Anodized parts can be stripped of the anodized layer and the color tinting. They are not always easy to restore because any surface corrosion

Cadmium is one of the least durable platings used in automotive applications. The gold cadmium plating has fallen off most of the underside of this two-year-old gas cap.

has to be sanded or buffed out, and that can change the appearance of the surface finish.

Chrome-Plating—Bright chrome-plating adds a special type of visual excitement to a car or truck. In the earliest years of automotive manufacture, brass was the brightwork of choice for enhancing the appearance of the motorcar. However, this "Brass Era" ended abruptly when Cadillac pioneered the successful application of nickel and chrome-plating. Although many other types and colors of brightwork have been tried on cars, chrome is still the king.

However, from a consumer's standpoint, all chrome-platings are definitely not equal. Almost like automotive painting, the quality of chrome-plating is dependent on the surface preparation, the underplatings, and the thickness of the surface layer.

Just like the top coat of paint, chrome does not adhere very well to the underlying metal. This is one reason why high quality chrome-plating has other metals plated underneath the chrome layer. The first layer plated over the steel is usually copper. Because copper is relatively soft, this layer permits the chroming shop to buff the surface smooth. Chrome-plating is so reflective that the slightest surface imperfections show up. The next layer of plating is nickel. Nickel itself appears very similar to chrome and, in fact, some of the parts that look chrome-plated are only nickel-plated because it is less expensive. The final layer is the chrome itself.

"Show" chrome has had the lower layers so carefully buffed that the final chrome layers are mirror-like in quality. Show chrome, or any chrome for that matter, can be easily scratched during cleaning or waxing. Make sure that the cleaning cloth and wax are completely free of sand and grit.

Inexpensive plating is often found on aftermarket parts. Although it looks good, it may not last very long. By skimping on the thickness of the plating, or even eliminating one of the lower layers, the cost of production is decreased. Unfortunately, you won't usually know until you see brown rust stains months later or you find the chrome beginning to peel. Ask if the chrome is covered by a warranty, and ask around to see how that manufacturer's products have held up.

Cadmium Plating

Cadmium plating is one of the most common types of metal plating found on cars today. It is one of the least expensive and least durable types of platings and therefore is seldom used on exterior car parts. Open the door or hood, and chances are that the gold or aluminum-colored plated parts you see are cadmium. Cadmium generally is not as shiny as chrome or nickel, and it discolors or corrodes away very easily. Although it is a very inexpensive form of plating, car restorers often go to great lengths to duplicate the original cadmium plating originally used by the manufacturers.

Why should you bother with a detailed inspection of the paint and body on a car, especially when it looks perfect and has only a few thousand miles on it? At the time the photo was taken, this car was less than a year old and did have only a few thousand miles on the odometer. Turn the page to see what it looked like a few weeks before.

When buying a vehicle, you want to know the answer to "Has it been in an accident?" and "Is its paint going to hold up?" These are also of interest for a vehicle you already own, but in addition you want to know how to prevent future paint problems. New methods of inspection can answer these questions and more.

Paint inspection is a powerful way to learn the history and condition of a vehicle. If it's been in an accident, it's been repainted. If it's rusted through and patched up, it's been repainted. If it has suffered delamination or another now-hidden paint failure, again, it's been repainted. Therefore, knowing that a body panel or entire vehicle has been repainted provides extremely valuable information and shows you the existence of potential problems.

Many times you can see evidence of repainting when you take the time to do a very thorough visual inspection of the paint itself and an inspection of the surrounding area for overspray. However when refinish work is good, it is difficult or impossible to spot using just your eyes.

The inevitable march of technology has provided instrumentation which can evaluate paint faster, easier, and more accurately than a person's subjective judgment. The three most valuable automotive paint measurements are thickness, surface finish and color.

Thickness—This is currently the best method of inspecting paint because it is the fastest, easiest and most affordable. Plus paint thickness tells more about the condition of the paint and what lies underneath it than the other measurements. It's discussed more fully below.

Surface Finish—A recent breakthrough in instrumentation enables this paint parameter to be now measured affordably. It can be used to measure the difference from one panel to another, or from one car to another, and therefore also helps spot repainted or buffed areas.

Color—The third instrument which can be used to spot paint differences between panels or cars, is a spectrophotometer. However it is expensive and is far more often used for paint matching than for paint

139

Yes this was the same car only weeks before. To "repair" it, it was cut in half, and the front of another car (which had a lot more miles on it) was welded in its place. This is called sectioning or clipping and most car buyers never know it's happened to their car. See the sidebar for a closer look at clipping.

This is the safest way to buy a car—with the paint stripped off. When a car is completely painted, you have to question what may be hiding under the shiny finish. Of course, you'd have to repaint this car, but at least you'd know up front what you're getting.

One of the best ways to examine the paint for surface damage and signs of underlying problems is under fluorescent light tubes. If you look closely, the reflection from the tubes will show every paint flaw and every dimple, ding or wave in the body panel.

inspection.

Thickness Tells

In less than two minutes, a person can walk around a car and take twenty paint thickness measurements with an electronic thickness gauge. This effectively tells if and where any

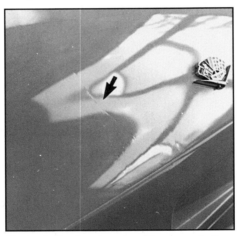

If you look closely you will see a shallow vertical line located about 10 inches forward of the emblem. That's a sink mark, and it shows that the front fender was cut and spliced here. That considerably devalues the car and is a warning to look closer for other major problems.

repainting exists. Look in the sidebar in this chapter for a guide to evaluating paint thickness measurements. Repainted areas can be more closely inspected to determine the extent of the damage which is covered up.

The electronic thickness gauge, and the new Paint and Body Gauge model which is designed specifically for automotive inspection, are now used by professional car buyers. Not only are they far more effective at spotting repaint, they enable buyers to inspect cars at under poor lighting conditions or at night, in the rain, or when the paint is covered with dirt or dust. Driver's Mart Worldwide, the first used car superstore to outfit their sourcing people with this new technology, reported that this cut inspection time in half,

It is also important to take measurements at the areas which are prime spots for finding serious collision damage or rust damage. These are described in detail in the following sections of this chapter and a photo sidebar shows where to look for evidence of perhaps the most serious collision repair, clipping or sectioning.

Hidden collision or rust damage can prove costly. So can repainting. Repainting was never cheap, but today it is even more expensive. A high quality paint job with a two-part enamel or pearl tri-coat can cost $3000 or more. The cost is even higher if bodywork is needed. The exotic chemicals and the equipment needed to control pollution have put

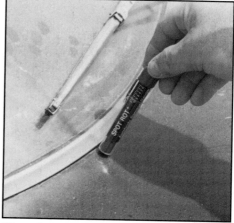

An inexpensive product is available to help you spot hidden rust or collision damage. It's an auto body damage gauge, and it is so sensitive that it will detect extra repainting or body fillers as thin as a piece of paper. The new gauge already has widespread use by insurance inspectors, police departments, and collector car buyers. You can obtain one from Pro Motorcar Products, Clearwater, FL 813-726-9225. Courtesy *Mopar Muscle* magazine.

Place the gauge on the area to be tested and pull it off by the cap. If the slider comes out to 10 or more, there is solid steel under one paint job. If it reads less, look for the reason why. Check the area near windshields because once rust starts here, it can be very hard to stop and it can cause other serious damage.

paint prices into the stratosphere while trying to keep the paint itself out of the atmosphere. Therefore, the condition of a vehicle's paint should be a critical factor in determining whether or not it is worth the purchase price. Quite often the paint is overlooked or given a cursory examination by an excited buyer, especially if it looks OK at first glance. The last section of this chapter looks closely at inspection and evaluation of the condition of the paint.

First we'll focus on problems under the paint, because a paint's future condition is dependent on the surface to which it is applied. If there are problems with the underlying sheet metal, plastic or fiberglass body panels, then problems will develop with the paint—no matter how it looks at the time of purchase. Therefore, it is essential that you carefully inspect the body of the car as well as the paint. Particularly with automotive paint, what you see today isn't always what you'll have in a year or two. No matter how good the paint,

in terms of preparation, application, or materials, it won't last when it's on a poorly prepared or damaged body. In some ways, inspecting the body is easier than inspecting the paint.

RUST INSPECTION

Generally, cars rust from the inside out. However, a thorough inspection of the outside can tell you if there is a rust problem because cars don't rust uniformly. Rust-through will first occur in certain pockets or areas of the body. In addition, cars that are located in the so-called "rust-belt" states of New England and throughout the Midwest will rust in different places than cars that are located near a coastline.

Detective Tools

There are a number of available tools designed to help inspect car bodies. A magnetic tool is an essential device for inspecting bodies for rust or repaired damage. A paint gauge will work well, but an auto body damage gauge is less expensive and

relatively new. This gauge is specifically designed to look for body filler. The old method of using a magnet can miss a lot, but a magnet is better than nothing if a gauge can't be borrowed or purchased.

If you're going to use a magnet, use the weakest one possible. A weak refrigerator-type or rubber magnet are good choices. The reason for this is that a strong magnet will stick on areas covered by thin coats of filler. It is important to detect those areas because they usually surround and extend out from areas that are rusted through. Because it's not practical to check every square inch of the car body with the magnet, the worst areas may go undetected unless you have a sensitive device that will detect the difference in the surrounding areas.

Another body shop trick to be aware of is the use of steel particles in body filler. Although no commercially available filler has steel particles as an ingredient, unscrupulous individuals have been known to add steel particles to fool people who later check the car with a magnet. Such tricks, however,

For the first time, the quality of the surface finish of automotive paint can be measured and evaluated. Previous to this, evaluation of finishes was only an opinion— and every person has a different one. The QFM optical instrument measures distinctness of image - gloss to provide an objective evaluation of finish quality. This will enable the setting of national quality standards and is already being used for this purpose by Driver's Mart Worldwide. Courtesy Pro Motorcar Products.

The newest technology for inspecting cars is the digital Paint & Body Gauge. It is already being used by Driver's Mart Worldwide to help their professional buyers inspect vehicles at big auto auction. Driver's Mart reported that the gauge not only identified previously repaired vehicles, it cut their inspection time in half. Courtesy Pro Motorcar Products.

"Bubble, bubble, toil, and trouble." That applies very well to auto paint. Take very seriously any tiny bubble you see because usually it is a sign that the car has already suffered significant corrosion damage. By the time it looks like this, you can be certain you're in for a lot of toil and trouble.

won't fool a gauge.

Rust–Belt Rust

Cars located in the so-called "rust-belt" states, meaning those states with heavy winter weather that requires salt to de-ice the roads, rust from the inside out and from the bottom up. That's because the moisture and salt act as catalysts and greatly accelerate the rusting process.

The lower parts of the car are exposed to the road spray and dirt kicked up by the tires. Inevitably, bodies have areas where this dirt collects under the car. Edges, ledges, and pockets provide resting areas for these rust fiends. Leaves, twigs, and debris also can fall onto a car and collect in doors, under the trunk lid, and under the hood near the windshield wipers or the air vent openings.

The dirt and debris themselves are not as much of a problem as the moisture they absorb. A rain storm can wet a car for a few minutes or a few hours, but pockets of dirt can hold that moisture against the underbody areas for days. Add salt to this combination and rust-through is assured. Invariably, the areas that rust first are areas that trap dirt and moisture. The only good aspect to this is that there are specific, identifiable areas most likely to rust through; you should always inspect these areas first to judge the condition of the body. When I mention "inspect" or "check," I mean to test the area with a magnet or gauge.

Front Fenders—First test the lowest portion of the fender in front of the door. In general, test the body panel about an inch in from any edge. Next, inspect the rear edge of the

This is the next stage of automobile rust, and it is literally just down the road from the appearance of the first bubbles in the paint. To repair damage like this, the rear quarter panel will have to be replaced, which is very costly. Remember this photo if you see any signs of rust damage on a car you are considering buying.

When it's time to get rid of a car, most sellers won't pay thousands of dollars for work that goes unseen. They'll just cover up the rust with fiberglass or plastic fillers. In fact, it's been done several times on this car.

The inside bottom edge of a car door is one of the best places to inspect the paint to get early notice of a rust problem. Look for metal that is puffing out or evidence of fillers or repainting.

Also inspect the inside lower lip of the trunk lid. The edge of the metal where it is folded over should be crisp and straight—with no blistering or bubbling of the paint.

fender that runs up along the side of the front of the door. Finally, check the top inner edge of the fender that runs along the sides of the hood. Inspect both front fenders before doing the doors. If you will be inspecting many cars, use the same system each time because it is very easy to forget where you've checked and thereby overlook a critical area.

Doors—Check the lower corners and the lower edge, again about an inch in from the actual edge. Next open the door and look at the door edge and corners from the inside. The outer piece of door sheet metal (called the door skin) usually wraps around and is folded over the inner piece of the door at the edge. Not only does debris collect at the bottom, but any part of the body where two layers of metal overlap "wicks" in water by capillary action and promotes rust-through. Some doors also have drain holes at the bottom that become clogged and allow moisture to accumulate. The edge of the door skin should appear crisp and uniform along

its length. If it is filled in, look for hidden rust damage.

Rear Quarter Panels—Again, check the lowest areas first. Start in front of the rear tire, then check the area behind the rear tire which is even more likely to rust through. Check the wheel well opening and the edges themselves.

Trunk—Open up the trunk or hatch lid and inspect the edges from the inside. Then pull up the mats and remove the spare tire, if necessary, to check all seams and low spots. Beware of any fresh undercoating or fresh paint.

Underbody—Check out all pockets or areas where dirt can collect. Again, be very suspicious of undercoating that appears freshly applied.

Interior—Always remove the floor mats and, whenever possible, unsnap or pull up the carpet. Water gets trapped under carpets or mats and especially under the cowl and foot well areas. The problem often goes unnoticed until it's too late.

Windows—It is critical to check the edges around the front and rear windshields. This is one of the hardest areas to stop rust because water

collects in the seams and edges under the molding. Therefore, the rust damage is often noticed too late, only after extensive rusting has occurred. Repairing such areas necessitates removing the windshields and welding in new metal. Seldom is the job done properly; and even when it is done carefully, it is difficult to permanently stop the rust.

Rust-through around the windshields can end up causing problems to the car's structural integrity. When the rust-through initially occurs, it

This rusted-through floorboard is the reason you want to check around the edges of windshields because water will seep into the car, collect under the carpets (or the trunk mat), and silently rust through the body. And the first warning sign is a blister in the paint around the windshield.

Also check the outside lower edge of the door, about 3/4 inch up from the edge. Like the bottom of the front fender, it is one of the first places to show evidence of rust damage. This photo shows where rust commonly occurs before it is covered up.

Why is it important to look at the paint under the rocker panel? It's not because you are so concerned about its appearance but that it can warn of serious collision damage. When modern unibody cars suffer severe collision damage, they must be pulled straight on a frame jig (as shown here). One of the points where the car body is clamped is the "pinch" weld lip under the rocker panel. If the paint or metal is damaged on this lip, it can be a sign that the car was wrecked severely enough to spend time on a jig.

allows water to seep into the trunk or under the carpets. It can be years before the problem is noticed, and by then the floorboard or trunk is severely rusted.

Coastal Rust

There are a lot of misconceptions about the effects salt water has on cars. To be sure, it will greatly accelerate rust, but just because you live near the ocean or the gulf does not mean your car will rust away.

Cars that are 10 to 20 miles away from the coasts are relatively unaffected by the salt air. The effect of the salt air becomes much stronger the closer the car is to the shore. A car or truck that actually has the salt water or spray blowing on it daily can quickly develop severe rust problems. However, a car shielded from direct ocean spray and mist can lead a long and rust-free life, even if it is within a block or two from the ocean.

Several factors can make a major difference in the level and rate of rusting in coastal cars. For example, if the car is usually garaged, rust will not be much of a problem. Frequent washing, particularly after windy or stormy days helps considerably, too. A carport can make a significant difference because it almost eliminates the soaking morning dew that wets the car's exterior. This is especially important on the coast because the salt comes primarily from the air and collects on the upper portions of the body. The locations where rust occurs on the car body are entirely different on coastal cars than on rust-belt cars.

Hood—Check the front edge of the hood, especially if it has a molding or chrome strip. This is a good example of how the region a car comes from affects where the rust occurs. Hoods and trunks are among the last body parts to rust on Midwestern cars, but they are among the first to rust on coastal cars.

Trunk—First check the rear edge from the outside; then open the trunk or hatchback to inspect the inner edge or seam.

Fenders—Check the upper areas, and particularly check around any moldings or emblems. In addition to checking with a gauge or magnet, look for signs of bubbling or blistering paint in these areas. If these kinds of paint problems occur here, they are a warning sign of serious rust damage.

Doors—It is always good to check the lower edges of the doors, but coastal cars should also be inspected at the upper edge, near the window molding and the door handles.

COLLISION DAMAGE

Inspecting for collision damage, like inspecting for rust damage, is helped by having a system. In fact, it is best to go around the car and inspect for rust damage, and then go around again and concentrate on collision damage. Start with the areas most likely to have been hit.

CLIPPED CARS

Few car owners realize that such a thing as clipping exists. Clipping refers to the "repair" of a severely crashed vehicle by cutting (clipping) it in half; discarding the crashed half, and welding the half of another vehicle in its place. The other vehicle was typically crashed on the other end, and it may be a different year or have higher mileage than the original vehicle. Clipping is popular because it is faster and easier than ordering and assembling all the different panels which make today's unitbody vehicles.

Although illegal in some countries, clipping occurs everyday in every state across the country. And often there is no mention of the severity of the collision damage or the repair on the vehicles title. Clipped vehicles were cut in half at places which are the least likely to be seen and require the least amount of finish work. The best way to spot these cars is to inspect the bodies at the common clipping points for signs of repainting (for example, thicker paint) or body filler.

The collision damaged rear half of the car is cut off (clipped).

The cuts were made on the windshield posts and under the carpet to minimize the body work and repainting.

A body with an undamaged rear half was bought from a salvage yard — it was even the same color!

The two halves were then welded together at the windshield posts, at the rocker panels and under the carpeting. Now only minor repainting is needed to hide the fact that this is two cars spliced together.

Hood—First check the center of the hood at the front, with the magnet or gauge, where collision damage is most likely to have occurred. Next

check the front corner and then the rear corner of the hood. If the rear corners or edges have evidence of body filler, check the adjoining area

on the cowl in front of the windshield. If you find repairs here, it means the crash was severe enough that the hood was pushed back.

Trunk—Inspect the trunk lid in the same manner as the hood, but check the rear most area first.

Roof—If damage exists here it is likely to have been caused by a falling tree limb, vandalism, or a roll-over.

Front Fenders—Check the front areas first. Note that the car may have a plastic or aluminum-molded housing at the front of the fender. If you can see a seam or distinguish a separate part here, don't be surprised that neither the gauge nor the magnet sticks. Check the middle areas of the fenders, particularly over the wheel well, because the fenders often bulge out here and this is the first area to get banged or scraped on the side of the car.

Doors—Again, check the middle areas but also give attention to the lower areas. Curbs or other low-lying objects often inflict damage here.

Rear Quarter Panels—Again, check the central areas first. Front fenders are often replaced when they are damaged in collisions because they can be easily unbolted. However, rear quarter panels are usually welded onto the body and require much more effort to replace. Therefore, body damage on rear quarter panels is commonly patched up and covered over.

PAINT INSPECTION

After inspecting that which supports the paint—the body—it's time to inspect the paint itself. The things to look for include thin paint, thick paint, cosmetic problems, and evidence of repainting.

A magnetic paint gauge is more than sufficient to inspect the thickness of paint on a car. Paint gauges can tell if there is too much paint, if a car actually was stripped before repainting or restoration, or if the paint is too thin. In effect, it tells a lot about the paint's past, present, and future. The US made Pro Gauge costs only about $50 and is the best selling paint gauge in the world. Courtesy Pro Motorcar Products.

Thin Clear Coats

The clear coat on modern cars protects the underlying paint by filtering out the damaging UV rays. If the clear coat is too thin, the entire paint job will be susceptible to damage. Unfortunately, there is no way to determine how thick the clear coat is just by looking at it. The finish can be immaculate, blemish-free and have an outstanding shine, without giving any indication that the clear coat is dangerously thin.

Clear coat paint jobs are often sanded down and buffed to remove damage such as acid rain or water spots. Although factory clear coats provide some degree of extra thickness to allow for this, if too much is removed the longevity of the paint job is jeopardized. For example, U.S. auto manufacturers recommend not sanding or buffing more than .0003 inch of clear coat. If more than this needs to be removed to eliminate surface defects such as scratches or water spots, repaint may be necessary.

PAINT THICKNESS READINGS

Measuring a vehicle's paint thickness will tell you much about its history and condition. The readings can tell if it has suffered collision damage, where it has been repainted, and if it has been buffed too thin. The following chart provides a rule of thumb for interpreting the readings.

2 - 3.5 mils: At two mils, the primer is about to show through on most cars and if it is a clear coated car, the clear coat is nearly gone. Even at 3 mils, the paint is fairly thin, and you would be well advised to be very careful with any polishing. If the paint looks good, it may have years of life left if you can avoid exposing it to the sun and elements for prolonged periods of time. One option: if the paint is in otherwise excellent shape, spray 1-1/2 to 2 mils of urethane clear coat over it.

4 - 5 mils: This is the normal range of most factory paint jobs. One of the most conclusive tests is to look for variation in the paint thickness around the car. Although it's possible to find as much as 1.5 mil variation on one panel (such as a door), if all of the car reads close to 4 mils but one fender reads 6, that is evidence that the fender was repainted.

5.5 - 7.5 mils: It still may be factory paint but, on many cars, paint that measures this thick indicates repainting has occurred. If it is a two-tone car, one color may have been painted over the other at the factory, and the thickness may exceed 6 mils on that overlaying color. Look closely for overspray on moldings or tape lines on door jams.

8 - 10 mils: It is almost certainly repainted, but the finish may last if the vehicle is garaged, is a northern car, or if it has urethane top coats over a good base. Few paint manufacturers would recommend painting over paint this thick.

10.5 - 12.5 mils: In most cases, you will only find paint this thick on a car that has at least three paint jobs on top of one another. Paint this thick is risky, particularly on a car that sits out in the sun. Ask yourself what went wrong with the first and the second paint jobs because there may be problems brewing under the current paint job. Again, if the repaints were urethanes applied over a good base, the paint job may last, especially if it is a garaged vehicle.

Over 13 mils: With few exceptions, automotive paint thicker than 13 mils is quite likely to crack, fade, or peel under constant exposure to the sun and weather.

Anti-Chip Paints: In the '90's, lower body panels and leading edges of fenders, hoods and roofs received thicker anti-chip primers on a number of models of cars and trucks. By 1997, Chrysler Corporation was implementing full body antichip primers on a number of their models.

Thin Paint

Fortunately, thin paint is one of the easiest problems to measure and detect. A paint thickness gauge can be used to determine when the thickness of an original paint job has decreased to the point were it can create problems. As a rule of thumb, paint thinner than 3.5 mils, especially on

Orange peel in the finish, like seen on this Cadillac, is evident on all new factory paint jobs. In fact, by closely examining the orange peel you can usually see where any repainting was done. Although it's difficult to match colors when repainting, it's even more difficult to match the orange peel and gloss.

top panels such as the hood, roof or trunk, is cause for concern. If the car is often uncovered or is in a sunny, southern part of the country, a thin paint job is of particular concern.

Nobody can tell how thick paint is by looking at it, and in fact, thin paint can look terrific. The problem is that a major portion of the protection from environmental stresses such as ultraviolet light and air-bore contaminants is lost when paint is worn off or over-buffed. Paint which looks great today can be cracking and flaking off in the near future. That's why all major auto manufacturers specify that paint thickness must be measured before and after any buffing or finessing. If as little as 1/2 of a thousand of an inch (which is only about one eighth the thickness of this page) is removed, repainting is recommended to preserve its protection and appearance.

If the paint is thinner than 3.0 mils, there is another danger: polishing through into the base coat or underlying primer layer. On non clear coat paint, even if you don't actually

polish into the primer, thin paint can cause problems because most paints aren't completely opaque. Lighter colors, such as yellow, will show different shading where it is thin because the primer shows through.

Thick Paint

Thick paint is as common a problem as thin paint, and its remedy can be more expensive. A thin paint job can

usually be sanded and repainted or just clear coated. However, when paint is too thick, the layers of old paint have to be stripped off. Stripping can increase the cost of a paint job by a thousand dollars or more.

Paint manufacturers generally agree that the optimum thickness for automotive paint is about 4 to 5 mils, which includes all primers and top coats. If paint is substantially thicker than this, cracking, checking, fading, and peeling are much more likely to occur. One reason is that paint tends to shrink as it ages. As solvents slowly evaporate out of the paint, the paint shrinks and contracts. If the paint layer is very thin and bonded closely to the underlying body panel, the shrinking can be accommodated. However, if the paint layer is thick, the surface splits and cracks as it contracts. The cracks and checks look like those of a dried river bed, and the physical principle is the same. In the case of paint, the solvents have evaporated. With the river bed or muddy areas, the water has evaporated.

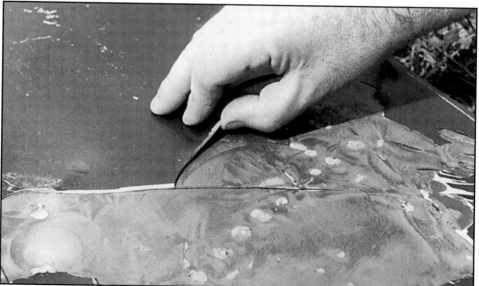

This is a graphic illustration of what can lurk beneath the paint. The thick plastic filler is being peeled off the body panel. The line of holes shows where the dent was drilled and then pulled out with a slide hammer before the plastic was applied.

Fortunately, thick paint can also be easily measured. A depth of more than 6 mils suggests that repainting has occurred. When prior repainting is evident on a car which needs to be painted, most paint manufacturers require that the paint be stripped, at least down to the original paint, or the new paint won't be warranted. Stripping the old repaint is especially desirable if there is reason to believe the repaint was lacquer based because lacquer paints are not a good foundation for a long-lasting paint job.

If the paint measures about 6 mils all around the car, it is also possible the paint was applied heavier at the factory. For example, many Buicks and Oldsmobiles or Cadillacs had an additional coat of primer-surfacer which some of their less expensive GM cousins didn't receive. Another thing to be aware of is that even though the paint is sprayed by robotic arms, it is not always consistent in thickness. I've seen paint thickness vary by 1.5 mils at different spots on the same door! However, if the paint measures consistently 4 mils on parts of the car and 6 mils on other parts, it is quite likely the 6 mil areas were repainted.

When a car has been repainted, you have no way of knowing the thickness of any of the top or underlying layers. The car could have been completely stripped of old paint (although this is not likely) and then had very thick layers of primer and paint sprayed on. Or there may be the full factory paint job with a thin layer of repaint over it. Or the dealership may have sanded out some paint defects and sprayed on a heavy layer of clear.

If the thickness of the paint surface is over 10 mils, this suggests that the paint has a substantial chance of

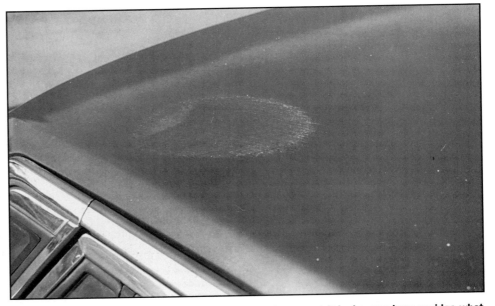

Be very cautious of a freshly painted car. No matter how great it looks, you have no idea what it will look like a few months or a year later. This patch of dying paint that covers a previous repair was not evident when the car was purchased; neither were numerous other paint problems that subsequently affected the surface.

deteriorating. However, if the paint is a high quality urethane or other high quality, two-part paint and if the car is garaged, paint this thick has a better chance of lasting.

Do more expensive cars have thicker paint? Not as a rule. You won't necessarily find thicker paint on a $95,000 Mercedes than on a basic Ford. There is some variation in the total paint thickness among manufacturers and among their models. However, the thickness of the paint has more to do with the type of paints they need to apply at those plants and the current recommendations of the paint experts, than with the final selling price of the car.

Determining Repaint

Why should a buyer care if a car was repainted? For one thing, repaint often doesn't last as long as factory paint. For another, a car buyer should find out why the car needed to be repainted. Was it in an accident? Was it rusted out? Did the underlying paint

go bad once already?

As was pointed at the beginning of this chapter, whenever a painter does a good job, it's difficult to detect whether or not a car has been repainted. Paint thickness gauges, whether the electronic model or the inexpensive pen type, are a big help. For example, if a vehicle has 4 mils of paint all around but the hood has 7 mils, it is very likely that the hood was repainted, even if there is no other evidence of repainting. Other evidence of repainting is poor color matching or metallic mismatching, tape lines, overspray, or differences in the surface finish such as the amount of gloss or orange peel.

The rules of "Never buy a car at night" and "Never buy a dirty car" certainly apply here. Try to examine a car outside to look for color matching or metallic problems. First, look at the car head-on and then at an angle when comparing the color and the metallic consistency. Looking down the sides of the car helps to spot differences in gloss and orange peel. Also, examining the paint under fluorescent lighting is one of the best ways to find minor pits or other flaws in the surface finish.

Overspray—Overspray is one of the easiest tell-tale signs of repainting to spot. Look closely at the edges of trim pieces where they come close to the painted parts of the car. If there is body color paint on the trim parts, you know the car has been repainted because these parts were not on the car when the car was painted at the factory. In particular, look closely at the lower moldings and undersides of moldings because people tend to get a little sloppier at masking these hard-to-reach areas.

If it sounds like inspecting the paint on a car is time-consuming, you're right. However, if you are spending many thousands of dollars for a car, you should take the time to inspect every square inch of the paint. Not only is repainting a clue that other problems may be covered up, but a paint job that goes bad in a few months will cost you more than most mechanical repairs would!

A blended area gone bad also can be seen in the upper middle of this rear pillar, between the two arrows. Be particularly vigilant in inspecting this area because it may show evidence of a clipped car.

New cars at the dealership can't possibly have body work and repaint. So most people think. These cars were dented by tent poles after a storm blew though. You can bet they were repaired, repainted and back out on lot in a matter of days. Unfortunately another storm came through a couple weeks later damaged another set of cars. Most states do not require that car buyers be informed that the new vehicle they are purchasing had body work or repainting.

13

PAINT TRAINING & CERTIFICATION

The level of technology in the auto refinishing industry has developed to the point where formal training and certification is necessary. All major parts manufacturers offer training courses and seminars.

Paint technology has progressed to the point where formal education and training are becoming necessary to become a professional. Although one can still find work in a body shop without formal education, it's now likely specialized education will be necessary during a career in bodywork and refinishing. To be sure, some painters have never taken a technical training course but this is not the pattern for the future.

Training is a hot issue in this field for another reason, there's a shortage of competent help at all levels. A number of things are needed: attracting young people to this profession, properly training them, and finding ways to keep them in the industry.

As shown in previous chapters, automotive paint has undergone radical changes in the chemistry of its materials. Perhaps the most profound changes in this industry from car owner's perspective will be in the delivery of services. Increased training and professionalism will be seen along with stricter regulations and new kinds of certification of products and services. Advancing technology and the new economic realities of car care have made possible a coming revolutionary change: the adoption of credible national standards for automotive refinish.

Automotive refinish has lagged behind nearly all other industries in one notable aspect: its lack of measuring its finished product. Think about it, almost every category of commerce uses measurements to assess the quality of its product.

Imagine optometrists without objective measuring equipment calibrated to international standards. Even in automotive refinishing's sister field of automotive repair, imagine an engine rebuilder without micrometers or an alignment shop without measuring equipment. And within the body shop, measuring equipment has become standard for collision repair now that unibody cars are the norm.

METRICS & NATIONAL STANDARDS

"Metrics" is a term used to describe the process of measuring important parameters so that the product or process can be evaluated, compared and improved. Advancement in any field is hastened by quantifying and measuring performance. Progress in established industries is generally accomplished in incremental steps. The improvements are typically small and difficult to see or accurately judge by subjective means. That's why measuring and objectively comparing the results is necessary. For example, without exhaust gas analyzers and timing lights, engineers and mechanics would be relying on trial and error to improve engine performance.

Automotive refinish, however, has been one of the last major industries to value the concept of "Metrics" to improve and certify its product. The evaluation of refinish work is still almost exclusively subjective, and comes down to nothing more than someone saying "I think it looks OK." Change, however, is coming rapidly to this profession in this new subject of metrics. This new need for measurement is spurred on by certification programs, OEM warranty requirements, elevated customer expectations, and good business sense. The fact that the price of measurement instrumentation for refinish has dropped hasn't hurt either.

When national standards are adopted, a consumer will be guaranteed that they will receive a consistent, measurable level of quality from any conforming businesses, whether it's a dealership in Arkansas or a specialty shop in Hawaii. To an extent, this has begun already. Lifetime paint warranties from paint manufacturers are given only when certain paint materials are used according to specifications and applied only by certified technicians in certified facilities.

TRAINING AND CERTIFICATION

A brief explanation of the types of training and certifications available today will not only benefit the do-it-yourself enthusiast or body shop customer, but the would-be professional as well. As a customer, knowing the types of certification a shop has or has not had will help you decide whether a certain shop is likely to deliver the quality paint job you desire.

The subjects of choosing a body shop and training of its painters go together because certificates of training are objective things a car owner can look for when evaluating the competency of a shop. But a training certificate on the wall is not positive proof that a painter or body shop will do good work any more than the lack of certification or formal training of a painter is proof that he won't do good work. Some of the best painters have never gone to classes. They've learned their trade by observation and experimentation. A bright painter who is always open to new ideas and is eager to learn about new products and methods can become one of the best in the field.

In the past, the majority of top painters were largely self-taught. Today, paint materials have become much more complex, and many of these self-taught, very experienced painters have now attended classes to become proficient in using modern paint systems.

ASE

You'll see the blue ASE gear-shaped logo on signs displayed at not

The ASE gear-shaped logo is one type of certification to look for when choosing a body shop or when choosing a mechanic, for that matter. The National Service for Automotive Service Excellence has offered testing for voluntary certification for automotive, truck, and collision repair technicians.

only body shops but also at shops that do mechanical repairs. For over 25 years, the National Institute for Automotive Service Excellence (ASE) has offered testing for voluntary certification for automotive, truck, and collision repair technicians.

Although ASE certification is probably the most widely found type of certification, (400,000 technicians have been certified over the years) it still is held by a relatively small percentage of body shop workers. The certification is, after all, voluntary. However, more employers and technicians are now viewing certification as a necessary step toward professionalism and quality. In addition, some proposed regional regulations for body shops require various types of objective certification. By comparison, the existing mandatory licensing in some states is

I-CAR Gold Certification is another important sign that the management and technicians are keeping current with paint and repair technology. Having such certification present indicates that the body shop cares enough about quality to stay current with the latest technological developments.

If you can't make it to a trade show or training seminar, some manufacturers bring the training to you. Meguiar's Mobile Training Centers are well equipped trailers set up as classrooms where refinishers are taught about the latest techniques and products in surface care.

often no more than a formality. Body shop workers are sometimes "grand fathered" in (automatically licensed) without having to prove their competence if they have been doing bodywork for a number of years.

Testing—To get tested by ASE, a person needs to complete and send in a registration form with a $25 fee and $20 for each test requested. The applicant must present proof of two years of relevant work experience or two years of formal education in this field plus one year of work experience. An admission ticket stating the time and location of the testing will then be mailed back to the applicant. Tests are given at the testing center nearest the applicant, and each test contains approximately 60 multiple choice questions. Samples of the questions are shown in a registration booklet. This registration booklet is free and can be obtained from ASE, 13505 Dulles Technology Drive, Herndon, VA 20171-3421. Phone 703-713-3800. Fax 703-713-

0727. WWW.asecert.org

Five tests apply to the autobody field: one for refinishers, three for repair technicians and one for estimators. The ASE Collision Repair and Refinish tests are offered every May and November at over 700 locations nationwide can be taken separately or on the same day. Help in studying for these tests can be obtained by sending for the "ASE Collision Repair Test Preparation Guide" which lists the tasks a body shop technician is expected to do and also provides sample questions.

The completed tests are sent to the same company that administers the college boards, American College Testing. Approximately eight weeks later the test results are sent to the technician. The results are confidential and help to show where improvement is needed, even if the person doesn't pass the first time. Those who pass the refinish test and the three repair tests become ASE certified Master Collision Repair/Re-

finishing technicians. Check the date of the certificate, technicians are supposed to be recertified every 5 years to keep up with new technology.

I-CAR

I-CAR goes a step further by providing technical education. I-CAR stands for Inter-Industry Conference on Auto Collision Repair and is a not-for-profit organization supported by auto manufacturers, body shops, insurance companies, and others who are interested in improving the level of technical skills of collision repair specialists. It is essentially a volunteer organization with over 3,000 volunteers organizing and teaching classes in every state and in the Canadian provinces.

I-CAR's stated goal is to "improve the quality, safety, and efficiency of auto collision repair for the ultimate benefit of the consumer." It was started in 1979 largely in response to the rapid increase in the unibody construction of cars. In earlier cars, a

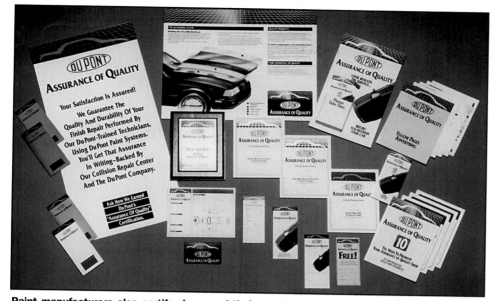

Paint manufacturers also certify shops and their employees. DuPont's "Assurance of Quality" certification aims for a level of excellence in the repainting work a shop delivers to the customer. It also includes marketing aids to help get the message out to car owners. Local body shops that are certified as AOQ can be found at www.dupont.com

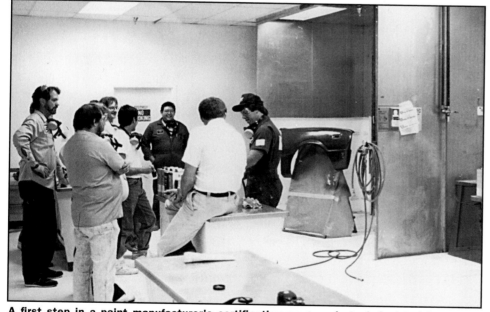

A first step in a paint manufacturer's certification program is technical training. Paint manufacturers offer workshops and training programs in a number of subjects. Seminars dealing with paint application include both classroom instruction and hands-on experience, like shown here at BASF's Orlando training center.

among the best in the country. Their student manual, for example, has over 140 pages filled with clear, concise technical information for automotive painters. The subjects range from consumer expectations and "Right to Know Laws" to the basics of tinting and color matching. The I-CAR Finish Matching Course is currently a three-unit course which was entirely rewritten in 1997.

The Uniform Procedures for Collision Repair, UPCR, were also introduced in 1997. These are very detailed step-by-step procedures for many different areas of collision repair, and are a big step toward national standards for collision repair work. Visit their web site for additional information at www.i-car.com.

Autobody repair shops and insurance claims offices can qualify as I-CAR Gold Class Professionals if 80% of their staff is I-CAR trained. Furthermore, they must be committed to on-going training and must requalify each year. If a shop is designated "Gold Class," car owners will know that the technicians are well trained and the manager or shop owner cares about keeping current with collision repair and refinishing technology. For more information, contact I-CAR, 3701 Algonquin Road, Suite 400, Rolling Meadows, IL 60008; phone 1-800-I-CAR-USA.

Paint Manufacturers

There has been a tremendous increase in the number of training and certification programs provided by the major paint manufacturers. Until recently, you were unlikely to find a body shop that displayed a certificate stating a painter was trained in the application of a certain type of paint.

strong steel frame provided most of the support for the drive train, wheels, and suspension. Unibody cars, however, are made of many separate pieces of steel welded together, and the repair of their bodies is more complex. With unibody cars, the sheet metal of the car actually holds the car together and therefore proper repair of collision damage is more critical to the car's structural integrity and safety.

In my opinion, I-CAR's training courses and training manuals are

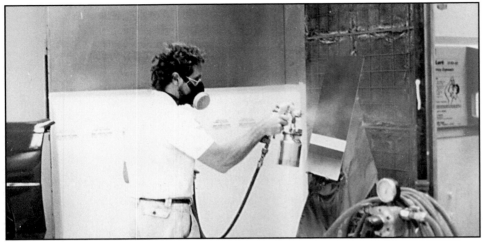

Painters get a chance to try new products and materials at the training centers. Here, the author is spraying urethane clear after experimenting with single-stage urethane and its tintable primer. The training session also included a thorough discussion of safety procedures. In addition to product information, the attendees were given a respirator with replaceable charcoal filter, gloves, and protective eye wear.

Today, every major paint manufacturer has an extensive training program available to body shop personal who wish to learn the specifics of a particular paint system.

The major paint manufacturers have established regional and national training centers, and offer a variety of courses ranging from color matching to plastics repair to complete paint systems to building your business. A course will occupy a full day or as many as four days for some of the more extensive subject areas. Typically, the courses will alternate between classroom-style presentations with audio/visual segments and actual hands-on experience in an adjoining workshop area.

Not surprisingly, the workshop or paint booth areas are clean, well-lit, and state-of-the art in terms of ventilation and temperature control. Throughout the courses, safety is a very strong theme. At the minimum, attendees wear new charcoal filter masks and safety goggles when spraying, and the instructors wear gloves when handling or mixing the paint materials. Some paint manufacturers give the masks, gloves, and safety glasses to the participants to take back and use at their shops.

Another valuable aspect of the training programs is that the instructors generally have many years of actual body shop and paint experience. They aren't chemists or sales people coming down from the national office to tell the body shop personnel how the paint materials are supposed to work. The instructors are painters who have dealt with the types of problems which occur out in the field when painting has to be done under less than laboratory conditions.

At one course I attended, the instructor was aided by the two local sales reps who each had many years of experience working in body shops. The course enabled the painters to get to know their local paint reps better so that they know who to call on when they have a problem or technical question. It also works in the other direction because if there are problems with the manufacturer's products, they will be better communicated to the research people since the manufacturer's employees will be in closer contact with the people who actually apply the paint. One result is the development of better paint systems and application techniques.

When choosing a body shop, there is good reason to look for a painter who has taken the time and effort to become certified by the paint manufacturer in the products he uses. Going one step beyond that, if you want your car's paint to be warranted by the paint manufacturer, the painter will have to be certified or the warranty won't be valid.

Car Manufacturers

Certification of body shops by car manufacturers is almost as new as certification by paint manufacturers. Saturn Corporation requires the technicians at its dealerships to be trained and certified in paint or body repair on Saturn cars. Lexus is another car manufacturer that has developed a very specific checklist with which a body shop must comply in order to be certified to perform warranty work on their cars.

This is a trend certain to gather momentum as the cost of automotive paint work increases. Car manufacturers and dealerships have become aware that it pays to train technicians in the application and repair of modern finishes because it is so much cheaper to do the job right the first time. New car sales and service has become an intensely competitive market and today's car buyer wants quality work.

PAINT WARRANTIES

A warranty on your paint job? Such a thing was virtually unheard of until the nineties. All the major paint

MANUFACTURER'S MAXIMUM PAINT WARRANTIES

Manufacturer	Paint	Warranty	Over Oem?	Over Any Repaints?
BASF	Glasurit, Diamont	Lifetime	If Good	Must Strip
DuPont	ChromaPremier,			
	ChromaBase	Lifetime	If Good	Must Strip
Herberts	Standox	Lifetime	If Good	Must Strip
ICI	Autocolor 2K			
	Aquabase	Lifetime	If Good	Must Strip
Martin-Senour	Tec-Base	Lifetime	If Good	Must Strip
PPG	Deltron, Global	Lifetime	If Good	Must Strip
Sherwin-Williams	Ultra System	Lifetime	If Good	Must Strip
Sikkens	Autocoat LV, Autocryl,			
	Autobase	Lifetime	If Good	If Good
Spies Hecker	Permacron	Lifetime	If Good	Must Strip

manufacturers now have warranties on their top-of-the-line paints. In the past, no paint manufacturers (and very few body shops) provided written warranties on their repaint work. Today's paint manufacturer warranties are a giant step forward for the car owner. And these warranty agreements are much more specific than those a body shop would offer.

Shop Certification—If you are spending a fair amount of money to have your car repainted or if you are planning to keep it for a number of years, it would be wise to find a shop certified to offer a warranty by a major paint manufacturer.

To be a certified shop, not only must the painters be trained and certified in the materials they are using, the shop itself must be certified. Certification of a shop usually requires that certain standards of cleanliness and safety are followed. Additionally, paint manufacturers may require an up-to-date spray booth and modern equipment and then make sure it's kept in good working order. The sales representative of the paint company may call on the shop regularly to make certain that high standards are maintained in both the work and the workplace.

Another way of looking at it is that the employees of a body shop certified to provide paint warranties have not only been factory trained but are also monitored by people with a lot of experience in the field. The paint manufacturer has enough faith in their knowledge and ability that it is risking its reputation and money to guarantee that that shop will provide high quality work. Therefore, even if you aren't looking for a paint warranty, there is good reason to seek out a shop that is certified to provide one.

Stipulations—Paint warranties have a number of stipulations. Warranties are only available on the top-of-the-line (read that as "most expensive") paints of that manufacturer. These are typically the urethane or other two-part paints.

Nearly all paint manufacturers require that the old paint be stripped to the bare metal or fiberglass if any previous refinish work has already been done. They will only allow the shop to paint over older paint if it is the original factory paint and if it is in good condition.

One paint manufacturer, Sikkens, will warranty the repainting even if it is over previously repainted areas if the underlying paint is in good condition. This can be very important to you if you don't want to go through the expense of stripping off the old paint. However, if problems develop in the paint, the warranty doesn't cover it if the painter or paint company representative says the problems were caused by the underlying paint and not by their paint. That may not be easy to disprove, and in such a situation you may be back to relying on goodwill of the body shop if the repainted areas aren't stripped to bare metal before the new paint is applied.

Paint warranties also require that the painter use only the materials recommended by the manufacturer. In some cases it may be necessary to have copies of the sales receipts for

APPROVED PAINTS

The field of automotive paint is moving rapidly toward national standards and true certification which is based on a high level of measurable performance. Perhaps the most significant recent advance in the field of automotive paint is the testing and approval of refinish paint systems by auto manufacturers. This had never occurred before. Dealerships were free to use whatever brand or quality of paint they chose for repainting. General Motors Service Technology Group (STG) tested the refinish paints submitted by all major paint manufacturers for hardness, humidity adhesion, chip resistance, hot-cold cycling, gasoline resistance, environmental chemical resistance and weather resistance.

The paint systems (specific products used from pretreatment through clearcoat) which passed all tests were listed in GM4901M. From 1997 on, dealerships had to use these paint systems or they could be charged back for warranty repairs. The effect of this is a breakthrough for car owners. The obvious benefit is that excellent quality paints will be used for all warranty repairs. Customers will be happier, and the paint is less likely to have to be redone in a few years, which saves money and the environment.

Another benefit is that for the first time, all body shops and painters, not just those at dealerships, have objective information on the performance of different paint brands. Before that, all they had were the claims of paint salesmen. Car owners and car collectors can use this information too to make sure an approved paint system is used on their vehicle. Painters can choose the approved paint system and know that they'll be putting a very durable paint on their customers cars. This also drives home how important it is to durability to use a paint system with specific products matched to one another.

Furthermore, dealerships now have to have an excellent paint system in their body shops. Because body shops typically only have one system, that means that even non-warranty repairs will receive top quality paint. And mega-dealerships often have many brands of cars but one body shop; now they are more likely to use only a top-quality paint on all repairs.

Another profound effect of this testing is that the bar has been set for performance of refinish paints. Paint manufacturers know what level their products need to perform at and in exactly which parameters (such as chip resistance) car manufactured want improvement. Plus it helps competition because there is a level playing field regardless of the company's size or prominence.

Ford has now completed its testing and approval of refinish paint systems too. Ford tested the paints in-house against the same very tough specifications they use for their OEM (factory applied) paints.

What's next? Certification or approval of paint systems for flexible plastics, certification of painters, paint shops, and equipment and global paint specifications. Not long ago, the only standard automotive painting needed to meet was "Can I get the customer to accept it the way it looks now." The new era where products and procedures need to meet measurable standards will make the field more efficient, more reliable and more cost-effective for body shops and car owners alike.

materials such as primer, sealer, base coat, clear, etc. attached to the warranty papers for the warranty to be valid. It is important for the car owner to read the fine print of the warranty and make certain that all stipulations are met.

Covered Damages—Paint warranties cover finish failures such as loss of gloss, peeling, checking, cracking, crazing, color fading, color chalking, or moisture blistering. If these conditions occur during the warranty period, the car must be inspected, typically by the body shop and by a paint company representative. If the paint failure is covered, the paint company will reimburse the body shop for the materials and labor needed to repair the problem.

The paint warranties do not cover rusting or other problems caused by the underlying body panel. Neither do they cover chips, scratches, or abrasions. Check the warranty to see the wording on chemical spotting and acid rain damage. The warranty may also exclude flexible parts and will exclude any problems deemed to be caused by breakdown of underlying paint if the car wasn't stripped before repainting.

Cost—Do paint warranties cost the car owner more? The answer is "yes and no." Paints generally covered by warranty are the best (most expensive) paints. However, even if that type of paint was already chosen to be used, some body shops will charge extra if an owner wants a warranty. Although the paint manufacturer doesn't charge the shop for each warranty, the shop has had the expenses of training and certification. And in fairness to the shop, there is additional paperwork and there can be additional paint preparation work needed to satisfy the stipulations of the warranty. Therefore, some shops will charge up to a few hundred dollars extra for the warranty.

CHOOSING A BODY SHOP

Referrals are one of the best means of finding a body shop and a painter who does high quality work. Asking friends and co-workers about their experiences with local shops will at least inform you of a few places not to go. Your insurance agent might also be able to suggest a few shops with a good reputation.

Car clubs can provide a wealth of information on local body and repair shops. Some marques, such as Corvette, have hundreds of local car clubs, making it likely that one is in your region. Ask around for the names of the contact people or officers of the local car clubs or look for directories of clubs in the back of major car magazines.

Car enthusiasts and street rodders are another visible (and vocal) source of information on paint and

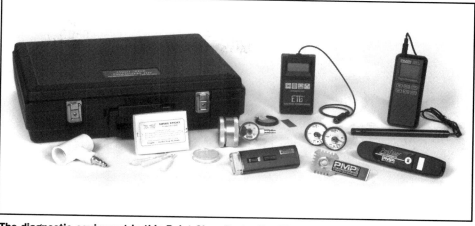

The diagnostic equipment in this Paint Shop Evaluation Kit was unknown to most painters five years ago, but these kits are now carried by the representatives and jobbers of most of the major paint manufacturers today. The tools are used to help troubleshoot problems in shops so that paint can be applied efficiently. Lifetime paint warranties are part of the reason for this; manufacturers want their paint to be applied properly to minimize problems and costly claims. The tools are: QAT air test system, wet film paint gauge, non-contact infrared thermometer, ETG electronic paint thickness gauge, digital hygrometer/thermometer and manifold to test humidity in air lines, smoke sticks and magnetic panel thermometers. It's available from Pro Motorcar Products, 813/726-9225

bodywork. Car shows are a good place to start and they are easy to find. At these shows, car owners are usually quite accessible. Don't hesitate to ask a car owner for the name of the person who painted his or her car. He or she will be flattered that you like the paint work and will be glad to fill you in on the experiences with that painter—good or bad.

Another source of referrals is the new car dealership. Sometimes the body shop at the dealership doesn't do certain types of paint work (tri-coats for example) but will give you the name of the shops they use.

Inspecting a Body Shop

Meet the shop owner or manager and then inspect the repair facility before entrusting your car to a body shop. Although remarkably good paint jobs can come out of dingy work areas and poor workmanship can just as easily take place in a clean environment, these are generally the exceptions. Look around to see if the shop is clean, organized, and well lit.

Also look at the tools and equipment to see if they appear to be in good condition. If the personnel don't take good care of their tools, they aren't likely to take good care of your car. Certificates of training should be displayed in the waiting room or elsewhere. Look for them; and if you don't see them, ask the shop owner or manager if the employees have completed such training.

Estimates

Generally, a body shop can't give an accurate estimate without first inspecting the car and its paint finish. The estimator will have to assess the condition of the underlying paint, the extent of dechroming and masking required, the amount of surface preparation that will have to be done, and whether or not any sheet metal will have to be repaired.

Comparing the prices quoted by different body shops can be difficult. The prices of the paints alone vary widely from the inexpensive synthetic enamels to the pricey two-part

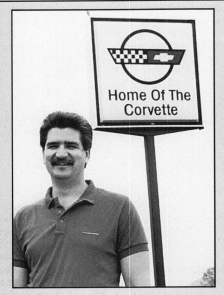

Home Of The
Corvette

TIPS ON SELECTING A GOOD PAINT SHOP
by Brian Dotterer, Senior Project Engineer, GM's Center for Paint Expertise

If you're reading this book, you've already begun to prepare yourself for choosing a good body shop, painter, or even the type of paint work you want done. It's valuable to read and learn what should be done in a good paint job. If you care about your car's paint, you should get educated about what to look for. Check around when it's time to paint your car. Prices can vary widely, and sometimes the price variations are due to the shop doing more preparation, disassembly, or finish work, or it is using more expensive materials. For example, the amount of disassembly of items such as molding, antenna masts, door handles, mirrors, etc. will affect the quality, appearance, and even the car's resale value. Find out exactly what the shop will do for the money it is charging.

If you are restoring a car, one of the first decisions to make is to define your objective. A flawless paint job is beautiful to look at but other considerations, such as judging in certain types of car shows, may favor a paint job which is representative of the production paint jobs of the time. You may have to take extra pains to match the original textures and overspray patterns, among other things. Some restorers favor lacquer paints for originality, although most would agree that urethanes are more durable. It might help to know that today you can also find urethane system base coat paints which are lacquer based.

Once you've decided what type of work you want done and you have narrowed the field to a few shops, visit and inspect them. See if they have a urethane paint system that enables them to mix the colors at the shop. If a color is a little off, a painter is much more likely to improve the match if it can be done there and not sent back to a paint supplier. See if the paint booth is clean, well lit, and up to date. A down-draft booth is certainly a plus, particularly when painting urethane clear coats. If the paint shop is separate from where the heavy work takes place, all the better because there's less chance of contamination during painting.

It's also good to see a paint prep area which has a dedicated rack or lift to help give proper attention to the lower panels on a car. Also, the general appearance tells a lot about the efficiency of the shop and how much the employees care about their work. Is it clean? Are there piles of rubbish or old parts lying about? If they don't care about keeping their work area looking nice, they may not care how your car will look.

That is one indication of the most important factor: the people who work on your car. If possible, talk to the painters. See if they are the kind of persons who take pride in their work.

See what kind of training they have had lately. Automotive paint has changed rapidly and radically. If they have made the effort to keep current in their industry, their training certificates usually will be prominently displayed in the shop or in the office. Don't hesitate to ask questions. It's your money—you have a right to know.

urethanes. If body panels have to be replaced, the shop's decision on whether to use new original equipment parts, new reproduction parts, or used parts can significantly affect the bill. The types of parts and paints can, however, be pinned down more easily than other factors which can greatly affect the cost of a paint job.

For example, a "strip and paint" on a Corvette at Final Finish in Branford, Connecticut starts at $4500. At many other shops across the nation, the price charged for a strip and paint on a Corvette can be $1500 or less, even when using the same types of paint. However, Final Finish doesn't just strip the old paint off and put new paint on, they do a complete cosmetic restoration to the external body panels which includes reworking and flattening all surfaces, refitting all panels, installing all new weather-strips, realigning doors, and perfecting gaps.

Because there is such a wide variety in the amount of work performed with a "strip and paint," a restoration, or even a simple repainting, it is wise to find out exactly what work is to be performed at what price. If the painter says the car will be dechromed before painting, ask which parts will be removed and which ones won't. Even when a painter says your car will be "completely dechromed," it doesn't always mean to him what you think that phrase implies. It often means removal of all chrome and trim pieces that aren't extremely difficult to remove but not those which are difficult to remove.

One of the most important things to do is to get a written agreement on how much the work will cost you, i.e., the formal estimate. And, make sure the body shop will call you beforehand for authorization if any extra work is found which will increase the price of the repair. Also, it is always a good idea to get a planned completion date in writing.

Replacement Parts—If body parts need to be replaced, you may want to specify which types are acceptable to you. Some body shops will bang out and reuse the damaged parts even when the insurance company is paying for new parts. They may even buy the new parts, show the receipts to the insurance company or customer, and later send the parts back for credit.

The type of new parts used to replace damaged panels is now a subject of controversy. There has been much discussion about the inferior quality of body parts made by some aftermarket and overseas manufacturers. Check to see if your car's rust-through warranty is still valid if non-factory made parts are used. Also, make sure you aren't being charged for new, original factory panels if overseas replacements are being used. If you haven't seen the part being installed before it is

repaired and repainted, use a thickness gauge or body gauge to make sure new parts were really used. Information on how inspect paint and body panels with those new instruments is in the previous chapter.

Inspecting the New Paint

Rule number one is: Don't take the car from the shop or pay for the repairs until you've thoroughly inspected the work. It is usually faster and easier to get problems fixed before the job is paid for than afterwards. If the repairs have been delayed and you really need the car, you are unfairly put under pressure to accept it as is. Be aware of this situation and try to avoid it. Also, make sure the person who dropped you off doesn't leave until you had a chance to inspect the work.

The second rule goes along with the first: Don't pick up the car at night or when it is left out in the parking lot in the rain (or snow). The car should be thoroughly cleaned so that you can properly inspect the bodywork and the paint. If a spot repair has been done, the car should be examined outside to see how well the colors match. Check to make sure that all trim and emblems have been reattached correctly and that they are clean and free of overspray. Look for overspray where it shouldn't be, such as in the engine compartment as well as in the interior. Take your time and don't let anyone rush you. The repairs or repainting undoubtedly cost a sizable amount of money, and you have every right to ensure that you received the quality that you paid for. It is best to have your copy of the written estimate listing all work to be done to refer to. Any disagreement about the quality of workmanship should be settled before

Body shops today are having to make sizable changes in areas beyond paint procedures and materials. Manufacturers are helping the shops to become more efficient in the design of their business. DeVilbiss has produced a book to assist in laying out and equipping a modern body shop. Courtesy ITW DeVilbiss.

you complete payment or take your vehicle.

TRADE PUBLICATIONS AND SHOWS

The courses offered by the major paint manufactures and I-CAR provide excellent training and education in specific areas. In addition to these, there are a number of resources that can provide continuing education in the field of automotive painting for not only body shop personnel but for automotive writers, car enthusiasts, and others interested in auto refinishing.

Publications

Two of the most widely distributed national trade publications are *Auto Body Repair News*, published by the Chilton Company, and *BodyShop Business* by Babcox Publications. These magazines are mailed free to body shops, warehouses, and jobbers (stores) in the paint and body field.

These publications provide tech-

Chilton's Auto Body Repair News (ABRN) is one of two major auto body shop trade magazines and contains a wealth of industry information and updates. Again, it's a good sign to see such trade magazines in a body shop; they do get read by the employees.

nical articles each month on subjects ranging from paint application and shop problems to business trends and efficient shop operation. They also furnish information on the latest developments in paint and equipment and show releases of new products in the field.

A number of publications, such as *Fuel Line* and *Midwest Automotive & Autobody News,* cover news of interest to both auto body and mechanical repair shops. Others publications such as the Collision Parts Journal are more specific and concentrate on news of interest to the Automotive Body Parts Association. Another useful source of information is available at stores that sell auto body supplies. Many have free catalogs on their counters which show new products and tools in the field.

Industrial Publications—For those people who want to get even deeper into the field of paints and coating, there are several industrial coatings

trade publications, such as Paint and Powder by the Hitchcock Publishing company and Products Finishing by Gardner Publications, Inc. These magazines also cover plating, anodizing, and powder coating technologies. Automotive applications are only part of the subject area they address, but they are an excellent window on new technologies that may make their way into automotive use in the near future.

Trade Shows

The single largest trade show for the automotive paint and body equipment (PBE) market is the NACE International Autobody Congress and Exposition. It goes beyond a typical trade show in two ways. First, it is an organized gathering for PBE business people to discuss the industry and its future. Secondly, unlike many trade shows, NACE is not just for the manufacturers and the distributors. The end users (the body shop painters and owners) are a welcomed and integral part of the trade show.

The NACE show, held once a year, is a tremendous educational opportunity for anyone in the trade. Painters can go from booth to booth to see the latest HVLP or other spray equipment from all the major manufacturers. They can learn of the advantages of each product, and they can directly question the manufacturers. Not only can they do hands-on inspection of every type of spray equipment in a single location, some manufacturers set up demonstrations so painters can actually try the equipment.

Under one roof at NACE, a body shop owner can walk around and examine 30 different types of frame or body straightening equipment. There is no other place I know of where a

Body Shop Business is the other major trade publication. In addition to serving the needs of the body shop, these trade magazines are of great value to anyone interested in automotive painting and, of course, to painters just learning the trade.

buyer has such a convenient opportunity to examine and compare this kind of large, expensive equipment.

All the major paint manufacturers are represented; in fact, some of their booths look like small cities. It's a great place to find out what each paint manufacturer offers in technical support, promotional programs, new products, etc. The same opportunity for comparison exists for the other staples of the paint and body trade such as sandpaper, tape, filters, and paint booths.

Regional Shows—Many areas of the country have large regional trade shows for the paint and body industry. In some regions, a PBE warehouse or jobber is big enough to hold a large show of its own and get major manufacturers to display their products and give demonstrations. One advantage of this type of show is that you can buy the product then and there. To find out what shows are scheduled in your region, ask the people at your local paint and body supply store.

Industrial Paint Shows—Shows such as the NSFT are more tailored for industrial uses of coatings and platings than for automotive paint refinishers. However, like the industrial trade publications, they do provide the opportunity to get deeper into the field of coatings. Along with the major paint manufacturers, you'll find the companies that supply the raw ingredients of paint, such as the resins and pigments.

Manufacturer Demos—Many manufacturers are pleased to send their technical people out to demonstrate their equipment and products. These smaller, private demonstrations are often set up by an auto body supply store or warehouse, so check with them. This is a good hands-on opportunity to try out particular brands of products or equipment such as spray guns. If you can get a half-dozen or more people together, a local store might be able to arrange this type of demonstration.

A few manufacturers consider this on-going training important enough to have mobile training centers which tour the country. Meguiar's mobile training centers are large, air conditioned trailers set up for classroom present-ations and demonstrations of their professional line of finish care products.

Body Shop Design

Another resource is now available to body shop owners to help them improve shop efficiency. Many of the major paint manufacturers have created a special service to aid body

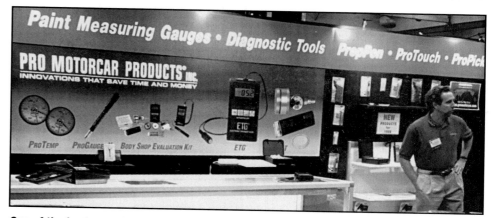

One of the best ways to keep up on the changes in the industry is to attend the yearly NACE trade show. In one location, you can see the very latest in paint, tools, and heavy equipment. Under one roof at NACE, a person can examine and compare body and frame straightening machines from thirty top manufactures. If your painter or body shop owner attends the NACE show, it's a good sign that he is interested in keeping up to date in his profession.

shops in the design and layout of their businesses. The service can help shop owners, whether they are building a new shop from the ground up or are planning a renovation or enlargement of their present facilities.

Although these services are not always free, they can provide a considerable savings in initial construction costs and in future efficiency and profit. Most body shop owners only plan a shop once or twice in their lives, so it makes sense to consult people who specialize in just this part of the business in order to take advantage of lessons other businesses around the country have learned.

Management & Marketing

In the past, most body shops were owned by someone who got into the field with little formal education, worked their way up and eventually had their own small to medium size shop. They liked working on cars and many were good painters or bodymen.

However, they weren't particularly interested or proficient at management or marketing.

The paint and body industry, like so many others have before, is undergoing consolidation and restructuring. The high cost of facilities, equipment, and procedures required by environmental regulations is part of the reason. Large shops run by professional managers who track closing ratios on estimates and CSI indexes are taking over.

Paint manufacturers are aware of how competitive this business is. Recently, their course offerings have grown to include business management and marketing. If the sales of a shop that uses their paint doubles, then their sales doubles. Instead of concentrating on getting shops to switch from another company's paint to theirs (which is becoming harder to do), several paint manufacturers are focusing on helping their existing customers grow through business and sales training.

AUTOMOTIVE PAINT SUPPLIERS

Akzo Nobel Coatings, Inc.
Product Line: Sikkens, Lesonal
Norcross, GA 30092
5555 Spalding Drive
770-662-8464
www.sikkensna.com

American Standox
Product Line: Standox, Standohyd
47802 W. Anchor Court
Plymouth, MI 48170
800-551-9296
www.standox.com

BASF - Automotive Refinishing
Product Lines: Glasurit, RM
(Diamont, Limco)
26701 Telegraph Rd
Southfield, MI 48034
800-825-3000
www.basf.com

DuPont
Product Lines: ChromaSystem,
ChromaPremier, Centari,
Lucite, Imron
PO Box 80021
Wilmington, DE 19880-0021
www.dupont.com

House of Kolor
(div of Valspar)
Product Line: Shimriní, Kosmic
Kolor, Kameleon Kolor
210 Crosby St
Picayune, MS 39466
601-729-1044 (techincal)
www.houseofkolor.com

ICI Autocolor
Product Line: Autocolor
801 Canterbury Road
Westlake, OH 44145
800-647-6050
www.ici.com

Napa/Martin-Senour Paints
Product Line: Tec/SYSTEM
101 Prospect Avve
Cleveland, OH 44115
216-566-1837

PPG Industries, Inc.
Product Line: Deltron, Global, Omni
19699 Progress Dr.
Strongsville, OH 44136
440-572-2800
www.ppg.com

Sherwin-Williams
Automotive Finishes
Product Line: Ultra System
101 Prospect Ave
Cleveland, OH 44115
216-566-3727
www.sherwin-williams.com

Spies Hecker
Product Line: Permacron
Permasolid, Permahyd
55 Sea Lane
Farmingdale, NY 1735
516-777-7100
www.spieshecker.com

Valspar Refinish
Product Line: ColorBase, Omega
2K, SupaFil
210 Crosby St
Picayune, MS 39466
601-798-4731
www.valsparrefinish.com

Appendix

Painting Problems

On the following pages — in alphabetical order — you will find a treatment of the most common painting problems. This format details the condition of the problem, its causes and prevention, and the best solution.

Bleeding

Condition:
Original finish discoloring — or color seeping through — the new topcoat color.

Causes:
1. Contamination — usually in the form of soluble dyes or pigments on the older finish before it was repainted. (This is especially true with older shades of red.)

Prevention:
1. Thoroughly clean areas to be painted before sanding — especially when applying lighter colors over darker colors. (Avoid using lighter colors over older shades of red without sealing first.)

Solution:
Apply two medium coats of 2184 S Bleeder-seal in accordance with label instructions. Then reapply color coat.

Blistering

Condition:
Bubbles or pimples appearing in the topcoat film, often months after application.

Causes:
1. Improper surface cleaning or preparation. Tiny specks of dirt left on the surface can act as a sponge and hold moisture. When the finish is exposed to the sun (or abrupt changes in atmospheric pressure), moisture expands and builds up pressure. If the pressure is great enough, blisters form.

2. Wrong thinner, reducer or BASEMAKER. Use of a fast-dry thinner or reducer, especially when the material is sprayed too dry or at an excessive pressure. Air or moisture can be trapped in the film.

3. Excessive film thickness. Insufficient drying time between coats or too heavy application of the undercoats may trap solvents which escape later and blister the color coat.

4. Contamination of compressed air lines. Oil, water or dirt in lines.

Prevention:
1. Thoroughly clean areas to be painted before sanding. Be sure surface is completely dry before applying either undercoats or topcoats. Don't touch a cleaned area as the oils in your hands will contaminate the surface.

2. Select the thinner, reducer or BASEMAKER most suitable for existing shop conditions.

3. Allow proper drying time for undercoats and topcoats. Be sure to let each coat flash before applying the next.

4. Drain and clean air pressure regulator *daily* to remove trapped moisture and dirt. Air compressor tank should also be drained daily.

Solution:
If damage is extensive and severe, paint must be removed down to undercoat or metal, depending on depth of blisters. Then refinish. In less severe cases, blisters may be sanded out, resurfaced and retopcoated.

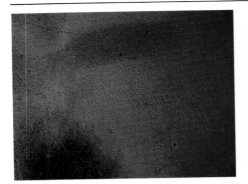

Blushing

Condition:
A milky white haze that appears on lacquer films.

Causes:
1. In hot humid weather, moisture droplets become trapped in the wet paint film. Air currents from the spray gun and the evaporation of the thinner tend to make the surface being sprayed lower in temperature than the surrounding atmosphere. This causes moisture in the air to condense on the wet paint film.
2. Excessive air pressure.
3. Too fast a thinner.

Prevention:
1. In hot humid weather try to schedule painting early in the morning when temperature and humidity conditions are more suitable, use 3602 S acrylic lacquer thinner. In very hot or humid conditions, use 3696 S.
2. Use proper gun adjustments and techniques.
3. Select the thinner that is suitable for existing shop conditions.

Solution:
Add 3979 S retarder to the thinned color and apply additional coats.

Chalking

Condition:
Formation on the finish caused by pigment powder no longer held by the binder, which makes the finish look dull.

Causes (other than normal exposure):
1. Wrong thinner or reducer, which can harm topcoat durability.
2. Materials not uniformly mixed.
3. Starved paint film.
4. Excessive mist coats when finishing a metallic color application.

Prevention:
1. Select the thinner or reducer that is best suited for existing shop conditions.
2. Stir all pigmented undercoats and topcoats thoroughly.
3. Meet or slightly exceed minimum film thicknesses.
4. Apply metallic color as evenly as possible so that misting is not required. When mist coats are necessary to even out flake, avoid using straight reducer.

Solution:
Remove surface in affected area by sanding. Then clean and refinish.

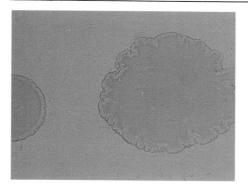

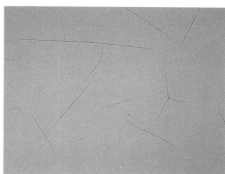

Chemical Staining

Condition:
Spotty discoloration of the surface.

Causes:
1. Atmospheric contamination falling on the finish in the presence of moisture or rain — usually due to adjacent industrial activity.

Prevention:
1. Avoid contaminated atmosphere, or wash surface with detergent and water as soon as possible after exposure.

2. Apply clear coat.

Solution:
After washing with detergent and water, rub affected area with rubbing compound and polish. In severe cases, sand to prime and refinish.

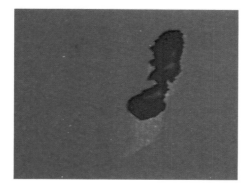

Chipping

Condition:
Small chips of a finish losing adhesion to the substrate — usually caused by impact of stones or hard objects. While the refinisher has no control over local road conditions — and thus cannot prevent such occurrences — he can take steps to minimize their effect if he knows beforehand that these conditions will exist.

Cracking
(Line Checking, Micro-Checking)

Conditions:
A series of deep cracks resembling mud cracks in a dry pond. Often in the form of three-legged stars and in no definite pattern, they are usually through the color coat and sometimes the undercoat as well.

Causes:
1. Excessive film thickness. (Excessively thick topcoats magnify normal stresses and strains which can result in cracking even under normal conditions.)

2. Materials not uniformly mixed.

3. Insufficient flash time.

4. Incorrect use of additive.

Prevention:
1. Don't pile on topcoats. Allow sufficient flash and dry time between coats. Do not dry by gun fanning.

2. Stir all pigmented undercoats and top-coats thoroughly. Strain and — where necessary — add Fish Eye Eliminator to topcoats.

3. Same as 1.

4. Read and carefully follow label instructions. (Additives not specifically designed for a color coat may weaken the final paint film and make it more sensitive to cracking.)

Solution:
The affected areas must be sanded to a smooth finish or in extreme cases removed down to the bare metal and refinished.

(The causes, prevention and solution for "Cracking," "Line Checking" and "Micro-Checking" are closely allied. For that reason, you will find information on the causes, prevention and solution for "Line Checking" and "Micro-Checking."

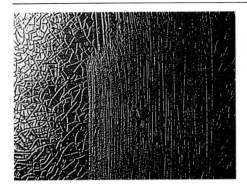

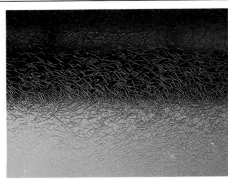

(Line Checking)

Condition:
Similar to cracking, except that the lines or cracks are more parallel and range from very short up to about 18 inches.

Causes:
1. Excessive film thickness.

2. Improper surface preparation. (Often times the application of a new finish over an old film which had cracked and was not completely removed.)

Prevention:
1. Don't pile on topcoats. Allow sufficient flash and dry time. Do not dry by gun fanning.

2. Thoroughly clean areas to be painted before sanding. Be sure surface is completely dry before applying undercoats or topcoats.

Solution:
Remove color coat down to primer and apply new color coat.

(Micro-Checking)

Condition:
Appears as severe dulling of the film, but when examined with a magnifying glass, it contains many small cracks that do not touch. Micro-checking is the beginning of film breakdown, and may be an indication that film failures such as cracking or crazing will develop.

Solution:
Sand off the color coat to remove the cracks, then recoat as required.

Crazing

Condition:
Fine splits or small cracks — often called "crowsfeet" — that completely checker an area in an irregular manner.

Causes:
1. Shop too cold. (Surface tension of original material is under stress and literally shatters under the softening action of the solvents being applied.)

Prevention:
1. Select the thinner, reducer or BASEMAKER that is suitable for existing shop conditions. Schedule painting to avoid temperature and humidity extremes in shop or between temperature of shop and the job. (Bring vehicle to room temperature before refinishing.)

Solution:
There are two ways to overcome crazing: (1) continue to apply wet coats of topcoat to melt the crazing and flow pattern together (using the wettest possible solvent shop conditions will allow); and (2) use a fast-flashing thinner such as 3613 S, which will allow a bridging of subsequent topcoats over the crazing area. For CRONAR applications, use 9355 S Non-Penetrating BASEMAKER. (This is one case where bridging is a *cure* and not a cause for trouble.)

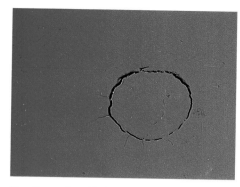

Featheredge Splitting

Condition:

Appears as stretch marks (or cracking) along the featheredge. Occurs during or shortly after the topcoat is applied over lacquer primer-surfacer.

Causes:

1. "Piling on" the undercoat in heavy and wet coats. (Solvent is trapped in undercoat layers which have not had sufficient time to set up.)

2. Material not uniformly mixed. (Because of the high pigment content of primer-surfacers, it is possible for settling to occur after it has been thinned. Delayed use of this material without restirring results in applying a film with loosely held pigment containing voids and crevices throughout, causing the film to act like a sponge.)

3. Wrong thinner.

4. Improper surface cleaning or preparation. (When not properly cleaned, primer-surfacer coats may crawl or draw away from the edge because of poor wetting and adhesion.)

5. Improper drying. (Fanning with a spray gun after the primer-surfacer is applied will result in drying the surface before solvent or air from the lower layers is released.)

6. Excessive use (and film build) of putty.

Prevention:

1. Apply properly reduced primer-surfacer in thin to medium coats (150% reduction preferably with 3661 S) with enough time between coats to allow solvents and air to escape.

2. Stir all pigmented undercoats and topcoats thoroughly. Select thinner that is suitable for existing shop conditions. (3661 S thinner in primer-surfacer greatly minimizes this possibility.)

3. Select only thinners that are recommended for existing shop conditions.

4. Thoroughly clean areas to be painted before sanding.

5. Apply primer-surfacer in thin to medium coats with enough time between coats to allow solvents and air to escape.

6. Lacquer putty should be limited to filling minor imperfections. Putty applied too heavily (or too thick) will eventually shrink causing featheredge splitting.

Solution:

Remove finish from the affected areas and refinish.

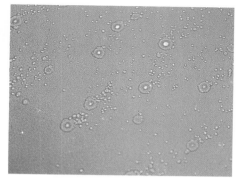

Fish Eyes

Condition:

Small, crater-like openings in the finish after it has been applied.

Causes:

1. Improper surface cleaning or preparation. (Many waxes and polishes contain silicone, *the most common cause of fish eyes.* Silicones adhere firmly to the paint film and require extra effort for their removal. Even small quantities in sanding dust, rags, or from cars being polished nearby can cause this failure.)

2. Effects of the old finish or previous repair. (Old finish or previous repair may contain excessive amounts of silicone from additives used during their application. Usually solvent wiping will not remove embedded silicone.)

3. Contamination of air lines.

Prevention:

1. Precautions should be taken to remove all traces of silicone by thoroughly cleaning with 3919 S PREPSOL or 3929 S PREP-SOL II. (The use of Fish Eye Eliminator is in no way a replacement for good surface preparation.)

2. Add Fish Eye Eliminator, 259 S or 9259 S CRONAR Fish Eye Eliminator.

3. Drain and clean air pressure regulator daily to remove trapped moisture and dirt. Air compressor tank should also be drained daily.

Solution:

After affected coat has set up, apply another double coat of color containing the recommended amount of Fish Eye Eliminator, 259 S or 9259 S CRONAR Fish Eye Eliminator. In severe cases, affected areas should be sanded down and refinished.

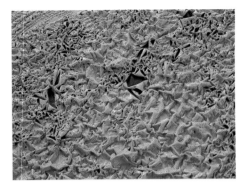

Lifting

Condition:
Surface distortion or shriveling, while the topcoat is being applied or while drying.

Causes:
1. Use of incompatible materials. (Solvents in new topcoat attack old surface which results in a distorted or wrinkled effect.)

2. Insufficient flash time. (Lifting will occur when the paint film is an alkyd enamel and is only partially cured. The solvents from the coat being applied cause localized swelling or partial dissolving which later distorts final surface.)

3. Improper dry. (When synthetic enamel-type undercoats are not thoroughly dry, topcoating with lacquer can result in lifting.)

4. Effect of old finish or previous repair. (Lacquer applied over a fresh air-dry enamel finish will cause lifting.)

5. Improper surface cleaning or preparation. (Use of an enamel-type primer or sealer over an original lacquer finish which is to be topcoated with a lacquer will result in lifting due to a sandwich effect.)

6. Wrong thinner, reducer or BASEMAKER. (The use of lacquer thinners in enamel increases the amount of substrate swelling and distortion which can lead to lifting, particularly when two-toning or recoating.)

Prevention:
1. Avoid incompatible materials such as a thinner with enamel products, or incompatible sealers and primers.

2. Don't pile on topcoats. Allow sufficient flash and dry time. Final topcoat should be applied when the previous coat is still soluble or after it has completely dried and is impervious to topcoat solvents.

3. Same as #1 and #2.

4. Same as #1.

5. Same as #1.

6. Select the thinner, reducer or BASEMAKER that is correct for the finish applied and suitable for existing shop conditions.

Solution:
Remove finish from affected areas and refinish.

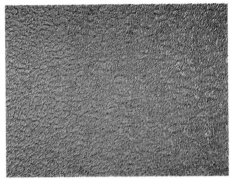

Mottling

Condition:
Occurs only in metallics when the flakes float together to form spotty or striped appearance.

Causes:
1. Wrong thinner, reducer or BASEMAKER.

2. Materials not uniformly mixed.

3. Spraying too wet.

4. Holding spray gun too close to work.

5. Uneven spray pattern.

6. Low shop temperature.

Prevention:
1. Select the thinner, reducer or BASEMAKER that is suitable for existing shop conditions *and mix properly.* (In cold, damp weather use a faster-dry solvent.)

2. Stir all pigmented topcoats — especially metallics — thoroughly.

3. Use proper gun adjustments, techniques, and air pressure.

4. Same as 3.

5. Keep your spray gun clean (especially the needle fluid tip and air cap) and in good working condition.

6. Same as 1.

Solution:
Allow color coat to set up and apply a drier double coat or two single coats, depending upon which topcoat you are applying.

Orange Peel

Condition:

Uneven surface formation — much like that of the skin of an orange — which results from poor coalescence of atomized paint droplets. Paint droplets dry out before they can flow out and level smoothly together.

Causes:

1. Improper gun adjustment and techniques. (Too little air pressure, wide fan patterns or spraying at excessive gun distances causes droplets to become too dry during their travel time to the work surface and they remain as formed by gun nozzle.)

2. Extreme shop temperature. (When air temperature is too high, droplets lose more solvent and dry out before they can flow and level properly.)

3. Improper dry. (Gun fanning before paint droplets have a chance to flow together will cause orange peel.)

4. Improper flash or recoat time between coats. (If first coats of enamel are allowed to become too dry, solvent in the paint droplets of following coats will be absorbed into the first coat before proper flow is achieved.)

5. Wrong thinner, reducer or BASEMAKER. (Under-diluted paint or paint thinner with fast evaporating solvents causes the atomized droplets to become too dry before reaching the surface.)

6. Too little thinner, reducer or BASEMAKER.

7. Materials not uniformly mixed. (Many finishes are formulated with components that aid coalescence. If these are not properly mixed, orange peel will result.)

Prevention:

1. Use proper gun adjustments, techniques, and air pressure.

2. Schedule painting to avoid temperature and humidity extremes. Select the thinner, reducer or BASEMAKER that is suitable for existing conditions. (The use of a slower evaporating solvent will overcome this.)

3. Allow sufficient flash and dry time. Do not dry by fanning.

4. Allow proper drying time for undercoats and topcoats. (Not too long or not too short.)

5. Select the thinner, reducer or BASEMAKER that is most suitable for existing shop conditions to provide good flow and leveling of the topcoat.

6. Reduce to recommended viscosity with proper thinner/reducer/BASEMAKER.

7. Stir all pigmented undercoats and topcoats thoroughly.

Solution:

Compounding may help — a mild polishing compound for enamel, rubbing compound for lacquer. In extreme cases, sand down to smooth surface and refinish, using a slower evaporating solvent at the correct air pressure.

Peeling

Condition:

Loss of adhesion between paint and substrate (topcoat to primer and/or old finish, or primer to metal).

Causes:

1. Improper cleaning or preparation. (Failure to remove sanding dust and other surface contaminants will keep the finish coat from coming into proper contact with the substrate.)

2. Improper metal treatment.

3. Materials not uniformly mixed.

4. Failure to use proper sealer.

Prevention:

Thoroughly clean areas to be painted. (It is always good shop practice to wash the sanding dust off the area to be refinished with 3812 S, 3919 S, 3929 S or 3939 S.)

2. Use correct metal conditioner and conversion coating.

3. Stir all pigmented undercoats and topcoats thoroughly.

4. In general, sealers are recommended to improve adhesion of topcoats. In certain cases (i.e., alkyd enamels over lacquer finishes) sealers are required to prevent peeling.

Solution:

Remove finish from an area slightly larger than the affected area and refinish.

 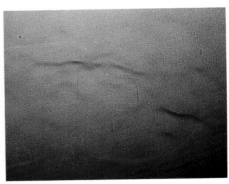

Pinholing

Condition:
Tiny holes or groups of holes in the finish, or in putty or body filler, usually the result of trapped solvents, air or moisture.

Causes:
1. Improper surface cleaning or preparation. (Moisture left on primer-surfacers will pass through the wet topcoat to cause pinholing.)
2. Contamination of air lines. (Moisture or oil in air lines will enter paint while being applied and cause pinholes when released during the drying stage.)
3. Wrong gun adjustment or technique. (If adjustments or techniques result in application which is too wet, or if the gun is held too close to the surface, pinholes will occur when the air or excessive solvent is released during dry.)
4. Wrong thinner, reducer or BASEMAKER. (The use of a solvent that is too fast for shop temperature tends to make the refinisher spray too close to the surface in order to get adequate flow. When the solvent is too slow, it is trapped by subsequent topcoats.)
5. Improper dry. (Fanning a newly applied finish can drive air into the surface or cause a skin dry — both of which result in pinholing when solvents retained in lower layers come to the surface.)

Prevention:
1. Thoroughly clean all areas to be painted. Be sure surface is completely dry before applying undercoats or topcoats.
2. Drain and clean air pressure regulator daily to remove trapped moisture and dirt. Air compressor tank should also be drained daily.
3. Use proper gun adjustments, techniques, and air pressure.
4. Select the thinner, reducer or BASEMAKER that is suitable for existing shop conditions.
5. Allow sufficient flash and dry time. Do not dry by fanning.

Solution:
Sand affected area down to smooth finish and refinish.

Runs or Sags

Condition:
Heavy application of sprayed material that fails to adhere uniformly to the surface.

Causes:
1. Too much thinner, reducer or BASEMAKER.
2. Wrong thinner, reducer or BASEMAKER.
3. Excessive film thickness without allowing proper dry time.
4. Low air pressure (causing lack of atomization), holding gun too close, or making too slow a gun pass.
5. Shop or surface too cold.

Prevention:
1. Read and carefully follow label instructions. Select the thinner, reducer or BASEMAKER that is suitable for existing shop conditions.
2. Select proper thinner/reducer/ BASEMAKER.
3. Don't pile on finishes. Allow sufficient flash and dry time in between coats.
4. Use proper gun adjustment, techniques, and air pressure.
5. Allow vehicle surface to warm up to at least room temperature before attempting to refinish. Try to maintain an appropriate shop temperature for paint areas.

Solution:
Wash off the affected area and let dry until you can sand affected area to a smooth surface and refinish.

Sandscratch Swelling

Condition:
Enlarged sandscratches caused by swelling action of topcoat solvents.

Causes:
1. Improper surface cleaning or preparation. (Use of too coarse sandpaper or omitting a sealer in panel repairs greatly exaggerates swelling caused by thinner penetration.)
2. Improper thinner, reducer or BASEMAKER (especially a slow-dry thinner, reducer or BASEMAKER when sealer has been omitted.)
3. Under-reduced or wrong thinner (too fast) used in primer-surfacer causes "bridging" of scratches.

Prevention:
1. Use appropriate grits of sanding materials for the topcoats you are using.
2. Seal to eliminate sandscratch swelling. Select thinner, reducer or BASEMAKER suitable for existing shop conditions.
3. Use proper thinner and reducer for primer-surfacer.

Solution:
Sand affected area down to smooth surface and apply appropriate sealer before refinishing.

Solvent Popping

Condition:
Blisters on the paint surface caused by trapped solvents in the topcoats or primer-surfacer — a situation which is further aggravated by force drying or uneven heating.

Causes:
1. Improper surface cleaning or preparation.
2. Wrong thinner, reducer or BASEMAKER. (Use of fast-dry thinner, reducer or BASEMAKER, especially when the material is sprayed too dry or at excessive pressure, can cause solvent popping by trapping air in the film.)
3. Excessive film thickness. (Insufficient drying time between coats and too heavy application of the undercoats may trap solvents causing popping of the color coat as they later escape.)

Prevention:
1. Thoroughly clean areas to be painted.
2. Select the thinner, reducer or BASEMAKER suitable for existing shop conditions.
3. Don't pile on undercoats or topcoats. Allow sufficient flash and dry time. Allow proper drying time for undercoats and topcoats. Allow each coat of primer-surfacer to flash naturally — do not fan.

Solution:
If damage is extensive and severe, paint must be removed down to undercoat or metal, depending on depth of blisters; then refinish. In less severe cases, sand out, resurface and retopcoat.

Water Spotting

Condition:
General dulling of gloss in spots or masses of spots.

Causes:
1. Water evaporating on finish before it is thoroughly dry.
2. Washing finish in bright sunlight.

Prevention
1. Do not apply water to fresh paint job and try to keep newly-finished car out of rain. Allow sufficient dry time before delivering car to customer.
2. Wash car in shade and wipe completely dry.

Solution:
Compound or polish with rubbing or polishing compound. In severe cases, sand affected areas and refinish.

Wet Spots

Condition:
Discoloration and/or the slow drying of various areas.

Causes:
1. Improper cleaning and preparation.
2. Improper drying of excessive undercoat film build.
3. Sanding with contaminated solvent.

Prevention:
1. Thoroughly clean all areas to be painted.
2. Allow proper drying time for undercoats.
3. Wet sand with clean water.

Solution:
Wash or sand affected areas thoroughly and refinish.

Wrinkling

Condition:
Surface distortions (or shriveling) that occurs while enamel topcoat is being applied (or later during the drying stage).

Causes:
1. Improper dry. (When a freshly applied topcoat is baked or force dried too soon, softening of the undercoats can occur. This increases topcoat solvent penetration and swelling. In addition, baking or force drying causes surface layers to dry too soon. The combination of these forces causes wrinkling.)
2. "Piling on" heavy or wet coats. (When enamel coats are too thick, the lower wet coats are not able to release their solvents and set-up at the same rate as the surface layer which results in wrinkling.)
3. Improper reducer or BASEMAKER or incompatible materials. (A fast-dry reducer or BASEMAKER or the use of a lacquer thinner in enamel can cause wrinkling.)
4. Improper or rapid change in shop temperature. (Drafts of warm air cause enamel surfaces to set up and shrink before sublayers have released their solvents, which results in localized skinning in uneven patterns.)

Prevention:
1. Allow proper drying time for undercoats and topcoats. (When force drying DULUX enamel, 7007 S Baking Additive is required to retard surface set up until lower layers harden. Lesser amounts can be used in hot weather. Read and carefully follow label instructions.)
2. Don't pile on topcoats. Allow sufficient flash and dry time.
3. Select proper reducer or BASEMAKER and avoid using incompatible materials such as a reducer with lacquer products, or thinner with enamel products.
4. Schedule painting to avoid temperature extremes or rapid changes.

Solution:
Remove wrinkled enamel and refinish.

Abrasion: Wearing away of paint film by some external force.

Accelerate: To speed up some process.

Acetone: A solvent, very fast evaporating, high solvency; little used except in certain special places. Has characteristic ether-like odor.

Acid: The opposite of base; gives a positive charge in solution; accepts electrons; donates protons; a chemical compound. Generally tastes sour. Neutralizes bases.

Acid Number: A measure of the acidity of a resin or a vehicle. Expressed as mgs. of KOH needed to neutralize one gram of solid resin or vehicle.

Activator: An additive needed to cure a two or multi-package enamel (See "Hardener").

Acrylate or Acrylic: A monomer or polymer polymers characterized by excellent durability; excellent gloss retention, crystal clarity, excellent color retention. Included should be acrylics, methacrylates, etc. Types: LUCITE. Acrylic widely used for painting automobiles.

Addition: A type of polymerization characterized by the formation of a polymer from one or more monomers without the loss of any atoms from the monomers or the formation of any by-product.

Additives: Chemical substances added to a finish in relatively small amounts to impart or improve desirable properties.

Adhesion: The property of "stick-to-it-ness." Difficult to measure. Most tests measure combination of adhesion, cohesion, toughness, hardness, etc.

Aging: To allow a material to stand for some time; growing old.

Agitator: A paint mixer of any type.

Air: Usually used under pressure as a propellent. Trapped air can cause bubbling, popping, foam, etc.

Air Dry: The ability of a coating to dry to its ultimate hardness under normal atmospheric conditions. Measurement of time required must state conditions of test, such as temperature and humidity.

Alcohol: A class of chemical compounds used as solvents, dilutents or co-solvents.

Aliphatic: A very low solvency hydrocarbon having an open chain structure. Typically these are saturated compounds.

Alkali: Opposite of an acid. Chemistry is like Iye or sodium bicarbonate.

Alkyd: The chemical combination of an alcohol, an acid and an oil. Widely useful vehicle for paint. Properties depend on ingredients. "DULUX," "GLYPTAL. A polymer, a polyester.

Alligatoring: A paint film failure resembling an alligator skin or a dried out river bed.

Alodizing: A chemical surface treatment for aluminum. "Alodine"

Aluminum: Metal useful as a substrate or pigment. When used as substrate requires paint to prevent corrosion.

Amberol: A resin or gum.

Amorphous: Having no definite crystalline structure.

Anatase: A form of titanium dioxide pigment—chalking type.

Aniline Point: A measure of solvency of a hydrocarbon solvent. Low numbers indicate high solvency and vice versa.

Anodizing: An electrolytic surface treatment for aluminum which builds up an aluminum oxide coating.

Antifouling: A paint which contains toxic substances to inhibit the growth of certain organisms on ship bottoms.

Banding: A single coat applied in a small spray pattern to frame in an area to be sprayed.

Base Coat: A color coat requiring a clear final coat.

Bleeding: Original finish discoloring—or color seeping through the new top coat color.

Blistering: Bubbles or pimples appearing in the topcoat film, often months after application.

Blushing: Hazing or whitening of a film caused by absorption and retention of moisture in a drying paint film.

Body: The consistency of a liquid.

Body Filler: A heavy-bodied plastic material which cures very hard and which is used to fill small dents in metal.

Bodying: An increase in viscosity or consistency.

Bridging: A characteristic of undercoat performance that occurs when a scratch or surface imperfection is not completely filled. Generally caused by under-reducing primers or using too fast a solvent.

Brittle: Lack of flexibility; usually combined with a lack of toughness.

Bronzing: The formation of a metallic appearing haze on a paint film.

Brush: A method of applying paint or an applicator for applying paint.

Brushing: The act of applying paint by a brush or the ability of a paint to be applied by a brush.

Bubble Test: A method of measuring the viscosity of clears or vehicles by observing the rate at which an air bubble rises in a tube of the liquid.

Build: The amount of paint film deposited (the depth or thickness of which is measured in mils).

Butadiene: A petroleum derivative capable of forming polymers such as artificial rubber.

Butanol: The chemical name for butyl alcohol. A solvent, cosolvent or diluent for paint. Medium evaporating.

Butyl Acetate: A solvent for paint. Commonly used in lacquers. Usually the base for comparing evaporation rates of organic liquids. Arbitrarily assigned the rate of 1 or 100.

Butyl Alcohol: See "Butanol."

Cadmium: A metal used to manufacture durable but expensive red and yellow pigments. The red is cadmium sulfide in conjunction with cadmium selenide. The yellow is basically cadmium sulfide.

Calcium: A metal component of driers and pigments.

Calcium Carbonate: An extender pigment. Whiting. Limestone is chiefly calcium carbonate.

Camphor: A volatile solid plasticizer for nitrocellulose.

Carbon Black: A black pigment manufactured by collecting the carbon resulting from incomplete combustion of natural gas.

Carbon Tetrachloride: A toxic solvent. Not to be recommended for use as a solvent or cleaner.

Casein: A component of emulsion paints.

Castor Oil: A natural vegetable oil used in the manufacture of alkyd resins and as a plasticizer.

Catalyst: Something which speeds up a chemical reaction without entering into the reaction.

Caulking: Sealing used in joints to prevent the passage of fluid (commonly moisture) or gas.

Cellulose: A natural polymer. From wood, cotton, etc. Composed of Repeating glucose units with three hydroxyl groups per glucose units available for reaction.

Cellulose Acetate: A chemically modified cellulose used as a binder in lacquers. Tough and horny Some rayon is cellulose acetate.

Cellulose Nitrate: Nitrocellulose, PX. A common ingredient for lacquers. A very useful binder. Tough, horny, easy to polish, durable when pigmented. Nitrocellulose lacquers widely used for automobiles prior to acrylics. "DUCO."

Centipoise: A unit of measurement of viscosity One centipoise is defined as the viscosity of water at 20.2 degrees C.

Chalking: A result of weathering of a paint film. Characterized by loose pigment particles on the surface of the paint. May be beneficial or harmful.

Check: A small crack.

Chemical Staining: Spotty discoloration of the topcoat caused by atmospheric conditions (usually near industrial activity).

Chinawood Oil: A common natural oil used in the manufacture of varnishes. Fast drying, good water resistance, poor color retention, excellent durability when properly compounded. Sometimes referred to as tung oil. Derived from the tung nut. The fastest drying vegetable oil.

Chipping: Small flakes of a finish losing adhesion from the substrate (usually caused by the impact of stones or hard objects).

Chlorinated Rubber: A chlorinated rubber used as a binder in lacquers. Very alkali resistant.

Chroma: The level of saturation or intensity and richness of a color Weak colors have less chroma, rich colors are more chromatic.

Chrome Oxide Green: A green pigment, good alkali resistance Very durable but little used. Commercially pure CR203.

Chrome Yellow: Widely used yellow pigment. Alkali-sensitive but good durability Darkens on exterior use. Lead chromate. Sometimes co precipitated with lead sulfate or lead oxide to give various shades.

Clean: A bright clear color. Also clean as after washing or cleaning.

Cleaner: Material used to clean a substrate.

Clear: A paint containing no pigment or only transparent pigments.

"Clorox": A bleach. An aqueous solution of NaOCl.

Clouding: The formation or presence of a haze in a liquid or in a film.

Coat (double): Two single coats, one followed by the other with little or no flash time.

Coat (single): A coat produced by two passes of a spray gun, one pass overlapping the other in half steps.

Coating: The act of applying paint or the actual film left on the substrate by a paint. A paint.

Cobalt: A metal component of some driers. Commonly cobalt naphthenate. Imparts rapid surface drying characteristics.

Coconut Oil: A natural vegetable oil used in the manufacture of alkyd resins. Non-drying. Good color retention and durability. Derived from the coconut.

Cohesion: The "stick togetherness" of a paint film.

Color: The visual appearance of a material. Red, blue, green, etc. Colors are seen differently by different people.

Color Retention: The permanence of a color under a set of conditions.

Compatibility: The ability of two or more materials to mix together and to form a homogeneous mixture.

Compounding: The action of using an abrasive material—either by hand or machine—to smooth and bring out the gloss of the applied lacquer topcoat.

Concrete: An alkaline substrate requiring special paint.

Concentration: The amount of any substance in a solution.

Condensation: A change from a vapor to a liquid on a cold surface (commonly moisture). A type of polymerization characterized by the reaction of two or more monomers to form a polymer plus some other product, usually water.

Consistency: The fluidity of a system.

Conversion Coating: Part of a metal pretreatment system that modifies a metal substrate for paint adhesion and corrosion protection.

Copolymer: A polymer made from two monomers.

Copper: A difficult metal substrate to paint. Used in the manufacture of pigments and driers.

Coverage: The amount of area a volume of paint will cover at a certain thickness.

Corrosion: Degradation of a metallic substrate by chemical agents in its environment.

Cosolvent: See "Latent Solvents."

Cracking: Formation of cracks in a paint film.

Cratering: Formation of holes in the paint film where paint fails to cover due to surface contamination.

Crawling: A wet film defect which results in the paint film pulling away from certain areas or not wetting certain areas, leaving those areas uncoated.

Crazing: A film failure which results in surface distortion or fine cracking.

Curing: The chemical reaction which takes place in the drying of paints that dry by chemical change.

Curtain Coating: A method of applying paint by passing a substrate through a curtain of paint.

Degradation: The gradual or rapid disintegration of a paint film.

Degreasing: Cleaning a substrate (usually metallic) by removing greases, oils and other surface contaminants.

Dehydration: The removal of water.

Dehydrated Castor Oil: A modified castor oil. A drying oil. Commonly used in the manufacture of alkyd resins. Good color retention.

Density: The weight of any material per unit of volume. Commonly grams per cubic centimeter.

Detearing: The removal of the bead or drips along the lower edge of a part coated by dripping.

Di: A prefix meaning two.

Diacetone Alcohol: A solvent for paint. Slow evaporating. Medium to high price.

Diamaceous Earth: A common extender pigment. Basically silica.

Dibutyl Phthalate: A plasticizer for lacquers. DBP.

Diluent: A liquid, not a true solvent, used to lower the cost of a paint thinner system. Generally cheap hydrocarbons.

Dirty: A color which is not bright and clean. A color which appears greyish. Also a condition requiring cleaning.

Dilution ratio: The amount of a diluent which can be added to any true solvent when the mixture is used to dissolve a certain weight of a polymer. Limits are determined by dissolving the polymer in the solvent and then adding diluent until gelation or kick-out occurs.

Dioctyl Phthalate: A commonly used plasticizer. DOP.

Dipentene: A very slow evaporating hydrocarbon used to control flow and skinning in certain types of finishes.

Dipping: To apply paint to an article by immersing the article in a container of the paint and then withdrawing the article and allowing the excess paint to drain from the part.

Dispersion: The act of distributing solid particles uniformly throughout a liquid. Commonly the dispersion of pigment in a vehicle. Does not imply the fracturing of individual particles, only their distribution. Also a mill base.

Distillation Range: The boiling range of a liquid.

Doctor Blade: An apparatus used to apply paint in a very uniform film thickness.

Drier: A catalyst added to a paint to speed up the cure or dry.

Dry: The change from a liquid to a solid which takes place after a paint is deposited on a surface. Included is the evaporation of the solvents and any chemical changes that occur. The result of drying is a useful film.

Drying Oil: A liquid (commonly a vegetable oil) that will change to a solid under normal atmospheric conditions when spread out in a thin film. Commonly triglycerides.

Dry-Spray: A condition in which the sprayed coat is short of liquid material in relation to the air pressure.

Durability: Length of life. Usually applies to a paint used for exterior purposes.

Electrostatic Spraying: The application of paint by high-voltage atomization. Different types: Ransburg, ionic, Ash Dee, etc.

Emulsion: A suspension of fine polymer particles in a liquid, usually water, dispersed particles may be binder, pigments or other ingredients. Emulsions can be made by certain polymerization techniques or by certain processes.

Enamel: Usually a pigmented gloss paint.

Epoxy: A class of resins characterized by good chemical resistance. These resins all contain oxirane oxygen.

Ester Gum: A hard brittle resin used in lacquers. The glycerol ester of resin.

Ester: A chemical compound. Technically the combination of an organic acid and an alcohol. Characterized by the suffix -ATE, i.e., acrylate, an acrylic ester.

Ethers: A class of compounds. Certain ones are used as solvents.

Ethyl Acetate: An ester solvent, fast evaporating. Commonly used in lacquers. Medium price.

Ethyl Alcohol: A solvent, cosolvent or diluent. Fast evaporating. Cheap. Commonly called alcohol. Whiskey is a mixture of ethyl alcohol, water and certain other ingredients.

Evaporation: The change from liquid to a gas. Commonly, when solvents leave a wet paint film, they do so by evaporation.

Evaporation Rate: The speed with which any liquid evaporates. Generally the rate is expressed as a number related to the evaporation rate of butyl acetate which is assigned the number 1 or 100.

Extender Pigment: An inert, usually colorless and semi-transparent pigment used in paints to fortify and lower the price of pigment systems.

Exterior: The outside. Usually refers to an area not protected from the weather or not in an enclosed area such as a building.

Fading: Loss of color.

Fan: The spray pattern of a spray gun.

Fanning: The use of pressurized air through a spray gun to speed up the drying time of a finish, which is not recommended!

Fatty Acid: An acid derived from a natural oil.

Ferrite Yellow: A commonly used, durable, yellowish-brown pigment. Very durable, lightfast and alkali-resistant. Hydrated iron oxide.

Featheredging: Tapering a paint edge from base metal to topcoat.

Featheredge Splitting: Stretch marks or cracks along the featheredge which occur during drying or shortly after the topcoat has been applied over primer-surfacer.

Filler: Commonly, a heavily pigmented paint used to fill imperfections or pores in a substrate.

Film: A very thin continuous sheet of material. Paint forms a film on the surface to which it is applied.

Fineness: The largest dimension size of the individual pigment particles in a dispersion, measured in mils.

Finish: A protective coating of paint; to apply a paint or paint system.

Fish Eyes: Small, crater-like openings in the finish after it has been applied.

Flag: The split-end of a bristle in a paint brush.

Flaking: A paint failure characterized by large pieces of the paint falling from the substrate.

Flash: The first stage of drying where some of the solvent evaporates which dulls the surface from an exceedingly high gloss to a normal gloss.

Flash Point: The temperature at which the vapor of a liquid will ignite when a spark is struck. There are various ways of measuring this.

Flat: Lacking in gloss.

Flexibility: The ability of a paint film to withstand dimensional changes.

Flocculation: Formation of clusters of pigment particles. Can cause changes in flow, gloss and setting.

Flooding: The phenomenon that occurs when color (pigments) accumulates at the surface of a wet paint film in a very nonuniform pattern.

Flop: The change in value, hue and chroma of a metallic car finish when it is viewed from different angles.

Flow: The leveling characteristics of a wet paint film. Also, the ability of a liquid to run evenly from a surface and to leave a smooth film behind.

Flow Coating: The application of paint to an article by pouring an excess of paint on the article and allowing the excess to drain from the work. Requires a paint with good flow.

Foots: Sludge formed in a container of a clear on aging.

Frosting: The formation of a surface haze or defects in a drying paint film.

Fungicide: An additive for paint used to prevent the growth of mold or fungus in the container or on a dry paint film.

Gas Proofing: The modification, usually by heat of tung oil to prevent the frosting or haze of the film formed by paints made from this oil.

Gelation: The development of insoluble polymers in resins, paints or other polymer solutions. Characterized by a jelly-like appearance; cannot be used. Normally irreversible. Cross-linking usually results in gelation of a resin solution.

Gilsonite: A grade of asphalt—occurs naturally.

Gloss: The ability of a surface to reflect light. Measured by determining the percentage of light reflected from a surface at certain angles.

Grinding: Term used to describe the dispersion of pigment in a vehicle. Does not imply reduction in particle size, only dispersion of the particles uniformly throughout the system. Methods of grinding vary. Examples—ball milling, roller milling, sand grinder, etc.

Gum: A solid resinous material which can be dissolved and which will form a film when the solution is spread on a surface and the solvent is allowed to evaporate. Usually a yellow or amber or clear solid. Also an ingredient of varnishes.

Hardener: An additive specifically designed to promote a faster cure of an enamel finish. (See "Activator").

Hardness: That quality of a dry paint film which gives the film resistance to surface damage or deformation. Hard to measure accurately or to separate from such other properties as adhesion, toughness, mar resistance, etc.

Haze: The development of a cloud in a film or in a clear liquid.

Hiding: The degree to which a paint obscures the surface to which it is applied.

Hiding Power: The ability of a paint film to obscure the substrate to which it is applied. May be measured while the paint is still wet or after it has dried, and these measurements may differ. Hiding power is measured by determining the minimum thickness at which a film will completely obscure a black and white pattern.

Hold Out: The ability of a surface to keep the topcoat from sinking in.

Holiday: An area which was accidentally missed when a surface was painted.

Hot-Melt: Generally an adhesive. A polymer applied to a substrate in its molten state. Dries by cooling to solid.

House paint: A pigmented paint designed to be applied by brush to the exterior surfaces of residential buildings. Commonly sold over the counter to the consumer.

Hue: The color we see: red, blue, green and yellow and all the shades in between.

Humidity: The amount of water vapor in the atmosphere. Relative humidity is the % of water vapor in the air at a temperature compared to the total which would be held by the atmosphere at that temperature.

Hydrocarbon: A compound which contains only carbon and hydrogen. Commonly applies to solvents either aliphatic or aromatic in nature.

Hydrometer: An instrument to measure the specific gravity (density of a liquid).

Induction Heating: The development of heat in a substrate by the application of an electromagnetic field to that substrate.

Infrared Baking: Drying a paint film by the heat developed by an infrared source.

Infrared Light: That portion of the spectrum responsible for most of the heating effects of the sun's light; 8000–100,000 Angstrom units.

Inhibitor: An additive to a paint which slows up some process, e.g., gelling, skinning, yellowing, etc.

Iodine Number: A method of measuring the drying potential of an oil or other reactive system. High numbers indicate fast drying potential. Actually determines amount of unsaturation.

Iron: A metallic substrate which requires painting to prevent corrosion. Also found as a component of driers and pigments.

Iron Blue: A widely used blue pigment.

Alkali sensitive. Durable. Made by oxidizing the ferrous ferrocyanide formed by precipitating a solution of a soluble ferrocyanide salt with iron sulfate.

Iron Oxide Red: A widely used red pigment. Durable. Very alkali resistant. Cheap. Mainly ferric oxide.

Isophorone: A very slow evaporating solvent. Expensive. Toxic.

Isopropyl Alcohol: A solvent, cosolvent or diluent. Cheap, fast evaporating. Used mainly in lacquers. Rubbing alcohol.

Kauri Butanol Value: A measure of the solvent power of a hydrocarbon. High numbers indicate high solvent power.

Ketones: A class of organic liquids. Very useful in the paint industry due to their high solvent power. Characterized by the suffix "one."

Krebs Unit: A measure of viscosity. Commonly used for those liquids which are thixotropic.

Lacquer: A paint which dries by solvent evaporation only. Usually it has been applied to nitrocellulose types only, but the term has a broad meaning.

Latent Solvents: A liquid which will not ordinarily dissolve a solid, but which develops solvency when it is mixed with another liquid.

Latex: An emulsion. A dispersion of a polymer in water.

Lead: A metal commonly used in the manufacture of driers and pigments. All lead compounds are extremely toxic. Lead driers promote thorough drying.

Leafing: The orientation of metal-flake pigments in a paint film which results in a bright metallic appearance and a concentration of the particles at the surface of the film.

Lifting: The attack by the solvent in a topcoat on the undercoat which results in distortion or wrinkling of the undercoat.

Lightness: The whiteness of a paint measured by the amount of light reflected by a surface. A perfect white is one which reflects 100% of the light in the visible spectrum.

Light Fastness: The ability of a paint to resist color changes caused by light.

Line Checking: Similar to cracking; lines or cracks are parallel and range from very short UD to about 18 inches.

Linseed Oil: A vegetable oil widely used in the manufacture of alkyd resins and also as a binder by itself. Poor color retention.

Livering: Gelation.

Lucite: DuPont's trademark for acrylics.

Luster: Gloss.

Magnesium: A very light, strong metal used mainly by the aircraft industry. Difficult to paint. Requires special surface preparation.

Manganese: A metal component of driers. Manganese driers are used mainly for baking products.

Masonite: A reconstituted wood product used as a building material

Masstone: The predominant or undiluted color a pigment produces.

Melamine: A hard resin used to modify alkyd resins and other film formers used in baking finishes. High quality, durable and lightfast

Metal Conditioner: An acid-type metal cleaner which removes rust and corrosion from bare metal, etches it for better adhesion, and forms a film which can inhibit further corrosion.

Metallics: Finishes which include metal flakes in addition to the pigment.

Methacrylate: A class of acrylic polymers.

Methyl Alcohol: A very low boiling, toxic alcohol. Very little use in the paint industry. Wood alcohol. Methanol.

MEK: Methyl ethyl ketone. A good solvent used mainly for lacquers. Fast evaporating. Almost the solvent power of acetone with a slower evaporation rate.

MIBK: Methyl isobutyl ketone. A good solvent used for a variety of resins. Medium fast evaporation rate.

Mica: An extender pigment. Essentially silicates of aluminum.

Micro-Checking: Appears as severe dulling of film, but when examined through a magnifying glass, film contains many small cracks that do not touch.

Mildew: The fungus growth which appears on substrates in warm, humid areas.

Milori Blue: An iron blue—durable blue pigment.

Mills: Equipment used to disperse pigments. Ball or pebble mill grinds by the action of large balls or pebbles impacting on the pigment groups. A roller mill grinds by the shearing action between two counter-rotating steel rolls. Sand mill grinds by the shearing action developed between moving particles of sand.

Mill Base: A colored paint containing a very large amount of pigment. Used to tint paint or to make paint. Product of grinding or dispersion.

Mist Coat: A coat of rich, slow-evaporating thinner with little or no color added.

Mixer: Any container containing an agitator of some type.

Molecule: The smallest possible unit or amount of any substance which retains the characteristics of that substance.

"Monastral": Blue green or red. Very durable, lightfast and alkali resistant. Phthalocyamine pigments.

Monomer: A chemical compound, usually simple, capable of reacting with itself or other monomers to form polymers.

Mottling: A film defect appearing as blotches or surface imperfections.

Nitrocellulose: See "Cellulose Nitrate."

Non-drying oil: A liquid (commonly a vegetable oil) which will not dry under normal atmospheric conditions, even when driers are added.

Oil Absorption: The amount of oil it takes to mix with a given pigment to yield a certain viscosity mixture. A measure of the surface area of a pigment.

Oil Length: The amount of oil in a varnish. Expressed as gallons of oil per 100 pounds of gum.

Oils: Commonly vegetable oils. Obtained from various natural sources. A relatively viscous liquid which has an oily or slippery feel. Technically, the reaction product of a fatty or long-chain acid and glycerol, a polyalcohol; also a hydrocarbon product having an oily feel and a very low or negligible evaporation rate. Used as modifiers for alkyd resins, as paint vehicles, as varnish constituents, as plasticizers, etc.

Orange Peel: A pattern developed in a film caused by improper formulation or application conditions and resulting from poor flow.

Oven: A piece of equipment used to bake finishes.

Overall Repainting: A type of refinish repair in which the car is completely repainted.

Overspray: An overlap of dry paint particles from the spray gun on areas that were not meant to be painted.

Oxidation: The chemical combination of oxygen and the vehicle of a paint which leads to drying. Also, the destructive combination of oxygen with a dry paint film leading to degradation. Also, the destructive combination of oxygen and a metal; for example, rusting.

P/B: Pigment—to—binder ratio. The ratio of the weight of pigment to the weight of binder in a paint.

pH: A measure of the acidity of a substance in an aqueous solution. 7 is neutral. Below 7 is acid and above 7 is basic. The scale is from O (strong acid) to 14 (strong alkaline).

PVA: Poly-vinyl acetate.

PVC: Pigment volume content. The percent by volume of pigment in the total volume of solid material in a paint.

Paint: All paint contains a carrier or solvent plus binder. Paints may or may not be colored by pigments or dyes.

Paint Remover: A chemical that breaks down an old finish by liquifying it.

Panel Repair: A type of refinish repair job in which a complete section (door, hood, rear deck, etc.) is repainted.

"PARLON": Chlorinated rubber.

Particle Size: The size of the pigment particles in a dispersion. Measured in mils.

Pastel: A light color. One containing a lot of white. A tint off white.

Pearls: Finishes which include mica flakes in addition to the pigment and binder.

Peeling: The loss of adhesion of a paint film which results in large pieces of film splitting away from the surface.

Phenolic: A class of resins. Characterized by very good chemical resistance and food color.

Phenylmercury Compounds: A class of materials used as fungicides. Very toxic but effective.

Phosphoric Acid: An acid commonly used as a catalyst to speed up the cure of some baking finishes, usually alkyd/nitrogen resin combinations.

Phthalic Anhydride: A white solid used in the manufacture of alkyd resins and other polyesters.

Pigments: An insoluble solid having a small particle size. Used to color paints and to impart either properties to paint. Pigments may be any colored semi-transparent, black, white or colorless. Incorporated into paint system by some dispersion process.

Pinholing: Holes left in a paint film by bubbles.

Pitting: The appearance of holes or pits in a paint film while it is wet. Related to crawling and poor wetting.

Plasticizer: A material which is added to a paint system to make the film more flexible.

Poise: A measure of viscosity. 100 centipoises = 1 poise.

Polar: Solvents or other organic materials which have strongly electronegative and electropositive areas in the molecule. Hydrocarbons are non-polar and oxygenated solvents are usually polar. Materials that are polar have high dielectric constants.

Poly: A prefix meaning many. Also implies repetition many times.

Polyester: A polymer formed from the reaction of a di- or polycarboxylic acid and a diol- or a polyol.

Polymer: A chain or network of repeating units combined chemically. Polymerization: The formation of a polymer from monomers. There are two types of polymerization— addition and condensation.

Polyoxithane: A polymer with an oxide ring that reacts with a polymer having a nitrogen group.

Polyurethane: A chemical structure used in the production of resins for enamel finishes.

Primer: The first coat of paint applied to a substrate: Often different from the following coats and often the most important coat for such things as corrosion resistance, adhesion, blister resistance, etc.

Primer-Sealer: An undercoat which improves adhesion of the topcoat, and which seals old painted surfaces that have been sanded.

Primer-Surfacer: A high-solids primer which fills small imperfections in the substrate and which usually must be sanded.

Printing: Permanent impression left in a film by something pressing on the film.

Putty: A high-viscosity, heavily pigmented paint used to fill holes or to smooth out a rough surface. Commonly linseed oil and calcium carbonate.

Ransburg: A method of applying paint electrostatically.

Reduce: To lower the viscosity of a paint by the addition of solvent or thinner.

Reducer: A solvent used to reduce or thin enamels.

Reflow: A heat process by which lacquers are melted to produce better flow "leveling".

Resin: A solid or semi-solid material, usually polymeric, which deposits a film and is the actual film forming ingredient in paint. See gum. Solutions of polymers are often called resins, but the term actually applies only to the film forming solids, not to the solution.

Respirator: A device worn over the mouth to filter particles and fumes out of the air being breathed.

Retarder: A solvent added to a paint to reduce the evaporation rate.

Roller Coating: A method of applying paint by means of a roll which transfers paint from a reservoir to the surface to be painted.

Rosin: A natural gum.

Rubbing (or polishing) Compounds: An abrasive that smoothes and polishes the paint film.

Runs & Sags: A heavy application of sprayed material that fails to adhere uniformly to the surface (the most common of application problems).

Rust: The corrosion product which forms on iron or steel when exposed to moisture.

Rutile: A form of titanium dioxide pigment relatively non-chalking.

Safflower: A vegetable oil similar to linseed oil in its uses and characteristics.

Sagging: Excessive flow on a vertical surface resulting in drips and other imperfections on the painted surface. Occurs not only when the paint is wet, but also during baking in certain types of paints.

Sandblasting: A method of cleaning metal, usually steel, by means of a blast with an abrasive.

Sandscratch Swelling: A swelling of sand scratches in the old surface caused by solvents in the topcoat.

Show Through: Sand scratches in the undercoat which are visible through the topcoat.

Saponification: The separation of esters into their components usually by alkaline attack. A destructive process when it occurs in a paint film.

Sealer: Provides uniform color hold out and an even, level surface for topcoat application.

Seeding: The development of tiny insoluble particles in a container of paint which results in a rough or gritty film.

Semi-Gloss: An intermediate gloss level between high and low gloss.

Settling: Gravity separation of one or more components from a paint and the resulting layer of material on the bottom of a container as a result of the separated material having sunk.

Sheen: The gloss or flatness of a film when viewed at a low angle.

Shellac: A natural gum useful in the manufacture of certain types of paint, chiefly lacquers.

Silicone: An ingredient in waxes and polishes which makes them feel smooth; also the primary cause of fish eyes.

Silking: Lines in a paint film resulting from the draining off of excess paint in a dip or flow coating process. A result of poor flow.

Skinning: The development of a solid layer on the top of the liquid in a container of paint.

Soap: The product formed by the reaction of a fatty acid and a base or the saponification of oil containing polymers by a base or an alkaline substrate.

Solids: The percentage, on a weight basis, of solid material in a paint after the solvents have evaporated.

Solvency: The measure of the ability of a liquid to dissolve a solid. Measured by the viscosity of a solution at a certain concentration of solid resin. The same solvent may have different solvency for different resins. The same as solvent power.

Solvent: A liquid which will dissolve something: commonly resins or gums or other binder constituents. Commonly an organic liquid.

Solvent Popping: Blisters that form on a paint film, which are caused by trapped solvents.

Soya Oil: A vegetable oil commonly used in the manufacture of alkyd resins. Cheap and durable. Fair color retention. A drying oil.

Spar Varnish: Commonly a clear varnish useful for use for exterior exposure, particularly for use on boats and other marine uses where a clear for wood is desired.

Specific Gravity: The ratio of the weight in air of a specific volume of a substance compared to the weight of an equal volume of water. Similar to density for practical purposes.

Spectrophotometer: An instrument to measure color. Compares the reflectance of a test sample to the reflectance of an MGO standard at all points of the visible spectrum.

Spewing: Spontaneous migration of a component of a paint film to a surface, either top or bottom.

Spot Repair: A type of refinish repair job in which a section of a car smaller than a panel is refinished (often called "ding" and "dent" work).

Squeegee: A rubber block used to wipe off wet-sanded areas and to apply putty.

Stabilizer: Something added to paint to prevent degradation.

Steel: A ferrous metal commonly used as a substrate for paint, which must be painted to prevent corrosion.

Strength: The opacity and/or tinting power of a pigment. The measure of the ability of a pigment to hide or to color.

Styrene: A useful monomer which polymerizes readily. Low cost and colorless. Vinyl benzene widely used to make plastic articles and polyester finishes.

Substrate: The piece or object which is to be painted.

Surfacer: A heavily-pigmented paint designed to be applied to a substrate for the purpose of smoothing or uniforming the surface for subsequent coats of paint.

Tack: The stickiness of a paint film or an adhesive. The time it takes for an air drying paint to reach a tack-free stage is a common measure of drying speed.

Tack Rag: A varnish-coated cheesecloth with a tacky surface used to remove dirt and lint before painting.

Talc: An extender pigment. Essentially magnesium silicate.

Tall Oil: A fatty acid obtained as a by-product in the production of wood pulp from pine trees. Useful in the manufacture of alkyd resins. Similar to soya oil in properties when made into an alkyd resin.

Thermoplastic: A polymer or other solid material which becomes soft or fluid when it is heated.

Thermosetting: A polymer or other solid which will not soften when it is heated. Thermosetting implies cross-linking and reaction on drying.

Thinner: One or a mixture of several solvents or diluents used to reduce the viscosity of paint or to lower the solids. Often used to mean the same as solvent or diluent.

Thixotropy: The development of high viscosity or apparent gelation in a standing liquid, which is reversible by the application of a sharing force.

Tint: A very light color, usually a pastel. To add color to another color or to white.

Titanium Dioxide: A white pigment. Most

generally useful white pigment. Has the greatest hiding power of all white pigments. Nontoxic and non-reactive.

Toluene: A solvent or diluent or a cosolvent. A fast-evaporating, high-solvency aromatic hydrocarbon. Widely used. Toluoi is a common name.

Topcoat: The final layer of paint applied to a substrate. Several coats of topcoat may be applied in some cases.

Traffic Paint: Paint designed to be used to mark numbers or lines on streets or curbs.

Trichlorethylene: A solvent used to degrease and clean metal substrates for painting.

Tumbling: A method of applying paint by placing a number of small parts in a barrel along with a small amount of paint and then rotating the barrel until the paint is spread uniformly over all the parts.

Turpentine: A solvent obtained from the distillate of the exudation of pine trees. Largely replaced by petroleum derivatives now.

Two-Tone: Two different colors on a single paint job; to apply two colors on the same paint job.

Ultraviolet Light: That portion of the spectrum which is largely responsible for the degradation of paints. Invisible to the eye. "Black light". 2000-4000 Angstrom units.

Undercoat: A first coat; primer, sealer or surfacer.

Undertone: The color of a pigment which shows up when that pigment is mixed with a lot of white pigment. For example, blues may be red toned, green toned or dirty.

Urea-Formaldehyde: A commonly used, hard colorless polymer used mainly to modify alkyd resins. A nitrogen resin.

Varnish: A clear resin solution made by the application of heat to a mixture of a hard gum and a vegetable oil and then dissolving the product formed in a suitable organic solvent.

Vehicle: All of a paint except the pigment. This includes solvents, diluents, resins, gums, driers, etc. The liquid portion of a paint.

Veiling: The formation of a web or strings in a paint as it emerges from a spray gun.

Vinyl: A class of monomers which can be combined to form vinyl polymers. Vinyl polymers are addition polymers, widely used to make chemical resistant finishes, tough plastic articles, phonograph records and floor tiles.

Viscosity: Determined by allowing a measured amount to flow through an orifice and measuring the time it takes for this amount to flow. There are also other methods of measurement. The unit of viscosity is the poise.

VOC Content: The measure of Volatile Organic Compounds in solvent-borne paints.

Water Spotting: A condition caused by water evaporating on a finish before it is thoroughly dry which results in a dulling of the gloss in spots.

Wax: A specially prepared material designed to shine or improve a surface. Waxes are usually paraffinic or esters of long chain fatty acids with long chain alcohols.

Weathering: The change in a paint film by the natural forces, such as sunlight, rain, dust, wind, etc.

Weatherometer: A machine designed to simulate the effects of weathering.

Wetting: The process by which a liquid forms intimate contact with the substrate to which it is applied.

Wet Spots: Discoloration caused where the paint fails to dry and adhere uniformly (usually caused by grease or finger marks).

Wrinkle: The pattern formed on the surface of a paint film by improperly formulated or by specially formulated coatings. The appearance of tiny ridges or folds in the film.

Wrinkling: Surface distortion (shriveling or skinning) that occurs in a thick coat of enamel before the underlayer has properly dried.

Xylene: An aromatic hydrocarbon. High solvency for a hydrocarbon and medium evaporation rate. Very useful. Commonly called Xylol.

Yellowing: A yellow discoloration to the paint color. Commonly caused by smoke, grease, certain gases—but more commonly, sunlight, or lack of light, i.e., in the dark.

Zinc: A difficult metal substrate to paint due to its reactivity A constituent of a drier. A pigment.

Zinc Chromate: A yellow, rust-preventing pigment useful on steel.

Zinc Oxide: A white pigment. Useful to prevent mold or mildew on paint films. Care must be taken in its use due to the embrittling action of this pigment in many vehicles.

INDEX

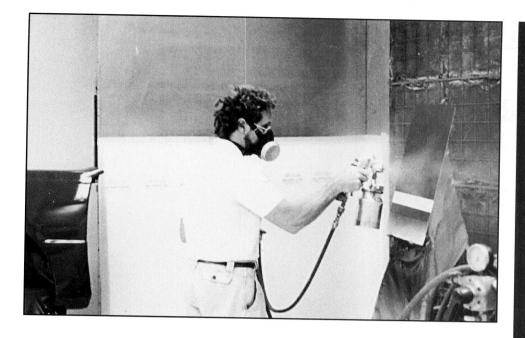

John Pfanstiehl has been involved in auto restoration and repair for the past 30 years. His technical articles have appeared in many national publications including *Automobile Magazine, Auto Body Repair News, BodyShop Business, Corvette Fever, Mopar Muscle*, and *Mustang Monthly*. He is author of *Used Car Buying Guide*, which has been published in four languages, and HPBooks' *Corvette Weekend Projects.*

In the early seventies, he worked at Corvette Center of Connecticut and later started his own specialty repair business. Pfanstiehl has designed a number of auto repair tools, and has patents on paint equipment and other products. His current business, Pro Motorcar Products, Inc. has introduced a number of breakthrough products which one major paint manufacturer said "has revolutionized the field of automotive refinishing." His U.S. manufactured automotive products have been repeatedly been chosen "New Product of the Year" by various trade organizations, and they are marketed throughout the world. He lives in Indian Rocks Beach, Florida.

OTHER BOOKS OF INTEREST

1,001 High Performance Tech Tips by Wayne Scraba 1-55788-199-5/$16.95

Auto Math Handbook by John Lawlor 1-55788-020-4/$16.95

Automotive Electrical Handbook by Jim Horner 0-89586-238-7/$16.95

Automotive Paint Handbook by Jim Pfanstiehl 1-55788-034-4/$16.95

Brake Handbook by Fred Puhn 0-89586-232-8/$16.95

Camaro Performance Handbook by David Shelby 1-55788-057-3/$16.95

Camaro Restoration Handbook by Tom Currao and Ron Sessions 0-89586-375-8/$16.95

Chevrolet Power edited by Rich Voegelin 1-55788-087-5/$19.95

Classic Car Restorer's Handbook by Jim Richardson 1-55788-194-4/$16.95

Holley Carburetors, Manifolds and Fuel Injection (Revised Edition) by Bill Fisher and Mike Urich 1-55788-052-2/$17.00

How to Make Your Car Handle by Fred Puhn 0-912-65646-8/$16.95

Metal Fabricator's Handbook by Ron Fournier 0-89586-870-9/$16.95

Mustang Performance Handbook by William R. Mathis 1-55788-193-6/$16.95

Mustang Performance Handbook 2 by William R. Mathis 1-55788-202-9/$16.95

Mustang Restoration Handbook by Don Taylor 0-89586-402-9/$16.95

Mustang Weekend Projects 1964½–1967 by Jerry Heasley 1-55788-230-4/$17.00

Paint & Body Handbook (Revised Edition) by Don Taylor and Larry Hofer 1-55788-082-4/$16.95

Race Car Engineering & Mechanics by Paul Van Valkenburgh 1-55788-064-6/$16.95

Sheet Metal Handbook by Ron and Sue Fournier 0-89586-757-5/$16.95

Street Rodder's Handbook by Frank Oddo 0-89586-369-3/$16.95

Turbo Hydra-matic 350 by Ron Sessions 0-89586-051-1/$16.95

Turbochargers by Hugh MacInnes 0-89586-135-6/$16.95

Understanding Automotive Emissions Control by Larry Carley and Bob Freudenberger 1-55788-201-0/$16.95

Welder's Handbook (Revised Edition) by Richard Finch 1-55788-264-9/$16.95

TO ORDER CALL: 1-800-788-6262, ext. 1, Refer to Ad #583b

HPBooks
A division of Penguin Putnam Inc.
375 Hudson Street
New York, NY 10014

*Prices subject to change